# How to Import Wine

## An Insider's Guide

3rd Edition

### Deborah M. Gray

Bluestone Wine Solutions

How To Import Wine – An Insider's Guide, Third Edition Copyright © 2022 by Deborah M. Gray

Publisher: Bluestone Wine Solutions

www.bluestonewinesolutions.com

howtoimportwine.com

Cover design: Rupa Limbu

All rights reserved. No part of this book may be reproduced or used in any manner without written permission of the copyright owner except for the use of quotations in a book review.

ISBN: 978-1-7371631-1-4

*In memory of my father and mother,*

*who both inspired me in different ways*

*Anthony Eric Gray*

*Mary Patricia Gray*

# CONTENTS

Introduction ... xi

## PART I

### Chapter 1  Initial Considerations ... 1

Portfolio — Options And Building ... 3
Sourcing Options ... 4
QPR – Quality Price Ratio ... 11
Packaging ... 12
Branding – Not Just About The Wine ... 15
Balancing The Portfolio ... 16

### Chapter 2  Building A Business Model ... 21

Company, Structure, Personnel, Partners ... 21
Office Requirements ... 22
Geography Decision : National Or Regional ... 24
Resources – Time And Money ... 25
Warehouse ... 28

### Chapter 3  Licensing, Permits And Definitions ... 35

The Importer In The Distribution Chain ... 35
Necessary Licenses And Other Licensing To Consider Now ... 39
COLAS Online ... 42
Power Of Attorney (POA) ... 44
Continuous Bond ... 45
Home State Licenses ... 45
California State License ... 46

| | |
|---|---|
| New Jersey/New York License | 47 |
| Other State Licenses | 47 |

## Chapter 4  Portfolio – Selections And Decisions — 49

| | |
|---|---|
| Narrowing The Field | 49 |
| Wine Industry Experience | 50 |
| Focused Research | 51 |
| Agents | 52 |
| Trade Associations | 54 |
| International Trade Shows | 55 |
| Personalities – A Relationship, Not A One Time Purchase | 56 |
| Contracts | 60 |
| Expectations – Yours And Theirs | 61 |
| References | 71 |

# PART II

## Chapter 5  Planning, Preparation And Preparedness — 77

| | |
|---|---|
| Purchase Orders | 77 |
| Food And Drug Administration (FDA) | 81 |
| Primary American Source (Appointment Letter) | 83 |
| COLA Guidelines And General Information About Labels | 86 |

## Chapter 6  Containers — 99

| | |
|---|---|
| Sizes And Weights | 99 |
| Pallets | 101 |
| Reefer Vs. Dry Vs. Blanket Vs. ... | 102 |
| CIF Vs. FOB | 105 |
| FCL Vs. LCL Summary | 110 |
| Controlled Consolidation (An FCL Hybrid) | 111 |

| | |
|---|---:|
| Freight Forwarder | *113* |
| Customs Broker | *115* |

## Chapter 7  The Next Steps · 119

| | |
|---|---:|
| First Container Budgeting | *119* |
| Pricing | *120* |
| Ratings | *120* |
| New Brand Demand | *121* |
| Old Brand Demand | *121* |
| QPR (Quality Price Ratio) | *122* |
| Timing | *122* |
| Seasonal Timing | *123* |
| Incentives | *124* |
| Pricing The Wine | *125* |

## Chapter 8  It's On The Water – Maximize Your Waiting Time · 139

| | |
|---|---:|
| Winery Marketing Materials | *139* |
| Setting Up A Website | *145* |
| Bookkeeping, Invoicing, Forms And Inventory Management | *147* |
| Warehouse And Customs Broker Notification And Arrangements | *151* |

# PART III

## Chapter 9  Distribution – The First Stages · 165

| | |
|---|---:|
| Narrowing The Search For The Right Distributor | *165* |
| Following The Distribution Trail | *171* |
| What A Distributor Looks For – Are You On The Same Page | *175* |
| Vetting The Distributor | *176* |
| Partnering With Your Distributor | *178* |
| States In General | *179* |

| | |
|---|---|
| *Franchise States* | *180* |
| *Control States* | *182* |
| *Territory Assignments And Restrictions* | *183* |
| *Brokers* | *184* |

## Chapter 10  Distribution – The Next Stage — 191

| | |
|---|---|
| *Incentives – Wine Launch* | *191* |
| *Incentives – Ongoing* | *195* |
| *Sample Allowance And Handling* | *199* |
| *Purchase Orders* | *202* |
| *Pickup And Delivery* | *204* |
| *Invoicing* | *205* |
| *Collecting* | *209* |

## Chapter 11  Tips For Distribution Success — 213

| | |
|---|---|
| *Communication* | *213* |
| *Travel Budgeting* | *214* |
| *Staff Training – In-House* | *216* |
| *Staff Training – On-Premise* | *218* |
| *Consistent Pricing* | *219* |
| *Relationships Outside The Wholesaler* | *220* |
| *Working Their Market Alone* | *221* |
| *Placement Reports* | *222* |
| *Depletion Reports* | *224* |

## Chapter 12  Marketing — 229

| | |
|---|---|
| *Website Trade Support* | *229* |
| *Wine Dinners* | *233* |
| *Trade Tastings* | *237* |

| | |
|---|---:|
| Consumer Tastings | *245* |
| Making The Best Use Of Press | *248* |
| Point Of Sale Material | *250* |
| According To Budget | *252* |

# PART IV

| | |
|---|---:|
| **Chapter 13  Inventory Control** | **259** |
| Reasonable Stock Levels | *259* |
| Vintage Management | *261* |
| Turnover | *263* |
| Reorder Timing From Winery | *264* |
| Container Consolidation | *265* |
| Direct Import (DI) | *266* |
| **Chapter 14  State Licensing** | **271** |
| In-House Or Outsourced | *272* |
| Compliance Issues | *273* |
| Saving Money – Using Others' Licenses | *274* |
| Monthly State Reporting | *276* |
| Change Of Importers | *277* |
| When To Say No To Distribution | *282* |

# PART V

| | |
|---|---:|
| **Chapter 15  Market Visits – Work-Withs And Ride-Withs** | **289** |
| Overall Preparation | *290* |
| Wine Dinners And Tasting Preparation | *291* |
| Time Scheduling | *293* |
| Account Protocol | *294* |

| | |
|---|---|
| *Expectations* | *295* |
| *Presentation Primer* | *296* |
| *Dos And Don'ts* | *303* |

## Chapter 16  Maintaining Distribution — 311

| | |
|---|---|
| *Ongoing Support And Communication* | *311* |
| *Expectations* | *313* |
| *Retail Support And Pull-Through* | *313* |
| *Diversifying Portfolio Placements* | *316* |
| *Winery Visits To The U.S.* | *317* |
| *Initial Planning* | *318* |
| *Trip Logistics* | *320* |
| *During The Trip* | *322* |
| *Winery Expectations Of The Trip* | *324* |

## Chapter 17  When It's Not Working — 329

| | |
|---|---|
| *During The Transition* | *331* |

# PART VI

## Chapter 18  Home State Distribution — 337

| | |
|---|---|
| *Distribution Basics* | *338* |
| *Sales Personnel* | *348* |
| *Office Personnel* | *353* |
| *Hiring Basics* | *355* |
| *Account Protocol* | *356* |
| *Outside The Single Account Model* | *358* |
| *Chains, Resorts And Country Clubs* | *358* |
| *Wine Clubs* | *360* |
| *Military Bases, Cruise Lines And Hotel Chains* | *361* |

## Chapter 19  Direct To Consumer — 365

*Where You Can And Where You Can't* — *365*

*Working Within The Three-Tier System* — *368*

## Chapter 20  Other Thoughts — 375

*Millennials* — *375*

*Current And Future Trends* — *377*

*Think Green* — *382*

*Clearing Wine* — *385*

*Export* — *387*

*Grey Market* — *388*

## Conclusion — 393

# INTRODUCTION

Each edition of this book has been written during, or following, a significant period in which economic changes have impacted the wine business. The first was the Great Recession, or Global Financial Crisis, as it is known elsewhere in the world, when high end, small vineyard Australian wines, which made up my entire portfolio, were suddenly unsaleable after fifteen years of growth in the US. In the process of putting together a different portfolio of wines during this extremely difficult time, I began writing the first *How to Import Wine – An Insider's Guide* to provide a roadmap for others who were considering importing alcoholic beverages into the US, based on my extensive experience. It was completed in 2010 and published in 2011.

In 2016, we emerged from the recession to find that much had changed, including how we did business. I had given up my own importing of wine as an evolving process and pivoted to full-time consulting. I found I gained an even broader range of knowledge from the clients who come to me for consulting, with far reaching wine brands from many different countries, along with beer, hard cider, mead and spirits. Their import issues and dilemmas have become my window into today's markets. After a long hiatus, Australian wines have emerged again in a sort of Australia 2.0 - a more thoughtful approach to the US market, with nuanced wines, new varieties and an emphasis on regional characteristics.

The second edition of this book incorporated new realities that came along with the changing economic times, together with the obvious impact of social media, emerging trends, and the influence of millennials. I updated some sections, particularly compliance and logistics and included real world issues that seem to be a recurring theme for many of my clients, and may be for you, if this becomes your chosen field.

This, the third edition, comes during the COVID-19 pandemic, which has altered once again the ways we do business, for now and perhaps forever. I have also revised the work once again, to address more fully the DtC market, which was growing in recent years, but has exploded during the pandemic. I have also corrected any errors in the previous works that were brought to my attention, and updated sections to reflect current regulations or prevailing trends.

* * *

Much of life is about timing. In the mid-1980's my father, Tony Gray, embarked on an ambitious plan to export wine to the U.S. He would be considered both foolhardy and a visionary in his lifetime and this venture was no exception. The 1980's saw the introduction of a few, mass produced Australian brands into the U.S. with some success, but very little wine from small, family-owned, single vineyard estates. Not only did Tony intend to take on the American wine buying public, but he had the temerity to call his wine brand *Australian Gold*. No quirky aboriginal dialect, no quaint vineyard scenes, or estates. This was guerrilla marketing positioning. *Let's take on all of America with something that embodied the best of Australia.* It was a bold idea and a progressive label.

Unfortunately, in this broad brush approach, he had not considered some of the more imperatives of export, such as appropriate importation, distribution, and a little matter of payment.

Phone calls and faxes found and secured an importer in California, a very short-lived arrangement that lasted until the importer's warehouse and all its contents were seized by the IRS for back taxes. In a protracted legal battle, the wine mysteriously disappeared. Tony lost both a container of wine and any hope of reimbursement.

Undaunted, he tried again. Better researching found a small importer in Florida, who was very enthusiastic and seemed to be a good fit. Tony made the trip over, met with the gentleman and sealed the deal with a handshake. Within six months of arrival of the first container, the importer had gone out of business, over 500 cases of

*Australian Gold* were still in storage, the new importer was behind on payments and once again any hope of recovery was gone.

My father, perennially optimistic and determined to find a way to crack the elusive U.S. market, turned to me for help. Which brings me to timing.

I had no experience in the wine business, and incidentally a demanding career, but the opportunity was irresistible. Here was the chance to help my Dad, represent my family's wine, and educate Americans about the Australian wine industry at a time when most people didn't even know we grew grapes. I was living in Tampa Bay, Florida and heard about a restaurant that was opening up nearby with an Australian theme. What better place to start.

It was easy to get a meeting with Tim Gannon. It was his first restaurant and he was personally involved in its physical creation. He hadn't yet been to Australia, but there were boomerangs on the wall, an Aussie themed menu and the partners were applying their previous corporate restaurant experience to a new concept on their own. The year was 1987.

Tim was gracious, and receptive to my proposal. The timing was perfect. But timing, however serendipitous or cosmically aligned, is only as good as one's preparedness for the situation. I presented a beautiful label, a brand name to fit their theme, terrific pricing, and a soft, fruity wine to complement the food and the prevailing palate. But the varietals, semillon and sauvignon blanc, were unfamiliar and unpronounceable and I had nothing in my nonexistent repertoire of experience to convince him otherwise. I thanked him for the meeting and left.

That restaurant was Outback Steakhouse. Today, according to Forbes, Outback Steakhouse has close to 1,000 restaurants worldwide. While sales were down in 2021 and food prices increased in both 2021 and 2022, they still report revenues in excess of $2.7B. If I had possessed the knowledge and experience during that most propitious of meetings, I would have had answers, options and alternatives that may have laid a foundation for a long, successful business alliance, propelling my father into the U.S. wine business far ahead of the curve. My subsequent, intermittent efforts around Tampa Bay were insufficient to sustain my father's dream and he withdrew from the U.S. It wasn't until 1992, when I established my own import company that he decided to tackle it again.

Yes, timing is everything, but in the wine industry timing has to be backed up with a plan. And that is where *How to Import Wine* can provide the foundational tools to begin the process to build your business. The rest is up to you. How much time and effort are you willing to expend in this endeavor? I always tell my clients that there is no substitute for hard work and being willing to accept setbacks to achieve your goals.

Most people, who gaze longingly across the fence at the wine business, seem to have their rose colored glasses perched firmly on their noses. When I tell people, with a sigh, that I have a stack of wine in my office for my palate to wade through, they mock-commiserate with me. "Oh, poor you," is the not uncommon response, which really means, "Wouldn't I love to have that problem." But, as you will discover in concrete terms, the tasting and enjoyment of wine is just the tip of the iceberg.

Years ago, when I started my import company, the only bit of advice anyone gave me was "don't do it." It was proffered by the head of a wine distribution company in Atlanta, and I've never figured out if he really thought it was a bad idea or was just afraid of the competition. Needless to say, I did not heed his warning. Since this was the only advice I received, I plunged blindly in and several years of trial and error ensued as I made my way up my own steep learning curve. Fortunately, this training I received in the trenches has enabled me to provide you with far more than a basic understanding or academic treatise on the importing and distribution of wine into the U.S. It is an exciting, rewarding, fascinating field if you know what you are doing. I really do want to reach back with a helping hand to those who are entering the field now. Each person shouldn't have to reinvent the wheel.

A plethora of wine books can be found on any bookstore shelf, with subjects ranging from the nuances of regions, tastes and food pairings by notable authors, to bicycle treks into bucolic countryside and in-depth texts on wine making and wine marketing. This book is unique in providing comprehensive step by step guidance through the importing process, from portfolio composition through distribution, presented in a practical, easily digested format.

Drawing on my thirty years hands-on career as a wine importer, consultant and university instructor, this book's primary purpose is to *demystify* importing wine into the U.S. For anyone considering this professional move, regardless of prior experience or education, this book will lay out specific guidelines and instructions for setting up and running a wine import business from the perspective of someone who is actually importing and distributing on a day-to-day basis.

Along the way, I'll share stories with you of actual experiences and advice on how to streamline your journey, alongside the more enjoyable aspects of successfully representing a product that brings people pleasure and enhances social settings. The prospective importer enters a world where tasting wine is part of business and business is often conducted under the olive tree overlooking rolling hills of trellised vines, or with a gourmet meal at the cellar door restaurant. But it is still a business and one that must be approached armed with the right tools.

In other words, this is a career choice from which you can derive much satisfaction and an enviable lifestyle. But first, you must do your homework. Or your business may become akin to the oft-repeated boater's lament "a big hole into which you pour money."

Figure I.1 Australian Gold poster

# Part I

# CHAPTER 1

# INITIAL CONSIDERATIONS

You may have picked up this book as a curiosity, considering what it might take to be a wine importer, or you may already have decided wine importing is definitely for you. But, like any business, being a wine importer is an entrepreneurial pursuit and takes a certain type of individual. Let's look at why you are considering undertaking this endeavor before we plunge into the nitty-gritty.

- **Do you have wine industry experience?**

This could be anything from retail to wholesale, or working in a winery; any such experience can bring knowledge to your venture and be very helpful, but be careful not to romanticize your experience or consider that one type of background prepares you fully for another.

- **Have you been in some other form of perishable goods import business?**

Any type of importing prepares you for the technical aspects of container management and logistics, but importing perishable goods – such as food and drink – extends this knowledge into a specialized arena, providing an understanding of timely product movement and budgeting.

- **Does it seem fun and exciting?**

This is not exactly an experiential reason, but one which will instill the necessary enthusiasm and desire to learn more about the business that will benefit you. Just don't allow yourself to get carried away with the idea that it is fun and exciting and forget about the real-world work and perseverance that will be necessary for the business to succeed.

- **Have you made money in an unrelated venture and now wish to invest?**

This can be a great reason, but the same caution as above can apply and that is to consider that an investment will only pay off if you have done your due diligence. This is not a hobby, or a business for the dabbler, unless you are only the investor and will surround yourself with knowledgeable, experienced people.

- **Have you always wanted to be an entrepreneur?**

This is not a bad reason, but be prepared to back it up with capital, a willingness to learn and an understanding that being an entrepreneur – unless you have considerable funds – does not mean being the boss and delegating everything to subordinates. It also means donning a variety of hats, including secretary, filing clerk and delivery person if that's what it takes to get the business off the ground.

- **Are you looking for a part-time or full-time operation?**

There is no reason not to approach this enterprise from either perspective, but recognize the ramifications and commitment of each before you proceed.

- **Is this a passion?**

This is very often the reason many people enter the wine business – from the perspective of loving wine and wanting to become more involved in the process. I applaud this motive, as long as it is combined with the real-world considerations outlined above.

## Portfolio — Options and Building

All of these may be legitimate reasons and ones that will serve you well, depending on your goals. If you are looking for a part-time occupation, be prepared to downsize your idea of number of brands and area of distribution. On the other hand, be aware of economies of scale. Due to office set-up, license fees, travel and other expenses, your business will not become cost-effective until you are at a certain volume level. If you don't have wine importing experience, reading this book will put you far ahead of the game. At the very least it will form the building blocks from which you can create your own wine import structure. A couple of other points to consider:

- Do you have the necessary self-discipline for a business that requires adherence to deadlines, such as state reporting, brand registrations and payment of fees and taxes in a timely manner?

- Are you a big picture person or detail-oriented? (You must be both!)

- Can you happily multi-task?

In other words, be prepared for coordinating container consolidation, submitting applications for label approval, keeping up with multiple license renewals, following government regulations regarding every aspect of wine, communicating with distributors, maintaining inventory levels and more…all at the same time.

Most importantly, if this is something you feel excited about, if your dream is to blanket the country with the next *Two Buck Chuck (Charles Shaw),* or source the unsung, artisanal finds of the wine world and lovingly hand sell each bottle, this may happen. Who's to say it cannot? Certainly not those who would seek to discourage you.

You may have uncovered that rare gem on a trip to Bordeaux or the Loire Valley and would love to make it available to wine devotees back home. Perhaps you have a passion for Argentine malbec or roussanne from the Côtes du Rhône and want to rush out and build a niche portfolio with all the distinctive qualities of your discoveries. But there are far broader, and narrower, considerations in selecting and building your portfolio beyond the initial catalyst that triggers you to consider a career, or adventure, as a wine importer. It would be helpful to examine that impetus within the framework of the various factors that can absolutely mean the difference between a financially viable, commercial entity and an expensive assortment of wines to add to your own cellar.

Let's say you have already decided exactly what type of wines you want to bring in and their origin, based on favorite vacations, palate preference or wines you enjoyed representing when you sold to retailers for a state distributor. There is nothing wrong with this approach. It is the way many highly profitable companies began. First and foremost, you should be excited about what you represent, just as in anything you undertake in life. Without passion, this will not be much fun and is far less likely to succeed and fulfill. But let's drill down a bit deeper and examine factors that may help you make alternate decisions, expand your thinking, or confirm your own choices, as you put together a workable portfolio.

# Sourcing Options

Some of these considerations would be:

### ❖A small collection of large brands or a large collection of small brands

When considering the overall makeup of your portfolio, the number of brands isn't necessarily the first decision you will make, but normally one brand does not generate sufficient interest from your prospective customers, nor sufficient income for you. Unless, of course, you have the great fortune to stumble upon a situation that proves to be the exception –a large production winery with many desirable wines, great reviews and impressive pricing. Or a high volume brand with established U.S. distribution that is looking for a new importer. Otherwise, this is all about how you want to spend your time, what interests you most and in general terms what you want your portfolio to look like. Sourcing small production gems from remote vineyard regions may be right up your alley, whereas someone else is all about landing a couple of big brand potentials and concentrating on building them towards large scale national distribution. This speaks somewhat to your personality and your long-range ambitions as well.

- **Specialization in one country - what does that represent to you**

If you choose to focus on France, for example, because elegant and restrained old world wines appeal to you personally, should this be limited to one of either Burgundy, Bordeaux, Loire Valley or Alsace, or encompass the whole country? Would you be able to find sufficient production from each region to complete a well-rounded selection? Are vintages in that one area so unpredictable that it is unlikely you will be able to procure adequate wine each season to make this a going concern? Undoubtedly, your endeavor should be a passion, you should represent what you believe in and enjoy, but presumably your ultimate goal is to build a thriving business as a successful importer.

- **Appreciation for the wines from that country, its regions and its classifications**

Using France, (although a particularly rigid example of vineyard designations, the principle could certainly apply to other countries), do you understand terms like *Appellation d'Origine Contrôlée* (AOC), or more commonly known as *Appellation Contrôlée* (AC) and their strict compliance laws regulating everything from vineyard to label specifications? Are you familiar with vintage conditions, relevant *terroir*, varietal and style that typify the finest offerings of the region? These would all be important considerations in successfully selecting, pricing and representing wine from that, and any other, locale.

Figure 1.1 Early morning overlooking a vineyard

❖ What about one hemisphere?

This can be a portfolio specialization decision, meaning a way to specialize in the regions of one hemisphere, still allowing you the diversification of different countries. When producers are within a reasonable distance, it can also help defray travel or container consolidation costs in putting together various brands by transporting to one origin port. Sourcing from "new world" or "old world" will tend to differentiate the wines as representative of particular styles. Not that either hemisphere produces one-dimensional wines – far from it – but it can be useful as a way to characterize the make-up of your portfolio, if that's your goal.

❖ Should it be made up of many countries or both hemispheres?

This is really another way to look at the previous issue and entails a personal decision based on the same factors and how you wish your portfolio to look, elements of travel, where you warehouse and, perhaps adding another item to that, what is being offered to you that you feel you cannot pass up.

- ❖ **Are you familiar with the up and coming or "hot" regions?**

Entering the market with product that is starting to gain considerable attention or recognized as a "must have" for a wholesaler's book may be a way to jump start your sales and achieve faster distribution, as long as you recognize what the current expectations are of that region in regard to pricing, styles, etc.

A few years ago, Chile was all the rage. While it remains popular, it was so successful at marketing itself at the lower end of the price spectrum that it has experienced difficulty raising the price bar. Argentina, on the other hand, which is one of the "hot" areas as of writing, recognized its niche - full-bodied malbec at great prices - but has managed to diversify its varietal offerings and price levels. Where is the next "hot" region? Can you be there ahead of the curve?

- ❖ **Conversely, have you become aware of what country origins may be over-saturated, ebbing in fashion, or no longer considered good value?**

Australia is the first example that comes to mind. During earlier days of less globalization and travel (pre internet) and a fascination with Australia from afar, it was considered exotic and romantic. Like Chile, it entered the market with inexpensive wines, mostly blends – familiar sounding varieties combined with unfamiliar names. Savvy vintners blended chardonnay with one of the most widely planted (but unfamiliar) white grapes at the time, semillon, and combined cabernet sauvignon with the most widely planted (but also unfamiliar) red grape, shiraz.

Consumers recognized at least one grape in each of the red and white and, priced at a retail of $5.99, were prepared to take a gamble on the wine. As fruit-forward, accessible wines reminiscent of California, these soon found a loyal consumer base and opened the door to other wines, and slightly higher price points.

Figure 1.2 Example of Australia's Unique Vineyard Wildlife

However, it was not until the *Wine Spectator* end of year issue of 1995, that Australian wines were firmly established at the next level. In that issue, Penfolds Grange, which sold for $100 a bottle, was featured on the cover, named *Red Wine of the Year* and awarded 98 points out of 100! Suddenly, Australia was anointed as a world class wine producing country and able to introduce wines to the U.S. consumer at every price point, with considerable acceptance.

The upward trend continued until the exchange rate, palate fatigue with high alcohol shiraz, massive planting, and over-proliferation of brands, particularly the "critter brands" (cute animal labels) that followed Yellow Tail, resulted in the consumer's waning interest in the crowded category. During the recession, high-end Australian wines all but disappeared from shelves.

Fast forward from the time of the first edition of this book and Australian wines at the mid to upper end of the quality and price scale are staging a carefully considered, successful comeback. Managed expectations, broader styles and a regional differentiation message that was missing the first time is the right formula. At a time of renewed distributor interest, this category could be a consideration for your portfolio. An appreciation of its current positioning will help you with your decision.

France is another example of waxing and waning popularity. Although, even during less popular times there are plenty of excellent examples of fine French table wine and lesser known Bordeaux. It requires, however, due diligence to identify those wines from well-represented regions that still offer great quality for good value, at any price level, and identify trends within the industry that do not depend upon region, but more on style, blend or character. Ultimately great wine is great wine, but if you look at Bordeaux en primeur (wine futures) today, it is a much bigger gamble than in the past. The future of futures seems to be in doubt.

❖ **Do you see a niche for esoteric wines, one that makes financial sense?**

What do I mean by that? You may, for example, love Moldovan cabernet, or Mexican carignan, and those would certainly represent a niche, but would a portfolio based on these wines, or these particular countries, be economically feasible? When I first wrote this book, those were the examples I used and I answered, probably not. At this time, Moldova is actually generating interest, and Mexico is vastly improving its vineyard management and winemaking capabilities. On the other hand, there are still other regions that remain relatively unknown, are newly established (thanks, climate change) or are reemerging. If you recognized a region or wineries of South Africa that produced fabulous pinotage, for example, and you saw little of it in the market, then this could be a good starter niche. Not something perhaps on which to build your empire, but South Africa is continuing to build a reputation for wines that are not yet fully realized in this market. Obviously, your own research, and current wine publications, will tell you more about the likelihood that pinotage, or any other grape finds, have either overtaken the market at the time you read this, or already fallen out of favor.

- ❖ **Are they wines that are so new they are likely to or may be misunderstood, or have not yet reached sufficient critical mass to be in demand?**

This overlaps somewhat with the previous area, but relates more to varietals, blend, style or packaging that is completely unfamiliar to the consumer, or may be too confusing for the consumer to appreciate. This can be overcome, as Chile and many others have done, by simplifying the label and westernizing it, if the winery agrees and it seems appropriate. Otherwise, if you love these wines, make them a small part of your portfolio or a hand-sell passion. If you plan on building your success around them and are just starting out, bear in mind it's difficult to be at the vanguard of change and innovation.

- ❖ **Will you have difficulty securing sufficient wines from this region or these brands?**

Something to consider when you've fallen in love with those fabulous dessert wines and discover that they are only made in vintages where botrytis occurs naturally, which the vineyard owner tells you averages every four years. Or the vines are never irrigated and the yields are so low that occasionally there isn't enough to sell. Or vintages all over the appellation are so variable that it is unlikely that you will want to bring in wines each year, because quality is not acceptable. You get the picture.

- ❖ **Will you encounter a language barrier?**

This is certainly something that can be overcome, through the use of agents, brokers, a trade organization, and/or people in the family or area who could serve as interpreter, but I only mention it to cover all those variables that can realistically come into play and may end up being a factor you would prefer to avoid.

- What impact does or might the exchange rate have on your purchases (based on historical, current and anticipated global trends)?

At the time of the first edition of this book (2010), the Euro and Australian and New Zealand dollars were all trading high against the American dollar. It is now back to historical norms of around 0.70 to 0.75 AUD to USD. This makes importing more desirable at a time when the category is recalibrating. The Euro was at around 1.4 in recent years, but has been back down to 1.1 Euro to the USD. If either one increases, does this mean you should stay away from all of Europe and most of the Southern Hemisphere? Of course not. This will change as the global currencies wax and wane. But be prepared to factor in fluctuating or increasing exchange rates into the price, or choose a region that represents the best value or most stable currency to you. Nothing can erode a margin – and your profit - faster than the exchange rate.

- Must each wine in each brand represent a superlative quality level, or are you more concerned with representing a region or country?

This is a subjective decision and not one based on what is correct or advisable. It speaks to branding, to some degree, which we will address later. It also takes into consideration your own preferences – country, palate, lifestyle, etc.

## QPR – Quality Price Ratio

This has become a key element in wine selection, representation and consumer decisions. To compete with, and rise above, all the brands from around the world already on the shelf, and all the brands on the horizon, your wines must be able to represent really good value. Even better if it can "over deliver." In other words, the sort of wine that makes the distributor or retailer say, "wow, I expected this to be a lot more money." The sort of wine that compels consumers to announce on Instagram, "you should check out what I just came across."

QPR becomes easier to find these days with markedly improved winemaking techniques, modern facilities and knowledgeable vineyard management. Which means wines of comparable quality are also available to everyone else in the field, and it becomes important to determine if your wine represents the best quality for the price *at each level.*

# Packaging

Another key element in the brand selection is packaging, and it cannot be ignored. Although numbers vary depending upon the survey, it has become evident that the vast majority of retail wine purchases are made by women and very often their choice of an unknown wine will be on the basis of overall visual impression. They may have narrowed it down to red or white, price or origin, but given the dizzying array of prospects - over 65,000 SKUs (stock keeping unit), with hundreds introduced every year - it often comes down to packaging or label.

Irrespective of gender, consumers will also often have preconceived notions of how a wine should taste, based on packaging. Items that will influence selection, even subliminally, are:

- bottle shape
- bottle quality – weight, feel, punt, etc.
- label graphics
- name
- back label story
- capsule
- quality of label
- cohesiveness of design and overall package

## Initial Considerations

First and foremost, a label must be eye-catching and not, as one distributor told me years ago when he declined one of my brands, "shelf recessive." In other words, not only did it not stand out on the shelf, it actually receded from view.

However, this does not mean eye-popping, garish and discordant. It cannot just demand attention. It has to be *meaningful* attention. Does it say fabulous at $5.99, but it's actually a $40 retail wine? Are the label graphics artfully blind embossed with gold leaf on linen weave, on a high shouldered bottle with a deep punt, at a retail of $5.99? Doesn't that sound more like the $40 wine? Aside from the expense involved (I exaggerated the example for the sake of making a point) consumers want any one or a combination of fun, bright, quirky, edgy, trendy and daring at $5.99. They also want a pronounceable name or at least a memorable label that's easy to describe when they return to the wine store and say they'd like "another bottle of that wine I got last time." Consider Rosemount's ubiquitous diamond label, Rex Goliath's *47 lb Rooster* or in the case of a name, *Fat Bastard,* one of the bestselling wines from France, originally because of the shock value of the name. It doesn't hurt that the wine, in each case, is sufficiently enjoyable to keep coming back for more. In fact, it is essential.

You will find that some wineries will be wedded to their dreadful label and cling to it as they would to a cherished family member. I have personal experience with these reactions, and more:

- *It's been in the family for generations,*
- *It's the ancestral crest.*
- *The Europeans have been behind it since we introduced it to the UK and Switzerland in 1988. (Translated as: it was old-fashioned then and it's now hopelessly out of style)*
- *We just spent considerable money redesigning the label and absolutely love it.*

More importantly, do *you* love it? Can you see it working in the U.S. market? At the risk of painting with too broad a brush, European labels have traditionally been more, well, traditional. Americans have embraced innovative and out-of-the-box for some time, almost to an extreme, and what works in Europe is no indication of what will work here.

Figure 1.3 A Story in Labels (Courtesy of Journey Wines)

The label must simply be something *you* feel can work. You don't *have* to love it, but the majority of those you show it to should at least like it. It can follow trends without necessarily being trendy. It can start its own trend even. As long as it's understood, enjoyed and seems to fulfill a reasonable expectation of price point and quality.

The exception to this would be the high end wine that has garnered enough accolades, awards, ratings and cult status they can pretty much do anything they want. The followers of these wines just want the wine.

## Branding – Not Just About the Wine

Branding usually does refer to the wine, or collection of wines under a brand, so the discussion begins there. A brand owner's ultimate goal is for the brand to be recognized and synonymous with something that makes it more desirable than other wines of its ilk, thereby making the job of selling the wine that much easier, with the benefit of image and prestige.

It could be the best of its appellation or varietal, the most food-friendly, the greatest value, the highest rating, the first from that region, the most highly touted. It can be identified with a name: Baron Philippe de Rothschild or Francis Ford Coppola. It can be the first New Zealand sauvignon blanc to rate above 90 in *Wine Spectator*. All these things sell and, if the brand continues to do its job, it will sell on the basis of those identifiers for a long time to come. It will even sell through variable vintages and wine quality that isn't quite up to scratch and ratings that occasionally disappoint. As long as the image remains intact and it can consistently perform to a certain level, or a perceived level. Possibly because of the confusing selection of wines on restaurant lists or retail shelves, it's an area to appropriately apply the old maxim, "there's no such thing as bad publicity." I've seen people seek out wines long after their star has faded - quality has deteriorated, because grapes are sourced instead of formerly estate grown, the winemaker has left, or the price has gone through the stratosphere - simply because of name brand familiarity.

Branding, for the purpose of this section, refers to you or your portfolio, or both. Are *you* the expert on petite sirah, riesling, viognier or malbec? Can you be? Do you want to be? Can you become the go-to person for esoteric, well-made varietals and blends? Wines that individually are not going to make up a successful wine business, but collectively start to build gravitas for your portfolio and you, as the acknowledged, savvy source of such wines.

Cool climate wines could be a branded portfolio specialty, or wines from around the world under $10, or ratings over 90 points in major U.S.-based magazines. Broad selections or great quality finds from Austria or Eastern Bloc countries or a concentration on small islands (Tasmania, Waiheke, Sicily, Sardinia, e.g.). Make up your own category, but continue to research and ask questions. It may seem like the best idea since sliced bread to you, only to find out that no one really cares if you're an expert on Eiswein.

But if you truly want to stand out, then branding might well be the way. It's an option you can explore down the road, but it can also be a goal as you put together your first portfolio.

## Balancing the Portfolio

Even if you've decided on specialization, think further about their overall salability. It would be difficult to stock your offerings with only wines above $30, or all cabernet sauvignon. A balanced, diverse portfolio can still be a specialized one that aims for branding, or limits its scope to certain regions.

If a distributor is looking at your price list and sees all wines of a particular price point or varietal, or too similar in style to differentiate, then you are effectively competing against yourself – cannibalizing your own portfolio. A distributor will not, no matter how desirable or highly rated each wine is individually, buy them all. If that were the case, then they would be asking their salespeople to do the same thing – present wines that compete against one another. It's not cost-effective and it wastes time. There is no time to waste in today's wine business.

*SUMMARY* — Bearing in mind what you want to represent and accomplish, aim for an exciting portfolio that offers a range of styles and price points to the distributor. Specialize in New Zealand if you wish, but include not just sauvignon blancs from Marlborough, but also pinot noirs from Central Otago and Martinborough, dessert wines from Waiheke, organic wines from Gisborne and Bordeaux blends from Gimblett Gravels. This way you are giving your potential customer an intriguing and well considered range of wines from which they can choose a broad selection.

# My Story

I will remind you occasionally of my early days as a new importer to illustrate a point and occasionally as a means for you to understand how easily one can make many different rookie mistakes I am hopeful you will avoid.

I have also added client stories from my consulting practice to provide another point of view on the subject.

One of the first shipments I brought in was an entire container of bone dry, moderately expensive Hunter Valley (Australia) semillon - around 800 cases. If you think bone dry, moderately expensive Hunter Valley semillon might be a difficult sell now, consider 1992. I believe it retailed for around $20. My motivation was this:

1. Extended terms of payment (very attractive for a new business with limited resources).
2. A winemaker held in high esteem who consistently won national awards and gold medals for his wines.
3. The wine's exceptional quality.
4. Varietal characteristics that exemplified the grape.
5. Introducing to the U.S. a varietal that was synonymous with the Hunter Valley (semillon was one of Australia's two most widely planted white grapes).

What could not be overcome was this:

1. Americans often *talk dry, but drink sweet*, but even more so back then, and this wine was almost devoid of residual sugar.
2. A price point that was way beyond anything the U.S. consumer was accustomed

17

to paying for Australian wines in general and semillon in particular.

3. No U.S. consumer experience with the grape, and unwillingness to embrace it.

4. Lack of knowledge of Australian regions.

5. Unfamiliarity with Australia's icon winemakers.

I sold three cases to a couple of local Atlanta restaurants, and the rest returned to the vineyard, after collecting warehousing fees for several months. Doing my due diligence in *this market*, (i.e., not the wine's origin country) could have averted this disaster.

## My Client's Story

Although there is an upcoming chapter about the mesh of personalities between importer and winery, the time to think about your own personality and what facet of the wine industry might suit you best is before you begin. Several years ago, a client came to me wanting to set up an importing business along with a wine store/tasting room, stocked with wines exclusively of his country of birth. After I explained the rules against having both a retail and wholesale license, he decided the store/tasting room would be his focus. The first obstacle to this was his desire to bring in wines that were not currently available, and stocking the store with one monolithic category. The bigger issue starting to take shape before me was how he saw his future, and future of the enterprise.

My client represented a not uncommon type of potential wine industry person: someone who has a passion for wine and perhaps some connections, but very little or no experience in the industry. To get to the heart of his vision, I asked him if he liked to travel, meet new people, actively recruit potential new business and educate others on the wines he would be representing. Or did he prefer to stay in one place, have people come to him and conduct business in one place? Oh, definitely the first one. Ok then, perhaps a store/tasting room is not quite the personality fit we were looking for. Today, this client has a rewarding career as an importer.

# CHAPTER 2

# BUILDING A BUSINESS MODEL

At this point, take a deep breath and look at this as a business, because to make it a success will require an investment of money, time and physical resources, and before you consider bringing in your first bottle you must build your foundation. First, decide what sort of an entity you will be.

## Company, Structure, Personnel, Partners

You must first decide how to structure your business and whether to bring in investors and partners. It can be an LLC, sole proprietorship, C Corporation, Partnership or S Corp. The decision is yours. There are many reasons for the choice of specific legal structure, and these are quite subjective, so I'm not going to attempt to advise you on this. They *are* decisions that have to be made with considerable forethought. If you have partners and investors, e.g., who will own the majority share, and what will be the delineation of roles? Even a "silent partner" often wants their say.

Based on my own experience, if you bring an investor as a working partner into your own endeavor, it is essential that they have either been in the wine business previously or have more than a rudimentary understanding of how it operates. Many of the tried-and-true business principles from the corporate world simply don't apply here, as much as the successful CEO from an unrelated sector might want to apply them. Additionally, the wine industry has changed dramatically in a relatively short time, and you must be flexible and continue to change with it. Someone who has worked within the industry will recognize this and be willing to make those adjustments with you, instead of trying to impose their own, unrelated, experience on your business model.

If a shareholder has over 50% stake in the company, they have, if they desire, *all* the say, not just a majority of the say. Should they wish to go down one path and you another, you lose. If they decide to bring in too much wine at too high a cost, spend money on staffing you don't need, guess who prevails? If you have confidence in your partner/investor and they bring so much to the table that you are happy to give up control, so be it. But make sure this is your carefully calculated decision beforehand, and not a shocking reality once you are in the midst of your venture.

Naming the business should take into consideration what you will become, not what you think you are now. To name it Joe's Fine Wines from Argentina is pretty limiting, even if you think you'll only ever want to represent fine wines from Argentina or never give up ownership. Similarly, calling yourself Hot Wines from Hot Regions may sound as if you have a handle on trends, but trust me, trends change in this arena too.

## Office Requirements

It is entirely possible for you to conduct your business from an office in your home, providing state laws allow it (some don't so please check). The wine will, by law or necessity, be stored elsewhere and, as this is a wholesale operation, there will be no retail traffic or surprise visitors. Just be sure your home office has privacy, a door to close, sufficient room to accommodate two people, and doesn't share space with the kid's game room or any other function of the house. It will be disruptive to you, and home noise will bleed over into professional conversations. It is one thing to have an office at home, quite another to let your suppliers and customers know they are competing for attention with the dog and X Box.

Initially, in a small enterprise, it can all be handled by one person. Part-time assistance, at least, is very helpful, especially if you are out of the office or traveling, but it is feasible to start alone if finances or personal inclination dictates. In either case, the size of the office can be reasonably small. The equipment you'll need will comprise:

- File cabinets - This is not entirely a paperless business. You must keep physical records in the event of a local license office audit, signed contracts, licenses, invoices, tasting notes and so on.

- Computer – either one laptop to take with you when you travel or one PC that remains in the office for personnel and one laptop for you.

- Dedicated phone line for the business – only really necessary if you have someone in the office handling calls for you while on the road; otherwise, your cell phone is sufficient.

- Copier and scanner– Most documents will be scanned and emailed. There are extremely efficient, inexpensive laser machines available today.

- Programs—Word, Excel and Quick Books, Adobe and Microsoft Publishing - Adobe and Microsoft Publishing are purchases that can be held off for a short while, if need be, but are extremely helpful in both creating and editing labels and POS (Point of Sale) material.

- Wine racks.

Wine racks? Didn't I just say the wine is stored elsewhere? Yes, but you need to organize the samples you'll receive to evaluate, and those you'll have shipped to you (by the 12 or 6 bottle case) from the warehouse to send to prospective customers and for publication review. Devise a system to categorize the cases that aren't in racks, from which you'll pull to replenish the racks or send out directly. Generally, have at least a case of each new item or new vintage sent immediately to you from the warehouse on container arrival. However, please be mindful that most state licenses do not allow for wine storage in your licensed office premises, so please factor that into your sample storage. Personally, I don't see how it is possible to have no wine at all in your office, either for personal evaluation or to send to potential distributors, but I must recommend compliance with state laws.

If you decide you can't or don't want to work from home, or are planning for the future, office space that can realistically handle even large-scale national distribution can be conducted in premises comprising:

- ✓ Reception – entry, waiting room or working space
- ✓ Two cubicles in a general space – one for compliance and one for invoicing/bookkeeping
- ✓ Conference room – doubles as meeting space and tasting room
- ✓ Your private office
- ✓ Storage room for wine samples

## Geography Decision : National or Regional

It's a good idea to consider what you want your business to look like, both to you and your potential supplier (the winery).

Do you intend to bring in wine just for distribution in your own state? Are you planning on blazing trails through all 50 states as soon as possible? The Federal Basic Permit (your import license) entitles you to import as an exclusive agent for the entire country. It doesn't require you to identify your intended market to obtain your license.

However, how you intend to operate impacts your business model. It could also impact the goals of the winery or vineyard you choose to represent (or have approached) and this should be communicated to them at the outset.

For instance, a winery may already have an importer for New York and New Jersey, but wish to broaden their distribution and add only a region, say Ohio, Indiana and Kentucky. That may work well for you, because you are in Indiana, but in general you may feel constrained by this arrangement. Illinois is adjacent to Indiana, and you may have contacts there, or because you intended to represent all brands in your portfolio for the whole country. National importing used to be the norm, but both my recent experience with clients and a more intimate understanding of the practices of other countries suggest otherwise. Some brand owners either already have distribution in some areas, as noted, or want to hedge their bets by doling out segments of the country to each new importer. One winery I've encountered keeps adding a state as their importer adds distribution, one state at a time.

If you really believe in the brand, always keep the lines of communication open. The importer covering New York and New Jersey may go out of business, fail to deliver on their sales or decide to give up the brand because it conflicts with something else in their portfolio. It happens all the time.

## Resources – Time and Money

The answer to how much time and money this will take cannot be arrived at through one formula. There are many variables to consider and evaluated as part of the whole picture. To a great extent it will depend on your personal aspirations, plus time and capital constraints. My goal in this book is to assist you, with as much expertise as possible, in the decision making and implementation required in setting up a viable import business. I hope it will read in a straightforward and easy-to-understand manner, but I would be remiss if I made it sound simple to execute and something to be undertaken as a frivolous diversion.

Therefore, I would suggest that importing is not necessarily something to be considered as a part-time occupation, unless you are doing this in conjunction with your state wholesale operation; that is, if you are importing wine solely to sell within your own local wine distribution company. Or if you are building the import company while working concurrently at another profession entirely, to keep the income flowing as you establish your wine business. As a long term prospect, there are too many licenses, logistical considerations, volume of wine, warehousing and other considerations that require *some* economies of scale, however minimal, to derive a profit from simply importing part-time. I believe you can be a part-time broker, distributor, retailer or salesperson, because all of these can be limited in all the ways that importing cannot. Limiting your business and limiting your scope is well within your purview, but if you truly wish to become a wine importer, treating it as a hobby or something in which to dabble will, in my opinion, result in poor results. Among many other considerations, alcohol is a heavily regulated industry and requires attention to reporting, license renewals, an understanding of laws and payment of duty and taxes. These activities become second nature to someone who is actively engaged in a flourishing wine company, but become onerous to someone who only occasionally has the time to devote to the pursuit.

There are still many other options for the aspiring importer. If you work well with others, then putting together a team of like-minded people who each bring value to the table, and perhaps needed capital, will spread the responsibility to the extent that your position may be occupied in a somewhat part-time fashion. The downside is that your share of the profits will most likely reflect this diminished role, unless the team you put together is utilizing *your* capital and you remain a majority shareholder.

Irrespective of the number of individuals running the company or occupying certain roles, or if you are doing it all yourself, there are certain overarching to consider in your initial and ongoing financial outlay:

- volume of wine on each container
- freight, duty and taxes
- quantity of wine to be stored
- warehousing fees
- licensing and brand registrations (varies by state)
- salaries, commission and taxes
- office overhead
- travel
- sample usage
- marketing and promotion
- insurance
- furniture, fixtures and equipment
- domestic freight (air, ground)

These are requisite expense categories, but the actual dollar amount of each and the extent to which you utilize various resources will be up to your business model, your aspirations and possibly your financial limitations. Preparing a business plan and budget incorporating these items will give you a much clearer picture of the financial outlay you can expect at the outset and moving forward, with adjustments for your own circumstances and goals.

# Warehouse

Where to warehouse is another decision affected somewhat by variables, covered below, and one to be made sooner, rather than later. This will determine where the container will arrive, what licenses you need, and how much it will cost.

**Geographical area** – if your licensed premises (your office) is on the East Coast and your immediate area of distribution will be New Jersey, New York, Connecticut and Pennsylvania, then warehousing at a licensed, bonded facility in New Jersey, where wine from various sources is stored, becomes a logical first choice for you. Containers regularly dock at Port Newark/Elizabeth, for example, unload and truck a short distance to area warehouses, minimizing transit time, cost and handling. Your distributors will be familiar with the warehouse location, able to pick up less expensively, and can consolidate orders with others at the same warehouse and replenish quickly when they run out. You won't have to wait as long for samples as when they are shipped from the West Coast and, if desired, you can visit the warehouse to interview the principals or for periodic physical inventory.

The caveat to this is that warehouses are generally more expensive on the East Coast, and this can complicate your search.

Figure 2.1 Groskopf Warehouse, Sonoma, California

Alternatively, if you live on the West Coast, or in a nearby state, warehousing in Northern California makes sense. Oakland is a shipping gateway to this region. Again, you select a licensed, bonded warehouse where distributors are as familiar with the name and location as they are with their own. They presumably have trucks going out to Napa or Sonoma once a week, or every two weeks, to pick up other wines stored at the same warehouse, and are well acquainted with the warehouse routines and requirements.

If you live anywhere in the mid or southern regions of the country, the decision can be dictated by where the majority of your distribution will take place or which wine region you source from, but should, in my opinion, be limited to a coastal choice.

The exception might be if you have concentrated your distribution in one state, or distributors are ordering by the container. Then the wine goes where the sales are.

**Wine sourcing regions** – where you intend to source your wine from will likely have a bearing on where you warehouse. In addition to your own geographical position, if your imported wines all come from Europe or South America, both of which are closer to the East Coast, it may be cost-effective to warehouse there. The transit time is shorter and less expensive. If the wines are from the Southern Hemisphere (Australia, New Zealand, South Africa) they are closer to the West Coast and for the same reasons it makes sense to warehouse there. Decide on the basis of both economic feasibility and personal choice.

**Business model** – if national distribution is your aim and you are building up significant business in states on both coasts, then warehousing in two places, one east and one west, could make sense for you, but this may be phase two of your plan. If you live on the West Coast and have a contract with a national chain with strong store business up and down the Eastern seaboard then you may choose to warehouse on the East Coast. The other alternative is to use that national contract, and a volume commitment from the chain, as a compelling argument to persuade distributors in each state to warehouse the wine for you, since they will have to ship directly to the chain's stores anyway.

**Fees** – nothing can eat up a margin faster than unanticipated expenses. All warehouses charge monthly storage, by the case. In addition, there will be a minimum charge each month – the "floor" – regardless of number of cases stored. This can be significant and require a large volume in storage at all times just to make this minimum, or your per case charge can go from affordable to exorbitant.

There are many other fees, including container unloading, in and out (when wine comes in or goes out), bill of lading, repackaging, rush orders, sending samples via UPS or FedEx, including a charge for the box and inserts, and other services that may be offered on demand, such as applying special labels to bottles (UPC codes, e.g.) or repackaging partial cases.

**Final questions** - Determine if the warehouse has a policy regarding returned goods (from the distributor), and whether they accept responsibility for breakages, incorrect vintages shipped or mistakes in general and how they handle them. Good, experienced warehouses will have online, private access for the importer to check inventory levels, shipped invoices, pending shipments and many other useful online tools for you to manage your warehouse business, in real time. In my opinion, this has become a barometer by which you determine the professionalism and transparency of the warehouse.

Make sure the warehouse is licensed as a wine warehouse facility. Not only will this determine the level of experience they have with this product, but also whether the warehouse is temperature-controlled, has sufficient access for wholesale trucking pickup and is open at the appropriate times.

Contact other customers for references.

Your relationship with the warehouse is one of the most important in your wine importing business and it should be an enduring one. It is far too expensive to store all your wine at one facility and have to move it to another and incur those charges all over again. I have warehoused at the same facility since 1993, and still recommend them today. The hallmark of our relationship is trust, respect and give and take. No relationship is perfect and the one you forge with your warehouse, by virtue of the volume of transactions, will be fraught with frustration, the occasional misunderstanding and mistakes. But everyone experiences these and it's the combination of realistic rates, quality of service, resolution of the missteps and how they treat their customer that counts.

*SUMMARY* — Aspects of the business that initially do not have anything to do with wine require deliberation and planning to effect a positive outcome for your business model. No one way is the right way. It has to suit your style and your circumstances. Making the most practical warehousing decision early on can actually keep the sales momentum going. Whichever option you choose, the warehouse should be affordable, responsive, on either coast, and readily recognizable to the wholesalers and truckers who will be coming to pick up your product. It should be licensed according to the laws of that state and bonded in the event you need to put goods into customs bond.

## My Story

I established my first import business in Atlanta, Georgia. Not having a clue as to how to proceed, I began by seeking out warehouses in Atlanta. Having secured one, I alerted my first two distributors, one in New Jersey and one in Georgia. The Georgia distributor was delighted because they could send a local truck to pick up small amounts whenever they wished, generating multiple invoices and incurring unnecessary charges at the warehouse for me, and it did not require the distributor to make a long-term commitment. The New Jersey distributor was horrified, as was every other distributor who followed. If they wanted my wine – and fortunately for me, this was an era of great interest in Australia and very few brands – they paid for the privilege with the inconvenience of diverting an entire truck to Atlanta solely to pick up my three or four brands, and sacrificed some of their margin, or increased the price of the wine. In turn, my margin was shrinking by paying more for a small, local warehouse and for the container to be trucked overland from California. I quickly learned that to remain financially viable and geographically competitive I had to choose a warehouse that met the criteria I've outlined in this chapter.

# My Client's Story

An east coast client bringing in his first shipment of wine had contacted a very conveniently located east coast warehouse for a quote. This was a well-known, temperature-controlled, wine storage facility, which was convenient for distributors and appropriately licensed. The quote was a not unreasonable monthly minimum, so the importer agreed to contract with this warehouse. The gaping hole in the communication between importer and warehouse was that the shipment was only 56 6 packs, which he intended to pick up within the month and he didn't have any timetable for importing more. The client thought it was a one month fee for the convenience of this arrangement. The warehouse, on the other hand, was quoting him a monthly minimum for a three year contracted commitment, which meant this new importer would be paying thousands of dollars for empty warehouse space. Once this was clarified, the importer had the pallet delivered to a local distributor with whom he had a relationship. No minimums, no contracts required. The importer could then test the market with the wines on this pallet, which was his intention all along, and contemplate the structure of his future business needs without warehouse budget constraints. In this case, the client/importer knew he was conducting an expensive exercise, which he had factored into his startup budget, but had not counted on warehouse contracts. Unfamiliarity with the nature of wine warehousing could have been his downfall.

# CHAPTER 3

# LICENSING, PERMITS AND DEFINITIONS

With all the detailed instructions and tips I have included, this section may appear overwhelming at first and have you chomping at the bit to get to the less mundane aspects. If you break down each piece in order, you'll find it will flow easily for you. You are building the foundation brick by solid brick, until you have a sturdy importing business structure on which to start layering your own individual design and flair. We simply have to remember that alcohol is a heavily regulated, closely monitored industry and adhering to these regulations allows us the freedom to do the part we really care about.

## The Importer in the Distribution Chain

I felt it was important to introduce this subject before we go any further, because so often to the uninitiated the term "importer" becomes indistinguishable from "distributor" and some use it interchangeably. In the U.S., the titles are as different as vigneron is from importer or distributor is from retailer, and must be understood from the outset. That's not to say an importer cannot also be a distributor – under certain circumstances – but to understand their roles, we must look at them in their discrete form.

**Importer** is the term used to define the licensed person or company who directly liaises with the winery (in most instances) and is the only entity authorized to import alcohol into the U.S.

**Distributor** is the licensed company in a given state that is authorized to buy alcohol from an importer and sell it to a retail store, restaurant, hotel, grocery store, casino or chain within their state boundaries. They are also known as a wholesaler or wholesale distributor.

**Retailer and restaurant** refers to the commercial enterprise that sells to the consumer. This covers all customers of the distributor including hotel, grocery store, casino or chain.

This is what is known as the **three-tier system,** which operates in every state and was written into law after the repeal of Prohibition in the U.S.

Figure 3.1 The three-tier System

The definitions are true no matter what the circumstances, but can be diluted or multiplied in a business model in different circumstances. For example:

- In Control states (discussed later) this model becomes more of a two-tier system, in that the State is both wholesaler and retailer. Although there are variations on this, depending on the state.

- National wholesale chains may appear to circumvent the laws of individual states, when in fact they are adhering to it by establishing brick and mortar businesses in each state in which they do business, and operating as licensed entities within the framework of that state's three-tier system. In many instances, they grow their national network by buying up existing distribution companies, which is again the same concept: a fully independently operated and licensed facility in each state in which they acquire a wholesale business.

- A distributor may choose to import one or more of the products in their portfolio (if the option is available to them) for several reasons: to have more control over a brand in their portfolio, to realize a double margin on a sale, ( i.e., importer > distributor and distributor > retailer), or possibly because they were approached by a winery to import their wines exclusively in that region. Normally, the distributor's general portfolio takes precedence over the importing aspect, because they choose to limit their importing to their local area. In other words, they will not be searching for distributors outside of their home state. It is up to the foreign supplier to choose to appoint them as their importer, knowing the limitations of the distribution region.

- An importer can (with a rare state exception) choose to distribute their own products in their home state, by applying for the correct licenses and establishing an office, warehouse and distribution system – i.e., sales and delivery mechanism – and paying the appropriate taxes. Generally, an importer will choose to distribute within their home state for some of the same reasons as the wholesaler, but their primary focus will be the inverse of that of the wholesaler who devotes a portion of their portfolio to importing, because when you are primarily an importer, then national or regional distribution will require the greater attention. If the importer has agreed to take on and import a brand for national distribution, expectations from the foreign producer will definitely be higher. They will expect you to appoint distributors in multiple states.

In California, for example, an importer can hold licenses for all tiers of the three-tier system and more. An importer may apply to the ABC (Alcoholic Beverage Control) for a retail license to sell from a bricks and mortar store, if they meet the state requirements. Additionally, or separately, an importer can sell over the internet, with the appropriate retail license. So, in effect, an import company can be its own self-contained entity from winery to consumer. But that is California!

> Tied-House Laws relate back to England and laws that were put into effect that regulated the sales of alcoholic beverages in bars, pubs and taverns, where the ownership of the entity was "tied" to a specific supplier of alcoholic beverages.

According to Wikipedia:

*Under the current post-Prohibition, alcoholic beverage regulatory regime, tied houses are generally illegal in the United States. Tied-house restrictions have been construed as forbidding virtually any form of vertical integration in the alcoholic beverage industry.*

This is no longer true. There have been numerous challenges to the tied-house laws. For examples, in 2009 legislation overturned these rules in Washington State, and more recently, a law was passed in Colorado to allow alcohol in grocery stores, and chains such as Walmart and Target to sell wine and beer. This was a state that formerly disallowed sales of alcohol where food was sold and vice versa, protecting the liquor stores' business. Signed into law by Gov. John Hickenlooper in June 2016, the Denver Post called it "the biggest change to alcohol sales in Colorado since Prohibition". There will no doubt be more to come as the climate of the wine industry, the business models and the available technology continue to evolve at rapid rates. It would therefore be reckless of me to set out more than a general overview of these laws. You should go to the individual State's websites for the most current legal requirements.

Since this is a book about importing, I am leaving out wineries, which have far greater leeway in many states and licenses that operate differently from an importer's license. Let me repeat this for emphasis, because it is a rule that is most often misinterpreted: *wineries have greater leeway in many states and licenses that operate differently from an importer's license.* In many cases, they are able to have a wholesale operation and a retail tasting room at the winery or off-site. State laws are significantly relaxed when it comes to interstate shipping to consumers by wineries. Do not confuse this with the ability, or lack thereof, of importers to operate within the three-tier system and ship to consumers.

## Necessary Licenses and Other licensing to Consider Now

### EIN – Employer Identification Number

This can be completed and submitted online at www.irs.gov and is a prerequisite for your import license. It is also essential for opening a bank account as any entity other than a sole proprietor, for which you can use your social security number. Obtaining an EIN is an easy, fast process.

### The Federal Importer Basic Permit "Basic Permit"

This is the first of the industry licenses you will require and the most important.

Even though at this stage it feels a bit like putting the cart before the horse, in that you may not yet have any wineries in mind for your venture, TTB (Alcohol and Tobacco Tax Trade Bureau) requires that you identify a winery willing to export to you before you can apply for a license, described as a **Letter of Intent with Foreign Suppliers**. I haven't found any examples of **Letter of Intent** on the website, but here is a perfectly acceptable, simple format. It should be on letterhead and signed by the winery or vineyard principal.

---

(Winery letterhead)

(date)

To Whom It May Concern:

It is our intention to supply Superior Wine Company, Inc. with wines from our company, Best Wines Vineyard in the U.S., pending all approvals.

Should you wish to verify this statement or request any further information, please do not hesitate to contact the undersigned.

Sincerely,

Pierre Marchand

Managing Director

---

Figure 3.2 Letter of Intent with Foreign Suppliers

It's a very general requirement, so it's possible to still be in discussions with a winery that may not ultimately sell to you and yet request a letter from them to enable you to obtain your Basic Permit. It does not obligate them to export to you, nor obligate you to purchase their wine, but simply states an intention. TTB just wants to know you're serious and intend to operate as an alcohol importer within a reasonable period of time.

TTB's website is straightforward and (somewhat) easy to navigate. The layout seems to be updated frequently and is now so chockablock with information, that it might be a bit dizzying. Originally, TTB had specific forms to complete and submit by mail. Then, those same forms were uploaded online, some of it in dropdown question and answer format. Although TTB does have these same instructions and forms on their website as examples of what will be asked, completing and uploading these forms is no longer required so please save yourself the trouble. All instructions are part of the registration and application process online. Requests for information, and some necessary uploaded documents, will be made as you proceed, depending upon the latest modifications they are making to simplify the process and which entity you use to establish your business. To emphasize, there is no "right" organizational choice: LLC, C Corp, S Corp, Partnership or Sole Proprietor. These choices are dictated by your own situation. Further advice, if necessary, should be from your attorney.

Whichever legal entity you choose, the essential first step (before EIN and Letter of Intent) is to make the choice. Not only will this determine the type of application you complete, but you will also have to reapply if the type of entity changes, so consider carefully. Long ago, when I first obtained my Basic Permit, there was extensive background checking, even extended through Interpol, because I had lived in several different countries. This may now be done behind the scenes to a minor degree, but I doubt it. TTB is overworked and understaffed these days, and everything is streamlined. Line up your sources of funding, even if it's a loan from Aunt Millie or the proceeds from a home equity line of credit, but there is no set amount of required initial investment. It just has to be sufficient to enable you to purchase wine and pay for initial expenses. This can fall into a modest category of volume and sales projections, depending upon your own situation. They recently reinstated a phone interview with the applicant, something they hadn't done in years. But this is a routine interview that shouldn't alarm anyone.

TTB can still tell you that processing of the application takes 90 days, but is generally only a matter of a week or so. It will depend upon TTB's caseload There is no route to expedite the process. Incomplete applications will not be processed until complete. At this writing, applications that are absent the required documentation will be considered abandoned after 15 days. It's best to start prepared.

The Federal Basic Permit is required to clear samples, as well as containers; therefore, unless you use someone else's license in the interim to clear them for you, have yours in place when requesting new vintages or first wines from your prospective wineries, vineyards or foreign brokers.

If you intend to sell domestic wines or wines you did not import, you will also need a Wholesaler's Permit. Both can be applied for at the same time on form 5100.4. There is currently no fee for the initial application.

The Basic Permit licenses your entity and *place* of business. Therefore, if your company configuration changes, e.g., from a sole proprietorship to a partnership or you form a corporation, or add or subtract members or stockholders, you will need to apply for and obtain a new license. The good news is that your existing license will remain in place (barring anything unforeseen) while this transition takes place.

## COLAs Online

When you receive your Basic Permit, you should apply for access to online submission of your COLA (Certificate of Label Application) on the TTB website and scroll down to "Create COLAs Online Account". TTB is constantly tweaking and overhauling its site, but at this writing, TTB has now consolidated all access to permits, formulas, registrations and label submissions on the same home page on their new website.

It's a simple one screen "form", there is no charge and there are no other requirements. A successful application will generate a "submission identification number", which you can give to someone on the phone if you need to follow up.

In the first edition of this book, I advised new importers to waste no time in registering, because it took an average of thirty days to receive approval, and this was potentially a thirty-day delay in starting a COLA application. However, as of writing, the average processing time is 2.5 days and I believe many applications are processed in one day. Applications may also be mailed to TTB's offices in Washington, DC, but unless you do not have access to a computer, I see no earthly reason to submit an application that will take longer and have no acknowledgment of receipt, nor indication of processing times.

TTB's website will not support older browsers, on the basis that they contain unacceptable vulnerabilities that can be exploited by malware. If your browser is not current you simply will not have access, so if this is a problem you encounter, check your browser.

Access to COLAs Online, allows you to begin submitting *online* label submissions (as opposed to paper) and this is now the only reasonable way to submit applications. The technology has been available for at fifteen years or more. I started using it from its inception and it instantly made my life easier. Prior to that, submissions were handwritten on a paper form, to which you glued actual labels or legible, full color label graphics and sent snail mail. Unless you incurred additional (unnecessary) expense sending each application via FedEx, you were left wondering whether TTB (or BATF at that time) had received it and what happened to it. I mention this here to both give historical perspective and to avoid confusion for you in the event you wonder whether label applications are best done online or via mail. As with the Basic Permit application, paper forms are still available on ttb.gov.

I don't want to get ahead of myself by further discussion of label approvals at this stage, but registering for COLAs Online as soon as you receive your Basic Permit is the right order in the sequence.

## Power of Attorney (POA)

There are a number of instances where a POA can be an asset to your business. Some optional uses of a POA are to outsource tasks, for example:

- authorize a compliance specialist to submit a Basic Permit application on your behalf.
- submit your label submissions via COLAs Online
- submit formulas, where required, in advance of obtaining a COLA

However, the essential use of a POA is to allow airfreight samples to be cleared through customs utilizing your newly minted Federal Basic Permit number, once your Permit is approved. I am not recommending any particular company, but DHL and FedEx are the most common carriers and it would be useful for you to contact them as soon as you have your Basic Permit to complete paperwork that allows them to clear for you. DHL and FedEx will also require a copy of your Basic Permit and state license. Once this paperwork is accessible throughout their systems (and you have to be patient; they don't all seem to talk to one another within the same company), the POA will expedite any shipments you receive. Otherwise, crucial samples may be held up indefinitely at customs and even returned to sender - not a good way to begin a relationship.

Additionally, FedEx will not allow you to ship domestically if you are not a licensed importer, with the appropriate state license. Once you establish both you will be able to submit an application for an account and begin to ship to potential distributors within the US.

## Continuous Bond

At some point, you will have to decide whether it makes sense to incur the expense of a "single bond" when clearing goods through US Customs and Border Protection or a "continuous bond" A single bond means a bond charge on each shipment, whether air or ocean freight. The continuous bond is an annual fee that allows you to clear multiple shipments at no additional cost. The purchase of an annual continuous bond may be premature at this stage, but I mention it as a consideration. If you are receiving multiple shipments of samples or anticipate a business in which you can realistically expect several containers of alcohol a year, because you have established chain business or have a specific, broad market business model, then it is much more economical to start out with a continuous bond and immediately start saving. If not, however, I suggest waiting. A continuous bond is obtained through an insurance company, freight forwarder or customs broker. I suggest comparing a couple of quotes. The cost should be no more than a few hundred dollars, but since the actual bond is identical there is no reason not to save money by shopping around for the company that charges the least expensive fees to process the bond.

## Home State Licenses

Each state has wildly disparate state licensing requirements, so much so that they are not variations, but appear entirely unrelated. The state in which you are federally licensed will be the state in which you must also comply with their particular regulations. Contact details for each state licensing agency, including links to each of their sites, are available on the TTB site. This is not only a helpful resource for your own state, but for all the states in which you seek to do business, which I will discuss further later. The hyperlink has changed so much, it is one of the reasons why I now have all link resources on my website. State board links also change from time to time, but I believe it is helpful to have them in one list on TTB, as a resource. Going to a state board link that is defunct will usually direct you to the correct site and likewise the phone number. I find it easier to use the TTB site in this way rather than to search the individual states by liquor licensing body. A Google search of each state can, and does, result in accidentally clicking on a non-government site that may charge you for processing your application or providing services above the state license fees.

## California State License

If your product is stored in California, you will be licensed by the California ABC (Alcoholic Beverage Control) to import into and warehouse in the state, irrespective of where you live or where your licensed premises are located. Processing an application for a CA state license takes about 90 days. It is essential that the public wine warehouse you choose is also independently licensed with the CA ABC. California, as with all states, will require that you obtain your Basic Permit before being issued a state license if you plan on importing wines. However, the California ABC will allow you to begin your application with them concurrent with the Basic Permit application. This way you can cut down on some of the processing time. If your business is also based in California, you will need other licenses, such as one to distribute, but there are several different "types", varying a little depending upon your situation. Two of the most common for an importer and distributor in California, useful as illustrations of types and their language, are the 09 and the 17:

09. A common license held by California importers, the type 09 is one of two licenses that govern the importation of wine to the United States. The 09 license lets an importer take possession of the imported wine as it enters the country and after it clears customs. Note that a type 09 license cannot stand alone, but must be held in tandem with either a type 17 or type 20 license.

17. One of the most versatile licenses, the type 17 is most commonly paired with a type 09, 10 or 20 license. The type 17 authorizes a person or entity to act as a

wholesaler and sell wine directly to retailers, thereby eliminating the need to locate another wholesaler.

## New Jersey/New York License

Only the Basic Permit is required to meet regulations for East Coast facility storage for sale to distributors. If your licensed premises are also located in the tri- state area, and you wish to distribute your own wines (sell to retailers), a separate wholesale license is mandatory through the respective New Jersey or New York agency in the state in which the warehouse is located.

## Other State Licenses

You are presumably just launching your enterprise, or you are just getting established and have limited distribution. Perhaps you are further along, but seeking advice on how to take a grassroots distribution enterprise to the next level. Regardless of your situation, *do not* go out and start getting licenses in every state, nor even in every state in which you wish to do business. This is not a case of *build it and they will come*. It is unnecessary and costly and ultimately a frustrating time waster. The majority of states will not allow you to obtain their version of a license, permit, registration, etc. without also identifying the distributor to whom you will be selling.

We will get into state licensing, brand registrations, outsourcing compliance vs. doing it yourself and related topics later in the book, but suffice to say, at this stage you should have only the essential licenses to begin to import and distribute your first container.

# CHAPTER 4

# PORTFOLIO – SELECTIONS AND DECISIONS

Throughout this section and the rest of the book, "vineyard," "winery," and "vigneron," will be used interchangeably to mean the supplier from which you purchase the wine. Now that you've conducted your research, settled on specialization or broad scope and identified the appellation or multiple appellations, you are ready to start selecting actual wines. There are a number of options to assist you with this process.

## Narrowing the Field

### On-site selection

If you regularly vacation in a country where you discovered an appealing selection of wines from a particular vineyard, you now have an owner with whom you can talk about exporting his wines. This establishes that you enjoy the wines of that region and appreciate the level of quality, so you might consider asking the vigneron if they have neighbors who could also be interested in exporting and, if so, ask for an introduction and an opportunity to try their wine. Driving to adjacent areas to expand your search could also prove fruitful and will broaden your familiarity with the region's topography, *terroir*, and other features that you will use in marketing your portfolio.

Family or close friends in the country of origin could assist with identifying and providing you with resources or setting up appointments so that you can optimize your time spent in the country when you do visit and meet with vineyard representatives personally.

## Wine industry experience

Employment with a distributor or retailer will have brought you into contact with wines, and even specific brands, that you would enjoy representing. I do not consider it good form to try to poach from another importer's portfolio, but this could give you the inside track to a brand who is already leaving (or being dropped by) an importer and therefore an acceptable opportunity. The ideal situation is if the brand already enjoys broad market distribution. However, it is unlikely that they would choose to go with a new, untried importer unless you have established a strong, long term connection to them, or they can secure a financially guaranteed commitment from you.

Don't be turned off by a brand that was not the one taking the initiative to end the relationship with their former importer. The importer may have a conflict within the portfolio, made a commitment to a new, larger brand that will compete with the prior brand, or the brand might not be a good fit for their personalities or the direction the portfolio is taking. One of the most successful brands I ever represented was previously with another importer who voluntarily gave up the brand, right on the cusp of greatness. Two years later, one of the brand's wines was the highest rated wine ever reviewed in the *Wine Spectator* for the price.

On the other hand, it may signal a deficit in the brand or a difficult personality and you should certainly take a hard look at this possibility.

Alternatively, you may find that your area of preference has either been honed through years representing a particular country and, while the actual wines you enjoy are taken, their neighbors may be available.

## Focused research

Your area of interest may lie in organic and biodynamic wines. It may be brands with 5- star ranking in an industry publication or regional recommendations of small, high-quality producers from a well-regarded wine book. Google your region of choice, based on your reading, and see where that leads. Are these brands already represented in the U.S.? If so, would they be amenable to considering distribution in your state, if it is available? More and more brand owners feel that having multiple importers in the U.S. is a reasonable and measured approach.

Figure 4.1 Biodynamic Wine from France

# Agents

What if you are unfamiliar with the country, its logistics, language and customs? What if you don't know how to find available wines? Do you travel all over the globe? Do you phone vineyards and introduce yourself over the phone, before finally discovering they are too small for export or already represented? Different approaches are dictated by your inclination, time, knowledge, capital and resources.

There are agents or export brokers in all countries who can assist you in your search or who already have a stable of brands for which they are looking for homes. This is their bread and butter after all, and they make their money either through commissions from the wineries or adding a commission or markup to the wine, in a price quoted to you. This adds yet another layer to the price structure (and the layers can start to add up) but they can often be worth it.

- An agent is very familiar with the region and available brands thereby saving you the trouble of excessive travel and the time commitment.

- They are fluent in the language (where applicable) and presumably have an established reputation or relationship as an export broker/agent. Even English-speaking Australia, South Africa and New Zealand have their distinct customs, idioms and idiosyncrasies and a broker/agent may well be an advantage if you are unfamiliar with the country.

- They can be contacted initially by phone and should be agreeable to sending samples for you to evaluate.

- Agents are also often much more familiar with the U.S. requirements than the wineries and can be your intermediary in explaining the situation to them. One of these areas is labels. Although most brand owners who have exported to the U.S. before will be receptive, I have often experienced situations where the winery resists working with me on immutable U.S. label regulations as if they think these laws are mere suggestions. One even told me that they could leave the organic leaf logo on the label, because "it doesn't mean anything in the U.S.". It most definitely does.

- They are in a position to convey expectations from you to the winery and vice versa.

- Agents may even be able to negotiate a better price for you, based on their relationship with the winery or familiarity with comparable wines and market conditions.

- The agent will presumably have experience with freight forwarders and shipping companies, which ports to use and even container consolidation of wines. This should not replace your relationships, which are important to build with your own freight forwarder, and an understanding of terms and charges but it does give you a basis for comparison and the benefit of the agent's experience.

The important point to take away from this section is to weigh the added cost of the agent and the distance it can create between you and the vineyard, against your time, resources, familiarity and ability to source the same quality – or any wine for that matter – through other means. As with anything else, there are good and bad agents, which should become readily apparent in the early stages of your association. There are also those who are just plain insecure and will try to be the buffer between you and the winery out of fear you will do an end run around them and cut them out when you've established the brand. Never do that. It's not ethical. But do make it clear that you also wish to initiate your own relationship with the winery. The closer you are to the supplier, the more opportunity you have to influence their supply, styles, labels and any other crucial aspects of your business. If they know and like you, they will be more concerned with your needs and building a long-term relationship.

# Trade Associations

Most countries from which you would be likely to import have trade associations established in the U.S. designed to assist with the marketing and exposure for their products, which often include indigenous or manufactured items of that country. Most of the trade organizations are based in New York but often have regional offices. Some have their own independent organizations to promote food and wine under the auspices of their country's embassy.

It is important to note that foreign trade associations vary significantly in their involvement in active promotion and should not necessarily be viewed as the best or likeliest avenue for import opportunities. However, they most certainly can provide an understanding of their respective country's regions and wines and may help you to narrow your focus by understanding the most popular and, conversely, the up-and-coming lesser-known areas. Some of them also actively seek importers for their winery clients, or retain a data base of wineries seeking representation. These organizations may not be acquainted with the wineries or their principals but are seeking to broaden market share for their country's products in general.

They are definitely worth contacting and a potentially valuable resource. They should be happy to assist you since your success is their success. They will also enable you to be in the loop of any trade shows, organized winemakers' trips or special events you may wish to attend.

Trade organizations go by varied names, depending on what the respective country wishes to call it, but will most often have the words Trade Commission in their name. There is a list of many different countries' trade organizations in the appendix.

# International Trade Shows

In considering advice, I am always mindful that most of you will be constrained by some type of budget, especially in the early days of your new business. Therefore, I would discourage you from attending just any trade shows within or outside the U.S. They can be very expensive and, as I will discuss more specifically later, can be useless if missing the right focus. There are several international trade shows that are very well regarded and draw a high caliber of potential prospects. After a hiatus of the first two years of the pandemic, they are back in full force. These are (in no particular order):

**VinExpo** – originated in Paris 40 years ago — and now held in Paris, Hong Kong, Bordeaux, Shanghai and New York. Now hosting over 78,000 visitors from 140 countries and 5,900 exhibitors annually. https://www.vinexposium.com/en/

**Prowein** – bills itself as the "World's Number One International Trade Fair for *Wine & Spirits*", begun in Dusseldorf, Germany 25 years ago and expanded to Singapore, Sao Paolo, Mumbai, Shanghai and Hong Kong. Dusseldorf remains the epicenter, but regional shows would still be worthwhile, depending on your focus. https://www.prowein.com/

**London Wine Fair** – calls itself "The Most Intelligent Wine Event in the World". A lot to live up to, but it's definitely up there with the best in global regard. Also 40 years old in 2022, it is held in London and attracts exhibitors and visitors from all over the world. As with all of these top events, it also offers master classes, industry briefings and wide-ranging tastings. https://www.londonwinefair.com/

**VinItaly** – is the grande dame of wine trade shows at 55 years old, begun in 1967. It also now includes international tasting events, road shows, education and extensive wine promotion throughout the year, but the main show is an annual event in Verona, Italy. https://www.vinitaly.com/en/

# Personalities – A Relationship, Not a One Time Purchase

This is the stage where that big funnel filled with so many choices and decisions, narrows down to specific countries, then regions, then vineyards, then brands and ultimately wines. You are at the point of discussing the representation and importation of wine with specific individuals and this becomes a very personal exercise.

"It's business", some will say, but it's so much more than that; it's a relationship. There are many more relationships you will develop throughout the importing and distribution of your wines, but this is clearly one of the most important.

In thinking about your commodity, you must consider the source. Wine is made from grapes, which are a harvested farm crop. Unless you happen upon the acquisition of wines from a large, international corporation, you will most likely be buying from someone who has tilled the soil, planted root stock, tended the crop, prayed for rain, wished for sun, harvested, pressed, fermented and waited years for the fruits of their labor. Their journey may have taken them through local sales at cellar door to national distribution to international sales…and then back again. This could be their first vintage or their one hundred and first. They could be naively embarking on their inaugural venture or been burned by the demise of their last importer. There are countless permutations but whatever their personal circumstance, they are looking for a representative – particularly someone from another country – to whom they can entrust their product with the desire, or the expectation, that it will become almost as important to you as it is to them.

On the other hand, you cannot afford to allow personal circumstances to cloud your judgment. This part *is* business. Remember your trips to Napa or Tuscany? The romantic chateaux, the charming cellar door experiences. How it was some of the best wine you had ever tasted, so good that you bought a case and had it shipped home? At home, it was still thoroughly enjoyable, but was it really the *best* you had ever tasted?

Did you really need *that* much sangiovese? Ambiance has a great deal to do with the perception of our experiences and wine may be one of the most compelling examples of this.

You will often find, as you sit on the terrace in the vigneron's backyard, surrounded by rose bushes and perhaps savoring aged cheese and homegrown olives, that you really want to represent these wines, you want to love them as much as your host does. You particularly want to be able to come back to this spot and experience the same thing again. This individual is happy to see you, will introduce you to the local bistro, café or watering hole and truly wants to entertain you and make you a part of an extended family. Not all the time, to be sure, but often enough. You are a potential purchaser of their product – and contributor to their livelihood – and these farmers, winemakers, landowners, will be strongly motivated to make sure that this *does* become a relationship.

Your job is to separate perception from reality and make decisions regarding the taste, selection, viability and all those aspects discussed in the previous chapter. It will also, let me tell you from experience, behoove you to be sure you can work with them. The effort you will put into developing the brands of your portfolio is not designed for a quick purchase and one time sale. A lot of the time and labor is frontend loaded when you select, introduce and promote a brand. Building on the initial order is where you have some economies of scale and where you can guarantee continuity to your customers and the assurance that the work *they* put into your portfolio is not misplaced.

Consider your own personality. Are you:

➢ driven

➢ goal oriented

➢ focused

- detail oriented
- resistant to deadlines imposed by others
- workaholic
- responsive to requests
- laid back
- communicative
- collaborative

Figure 4.2 Waitiri Creek Vineyard, Central Otago, New Zealand

This would be the time to consider whether you can work with the autocratic, new vineyard owner who retired from a vice presidency with SONY and cashed out his stock to start an expensive project on prime land, using state of the art equipment, having hired the local hotshot winemaker. He still wants to get his hands dirty (that's part of the appeal: "getting back to the land" after a lifetime of corporate sterility), he knows he has become a farmer, but he's going to be the best darned farmer in his hemisphere, producing wine the likes of which the world has never seen. And maybe he is. Are *you* the retired or cashed out IBM exec who understands exactly how he feels and is a perfect fit? Do you understand his need for detailed graphs and regular reports on your progress, his confidence that he has done his due diligence on the market and knows exactly what his pricing should be and his expectation that he can contribute a good deal to your enterprise including a semi-annual trip to work the market?

What about the local hippie winemaker who makes wines utilizing what the *terroir* gives her that vintage – and it's very good – but doesn't know a graph from a graft and really isn't interested. She wants to make her 800 to 1,000 cases of wine – depending upon the year – and find good homes for them. If you don't commit to the wine quickly enough, it may be sold elsewhere, because with her it's *the quick or the dead*, and she most likely won't come over to visit because she can't afford to and the dogs would miss her. But she's not going to compromise on quality and she will supply you with whatever you need, *as long as you speak up quickly and without equivocation.*

These might sound like extremes, or caricatures, but I can assure you I know people exactly like this and about fifty other different, but equally quirky, challenging, interesting, entertaining, frustrating and ultimately extremely rewarding people who populate the wine industry, and whom you will inevitably come across. The issue is whether you can work with a particular personality type and who best suits your style. Can you modify yours and can they modify theirs and meet somewhere in the middle? Occasionally, it's not so much about the style, as the character traits. If the individual is purely ego driven, greedy and untrustworthy, it doesn't matter how good their wines are. Inevitably, this will become a nightmare and you will regret the decision to override your gut.

## Contracts

Personally, I have rarely had a contract with a winery but this is a product of starting my own import business in 1992 when contracts were not common and because this has traditionally been an industry of handshake agreements. However, based on my experience and that of others, I *do* recommend a contract of some sort — a simple, but comprehensive, agreement that covers responsibilities and expectations — the salient points of your working partnership. I would be careful not to prolong the process, and possibly delaying getting started, with a league of attorneys taking weeks to construct a document that takes weeks for each side to decipher. It can also depend somewhat on the country of wine origin. Inexperienced suppliers, for example in many small regions of Europe, may not want to become mired in contracts they will have trouble deciphering or collecting on if things should go sour. They often have their own way of vetting their importer – you – through requiring payment up front and doling out the rights to a state or two at first. There is nothing wrong with this cautiously optimistic approach. After all, they're still willing to entrust their wine with an unknown entity at this stage. It's up to you to build trust, terms and a business from that base.

Quite frankly, I believe a written agreement protects the importer more than the brand owner, although it would depend upon their idea of an agreement and their own individual expertise or experience in the matter. They will want assurances that you will pay them, of course, and available recourse in the event you do not. Most significantly, the agreement defines, in written form, the areas you have already agreed upon and leaves less to subjective interpretation. I am not an attorney, and would not presume to advise you as such, but simply put: it should include what you intend to do for them and what they agree to provide for you. This will be expanded on under the expectations section ahead so that you have a clearer picture of just what areas should be covered. Some expectations on either side do not have to be more than verbal acknowledgments, clearing the way for more discussion, but it allows you to incorporate those points that are most meaningful to you and give both sides a measure of confidence moving forward.

I also believe an agreement should afford you some protection if the winery decides to change importers after you have built the brand's sales and distribution to a measurable degree of success. This has been accomplished through your considerable time and expense. Nonetheless, the brand owner is always just that – the brand *owner*. You have agreed to be their representative in the U.S. but at no time do you own the rights to the brand and its supply and distribution. It can be taken from you at any time irrespective of your understanding. Therefore, some compensation for future earnings, at a level you both agree, is reasonable. And I stress *reasonable*. The beginning of this relationship should ideally be on a congenial footing and one in which each party feels they are being justly represented by the contract.

## Expectations – Yours and Theirs

Irrespective of style and approach, it is imperative to establish, in the early stages, what the expectations are on both sides. Leave no aspect to chance and assume nothing. You would be surprised at the extent of time, energy and resources that can be spent on securing a particular brand, only to become aware of a deal breaking requirement on their part, or an assumption on yours that was never addressed. Some of these would be:

- ❖ national vs. regional appointment
- ❖ terms
- ❖ which wines
- ❖ first year volume
- ❖ allocation

- sample allowance
- payment currency
- price increases
- long term goal
- first purchase

## ◆ National vs. Regional

As discussed earlier, since national and regional importing are so different, and critical to the future of the brand, it is in your best interests to determine, from the commencement of your business, which model to choose. However, if the brand you fall in love with belongs to someone who only wants national distribution through one importer or, alternatively, multiple importers, this should be discussed in the beginning either to avoid misunderstanding or perhaps early enough to change the mind of either party.

## ◆ Terms

Although it used to be common to extend terms to U.S. importers for wine purchases from the first shipment, I can see from my own experience as a consultant to other importers that this is the exception rather than the norm. More likely, terms will require payment up front, e.g., for Europe, for the first shipment or two, with variations that include half up front and half on delivery. Terms are likely to be relaxed later, with a proven payment history and substantial increase in orders.

Hopefully, you can work towards arrangements that make it possible for you to ship, sell and collect on your investment. A reasonable goal for payment terms from the winery could be 60 to 90 days from B/L (Bill of Lading), FOB (Freight on Board) port of origin. In other words, the winery gets the wine to the port nearest to them (FOB), or the one nearest to them that ships to the U.S., and the date on the B/L provided by the shipping company is when the clock starts ticking on terms. To put it another way: if the wine is loaded on the ship at port of origin on January 1st, payment is due on March 1st for 60 day terms and April 1st for 90 day terms.

It is not necessarily customary but not unusual for a winery to want to have the first shipment under LC (Letter of Credit) to ensure payment. This requires a guarantee from you, through a letter from your bank, to ensure sufficient funds will be on deposit to pay the invoice at the close of terms.

## ◆ Which Wines

You would be surprised at how often the vineyard owner, with a quiver full of varieties produced on their property, will automatically assume you will take them all. It doesn't matter what they are or how many - if you agreed to bring their wines to the U.S. you agreed to bring them *all*. Just like children - no favorites! It is up to you to explain, as diplomatically as possible, that while they are all lovely in their own inimitable ways, the ones you feel best equipped to begin with, based on market research, style, price, or whatever the reason, are, for example, these three wines. You will necessarily need to start slowly, to establish the brand carefully and not overwhelm distributors. Fostering a warm and collaborative relationship is crucial but this is your business, and you have to purchase according to common sense and fiscal constraints.

It may not be the conventional varietals that win over the esoteric or funky. It could be that *that* style of merlot from France won't sell, or the Bordeaux blend from New Zealand will be too difficult at that price point. They may be beautifully made wines, with structural integrity and recognizable grape names, but if it doesn't appear to be the right time, then don't do it. Find at least two wines from the brand (unless they only make one) that will complement one another and provide the best entrée into the market. They don't have to be red and white, or even both table wines. It could be a Tawny Port and a sparkling. Just make them "best foot forward", as you see it. You can always add later.

Figure 4.3 Mark Creed of Creed Wines

## ◆ First Year Volume

This is a critical element. It is not uncommon to reach an accord with a vigneron on all levels only to discover that this individual thinks that 5,000 cases for the first year would be a perfectly reasonable "starting" volume. After all, there are over 330 million people in the United States. That paltry drop would be absorbed in no time. That's when you groan and try to explain (again) that of those multi-millions, only a certain percentage drink wine, of those a smaller percentage drink regularly, a number of people only drink *Two Buck Chuck*, or wines of a certain country…and on it goes. Yes, U.S. wine drinking percentages are increasing in both number and annual per capita consumption and the right wine, marketed properly, can certainly succeed. But add to the mix the sheer volume of international imports, America's own thriving wine production, increased plantings everywhere and the consolidation of wholesalers and you have a situation that requires a skillful, savvy approach. Which is where you come in and why they need you. For your sake, do not promise something you can't deliver or commit to wine that puts you out of business. It's far better to set conservative expectations and exceed them, to the delight of your supplier, than find yourself backpedaling or, worse, being confronted by an angry vigneron who, having bottled and labeled all his production just for you, is in financial ruin!

On the other hand, if you have reached an agreement with Trader Joe's or Whole Foods to supply wine to all their stores, that's a different story. But not usually the way it goes out of the gate.

## ◆ First Purchase

I'm now referring to the actual first container commitment from any and all sources, as opposed to the volume you are tentatively committing to over the first year to an individual vineyard. As with everything else, a good deal of thought should go into the size and composition of this first container. Unless you have lined up some large pre-orders, you are at the starting gate, hoping your horse is a winner, but not actually sure how he's going to run that day.

There is no one right way to launch and manage your wine import business but there are certain considerations that make the difference between success and failure or profit and loss. Aside from the obvious failure I outlined in Chapter I – the 800 cases of high priced semillon – there are other ways in which wine will languish in the warehouse.

Let's assume you have put together an appealing group of brands from one country. Whether you are immediately importing from several countries or decide to branch out later, you can only fill the container at one port. After that, it's sealed and on its way.

Unless you are starting with a big budget and expect to hire a full complement of sales people as soon as possible, my recommendation is to estimate how much you can sell within a three-month period and take this as the approximate quantity you should put on the first container. Any more and you have mounting warehouse fees for wine already paid for – but not sold. Any less and you run out before a new container arrives. If it moves faster than expected you can always order more but wine that does not sell quickly also runs the risk of not selling at all, because you have overestimated the demand or time works against it in vintage change expectations.

I have always started out slowly with wineries, explaining that this is the "test" shipment. Throw it against the wall, see what sticks and proceed from there to build an increasing, but manageable, volume. I'm actually more diplomatic about it – after all, these are all wines they are proud of and expect to sell well – but essentially, that's the bottom line.

## ◆ Allocation

Although the early stages are all about lowered expectations and conservative commitments, you still want to know how much the vineyard is willing to allocate to you for either your region or the entire U.S. They may have an almost limitless supply and allocations are not really an issue but what of the special place of old vines that produces only 300 cases of each wine in a vintage? You will need to know whether you can have 290 cases or 50 and whether this is a fluid allocation or static. If the wines garner amazing press or achieve cult status you will want your allocation protected and if you are splitting the country you will need to know that the wines are split equitably with the other importer. Make sure the winery does not confuse allocation from *them* with commitment from *you*, unless you want it to mean the same thing.

## ◆ Sample Allowance

This is a significant consideration so often ignored but one which can have a major impact on your net profit and your ability or willingness to utilize samples to increase sales.

In my opinion, any supplier of wine – vineyard or winery – should provide a sample allowance even if their production is small. The smaller they are, the less wine they produce, and they may be resistant to the concept. But the smaller they are, the smaller the sample allowance will be and if they understand the importance of sample usage at all stages of their brand development, they will willingly acquiesce.

Samples are used for many purposes, some of which are:

- publication and competition submission
- prospective distributors/wholesalers evaluation
- trade shows
- prospective chain buyer evaluation
- wine dinners
- wine tastings
- distributor's sales meetings
- distributor's sales staff for sales calls

Some of the uses are expanded later in the book but for purposes of discussion with the supplier, these are all viable reasons for a sample consideration.

There is a good deal of the subjective about sample allowances, but it is usually expressed in a percentage discount off the invoice. While generalities are helpful to a degree, I recognize it is the specifics that will be important to you on this subject so I offer a series of suggestions and from those you can distill what feels comfortable to you or what works for your supplier. These are all examples of actual allowances that I have worked with in the past:

- ➢ 5% on the first container and 2% on subsequent shipments
- ➢ 3% across the board on all shipments

- 2% across the board on all shipments and in addition a free case of each new wine or new vintage to be reviewed by press

- 5% on all new vintages, 3% on shipments of the same vintage

- 5% on new and old vintages until a satisfactory sales level is reached

- 2-5% based on cost and rarity of wine and varying with the shipment

- 2.5% across the board and free cases of new wines or new vintages for *you* to evaluate and pre-sell

- 0% off invoice, but additional wine on a container order to use as samples.

I have encountered resistance to providing samples on several occasions, usually from very small or inexperienced vineyard owners, but once I explain the scope of sample usage and their absolute necessity, this resistance lessens, if not disappears. I also let the brand owner know that this is not just their investment; the wine I send out and use is in excess of most sample allowances. They are helping me defray my costs and giving me far more latitude in utilizing samples to secure and increase sales.

Sample allowances are not to be confused with incentives, in which suppliers offer periodic deals and incentives to affect price and stimulate sales. This is a separate discussion to have with the winery. Although this is a conversation that can well be had during the first negotiations, I have saved the topic for a later section of the book where the incentives can be illustrated within the relevant framework.

## ◆ Payment Currency

The question of currency in the payment of invoices should be raised but there are no hard and fast rules on this. If you feel the currency of the country of the wine's origin is stable, the exchange rate is very good and unlikely to fluctuate, or you can build in sufficient margin to allow you a degree of comfort, then operating within that currency is not a problem and usually the way I prefer to work.

One option is to build in *forward contracts* on currency, when considerable fluctuation is already taking place or the prevailing feeling is that the value of the currency of the country of origin will likely increase. This requires speculation on your part and, although you have stabilized the price for the foreseeable future, the contract stipulates a specific quantity of currency and a rate you agreed to at the time of the contract. It locks in the rate at the current value but requires considerable insight on your part into your future needs.

The winery may have its own preference. I have known suppliers with personal or business ties to the U.S. who prefer wires into their U.S. bank accounts. Not uncommonly, a supplier with no U.S. connections will quote in USD because they feel it keeps their wine at a specific price, such as retailing under $10 or under $20 (both important price levels) but this is a topic for the next chapter.

Whatever your choice or the winery's, factor it into your pricing and you will be better prepared in the event of changes in exchange rates and market conditions.

## ◆ Price Increases

As a rule, price increases from the winery should not be automatically triggered by each vintage, or the start of a new year. However, there are certainly circumstances that do precipitate an increase – e.g. a lower introductory price for the first shipment, unexpected costs of doing business or the winery's USD currency choice eroded by a devalued dollar.

The winery cannot anticipate some of these events, but can address, at the outset, whether they intend to increase pricing on an arbitrary basis or as a result of certain events. It is not the most critical aspect of your early negotiations but one I mention to keep you informed about what may be customary and what you could expect.

## ◆ Long Term Goals

My emphasis in this section is on the winery's goals more than your own although you may have very specific and easily articulated ambitions, which will be important for the winery to hear. If you do, be sure you can back them up and that you haven't sent them happily running out to buy more French oak barrels at $1,000 a pop based on your unsubstantiated projections.

Some wineries only want to know you will do your best and will take as much wine as you can sell and see where it goes. This gives you a certain peace of mind at first, but does not guarantee supply in the long term. You may find yourself in the fortunate position of rapid growth where the winery cannot keep up with demand. This leaves you with dissatisfied customers and lost sales and momentum.

Others want to determine how much you can purchase over a five year term, down to the last case. It is very difficult for you to make projections based on no historical reference. I find myself in this position all the time and I do understand the motivation behind each person's request for this information. After all, their own long range plans — and perhaps the livelihood of their entire family — hinge on what you anticipate the sales and growth will be over time. However, I don't want to be put in a position of committing to something I can't deliver, based on information I just don't have, and neither should you. I think it is reasonable to explain that you want this to be an honest and successful *long term* partnership and you will be in a better position to give them your anticipated needs and objectives after the first few months or the first year.

You will at least want to ensure that your first few months can provide you with sufficient wine to back up the first orders but don't let them think they should have the wines all labeled for the U.S. requirements, ready and waiting for an order. If they find this more cost-efficient, then by all means, but otherwise the advice I have just given should dictate how they will approach the beginning stages of this endeavor and that is: *softly, softly*.

# References

It would be helpful to line up references, if at all possible, from within the wine, banking and professional industries, to offer peace of mind to the winery who will be across an ocean from you and their goods. It is understood you are new, but if you are funded by, or partnered with, someone with an established reputation or if you come from a successful financial or corporate background, this will be helpful in establishing credibility. It then just takes one winery or vineyard who has taken a chance on you. Assuming you have performed well for them and paid on time, they can become the reference to which you turn when looking to secure the next brand.

*SUMMARY*—From the time you start speaking seriously with your prospective supplier is the perfect time to establish the ground rules, expectations, commitments and the framework of the working relationship. But never forget that it is a relationship and that this will be the true basis of your collaboration. The tone you both set will see you through good times and bad, through misunderstandings and through the inevitable time when, if you are successful, someone will come along and promise your supplier a better import experience through *their* company!

## My Story

I had not usually found the absence of a contract to be an impediment in doing business but about six years into national representation for two brands owned by the same person – an ego-driven man who was dissatisfied with the level of U.S. sales – I was abruptly told that he was switching to a New York importer because he thought New York was *the* place to be. These brands unfortunately represented about 45% of my portfolio at the time. The owner flew to the States and met with me for fifteen minutes to give me the news before flying on to New York, and that was that. I had no contract and therefore neither notice nor compensation was contractually required and none was offered. It was a significant blow and although I did recover from it, it was not without extreme difficulty. Others in the same position have not.

The ending for this story is that the two brands did very poorly with the new importer and disappeared from the States and the owner went bankrupt after defrauding his creditors in the amount of 60 million dollars. Some satisfaction, but I would have preferred the notice and the compensation to allow me some time to replace the lost sales and income.

## My Client's Story

This savvy businessman, brand new to the wine business but clearly well-versed in delegation, took a three-pronged approach: he lined up a Master of Wine in the country of wine origin who was able to source superb quality wines and provide the credibility that I referenced above; he hired a young, eager sommelier in the U.S. with a good palate and the energy and personality to make sales and secure accounts, and he retained my services to help him launch the business and avoid delays in his learning curve. As a result, I've watched him build a difficult category in less than two years into something viable with growth potential. Not everyone has those kinds of resources or opportunity but making the most of your strengths and taking advantage of opportunities for portfolio selection and exponential sales growth will build your business faster than just waiting for it to happen.

# PART II

# CHAPTER 5

# PLANNING, PREPARATION AND PREPAREDNESS

There are several tasks that should be undertaken pre container shipment arrival, some of which are required, and some of which are advisable. Taking care of them at this stage will save you time and possibly money, assuming you have reached agreement with wineries, vineyards or agents for specific wine to be bought and transported in the foreseeable future.

## Purchase Orders

Before a winery will be willing to commit resources towards U.S. compliant labeling, allocating wine to you and all the logistical considerations, they understandably will want a commitment from you in the form of a purchase order.

A purchase order also protects you by the specificity of its content, which should comprise the following:

- purchase order number (for tracking)
- date
- terms
- price
- currency of payment
- shipping point
- vintage
- consignor (the supplier, with contact details)
- consignee (your contact details)
- quantity
- sample allowance.

QuickBooks has an example of a purchase order that can easily be modified to suit your needs. Most of this example is self-explanatory and easily understood. However – and you will be glad of this advice – be sure that you stress the vintage must be strictly as ordered. Too often, without any ulterior motive, a winery will ship wine to you that you neither ordered, nor ultimately will be able to sell, based on their misunderstanding of your market.

## Purchase Order

**Bluestone Wine Solutions**
1671 James Drive
Carlsbad, CA, 92008

| Date | P.O. No. |
|---|---|
| 11/4/2022 | 064 |

**Vendor**
Mountain Top Winery
1 Mountain Top Rd
McLaren Vale 5171

**Ship To**
Wine Warehouse,
100 Wine Warehouse Rd,
SONOMA, CA, 95476

**Terms**

| Item | Description | Qty | Rate | Amount |
|---|---|---|---|---|
| BWPRGMS19 | Grenache Mataro Shiraz 2020 12/750ml | 250 | 80.00 | 20,000.00 |
| BWSPBVS18 | Single Vineyard Shiraz 2020 12/750ml | 100 | 110.00 | 11,000.00 |
| BWPEVR18 | Eden Valley Riesling 2021 12/750ml | 75 | 80.00 | 6,000.00 |
| BWPBRS16 | Estate Grenache 2020 6/750ml | 150 | 60.00 | 9,000.00 |

all vintages and samples to remain as ordered, unless discussed prior to shipment.
Sample allowance as agreed.

**Total** $46,000.00

| Phone # | Fax # |
|---|---|
| (760) 519-7343 | |

**Web Site**
www.bluestonewinesolutions.com

Figure 5.1 Purchase Order example

Imagine that you tasted a particular wine, learned that it was a gold medal winner and loved the particular style that vintage produced. You order it and receive the previous vintage. Huh? No gold medal, different taste and a tough sell. The winery, in their defense, may have thought you were aware that they would ship you the vintage they were currently working through, not the one they were releasing in two months. They could also have a difficult time selling this vintage domestically, but don't think it will be a problem to move such a small quantity in the vast United States. Either way, it could be devastating to your sales.

Imagine that you were expecting the latest sauvignon blanc release – fresh, lively, aromatic and just released, everything the U.S. consumer is expecting. Only, the winery still has 150 cases of the previous vintage in stock and, since your order was for 250 cases, it made sense to them to deplete the previous vintage and make up the difference with the new. But now, instead of 250 cases of the current release, you have to list two different vintages on your price sheet, submit both to publications for review and presumably deal with the concern of having everyone choose the new over the old – U.S. tastes and expectations being what they are.

The exception to the above would be if the winery sold out of the vintage you were expecting prior to the purchase order. This is still something that should be discussed at the time of the purchase order and certainly prior to shipment. If you have not tasted the new vintage, the winery should send you samples immediately. Vintage variation for estate grown, smaller vineyards is the norm, rather than the exception. This does not mean it will be inferior of course; it may even be better. It gives you the opportunity to determine if you feel it meets the price point, consumer tastes and your requirements. If it does not, but is still marketable, then you can reduce the order. Conversely, it may be even better and you want to increase the order in anticipation of higher sales.

In recent years, countries other than the U.S. have started packaging in six-packs, rather than twelve-packs. I have been told two different reasons for this: the first is that it is a weight issue, with the potential for back injuries greater with the larger case; the second is that there is a perception that lower priced wines – the generic supermarket wines – are packaged in twelve-packs. To differentiate, wineries started packing higher end wines in six-packs. Whatever the reason, the U.S. continues to sell in a twelve bottle case format and is happy to do so. Shipping in six-packs from your supplier (unless requested) can be potentially expensive, time consuming and resulting in lost sales. This is why:

- shipping in six-packs is bulkier on pallets, resulting in less wines per pallet
- storage in a warehouse is most often priced per item, so this doubles the cost
- orders from distributors may limit the number of cases (six-packs) from you. If they can order less, why not?
- orders from retailers to the distributor may be less; they have limited storage, and often limited budgets, so it can make sense to order a six-pack of an item.

If you ordered in twelve bottle cases, and the winery only make six-packs, have them strap two cases together at the vineyard or winery to make a twelve bottle case. This minimizes their investment in complying with your order, because they don't have to have larger boxes bought and printed with brand identifiers, and saves you money at the U.S. end. Wine warehouse are accustomed to strapping cases together for this purpose, but will charge per case.

# Food and Drug Administration (FDA)

Both you and your winery will have to register with the FDA [www.fda.gov](www.fda.gov) in the country of origin of the wine. This is a post 9/11 requirement covered under the *Bioterrorism Act of 2002*. In the event of a threat to the food or beverage supply, the FDA has access to your winery's contact information to advise them of the threat, trace the source or eliminate them as a threat in the event of a trace.

Your registration is as the importer who will warehouse the wine. Registration is done on the FDA website, under the section titled Registration of Food Facilities. The US FDA considers all alcoholic beverages under the "food" umbrella. The link for this section, at the time of writing (it does change and did change from the first edition of this book) is:

http://www.fda.gov/Food/GuidanceRegulation/FoodFacilityRegistration/default.htm

At the time of their registration, the winery will assign an agent in the U.S. This can be anyone with a U.S. address, but I certainly advise having your winery assign you as their agent of record, since you then have access to their information, their registered number and notification of prior entry submissions. It also allows you to confirm that they have assigned an agent correctly because their registration will trigger an automatic email from FDA to authorize and confirm your agent of record status. Carefully check your company's name and address as they will now be used on all prior notifications and any notices issued by the FDA.

Prior notice is required for all shipments entering the U.S. The FDA site is not as user-friendly as, for example, the TTB site, but there is a lot of good information once you recognize where to look for it. In the case of prior notice regulations, there are FAQs, helpful background information, and tutorials under this section, which has also changed since the last edition (please remember to check with my website for periodic updates on all mentioned links):

http://www.fda.gov/Food/GuidanceRegulation/ImportsExports/Importing/ucm2006836.htm  Prior notice for all shipments is required no more than 5 days before arrival and, in the case of air shipments (samples), no less than 4 hours, and for water shipments (containers) the minimum time is 8 hours. My advice in the case of ocean freight is to leave it to the customs broker to incorporate this prior notice notification into their routine. It is something they do as a matter of course and the cost is nominal. You could drive yourself crazy trying to track the timelines on these shipments and there are far more important uses of your time ahead!

Please note that FDA registration renewal became a requirement in 2014. "Food facilities", i.e. wineries, breweries, meaderies, etc., that are required to register with FDA are now required to renew the registrations during the period beginning on October 1 and ending on December 31 of each even-numbered year. Therefore, even if your winery registered on September 30, 2022, for example, they will still need to renew between the Oct-Dec, 2022 renewal period. As another example, if they registered for the first time on February 4, 2020, they will not need to renew until the Oct-Dec 2022 renewal period. If they fail to renew in the mandated period, the facility will need to register again as a new facility. At that point, a renewal is no longer possible.

## Primary American Source (Appointment Letter)

Although Federal guidelines do not specify exclusivity on any products you import, each state has a different set of guidelines (as outlined in the state license overview in Chapter I). I used the words "wildly disparate" to characterize their differences, and I don't believe this was hyperbole on my part. All fifty states behave as if they are fifty different countries, due in great part to the stringent lobbying by distributors in the years following Prohibition. How successful they were, and remain, is evident in the resulting laws.

One requirement that will come up time and again is that you prove you are the Primary American Source of this wine (authorized by the winery). This is also called an Appointment Letter. I strongly advise you to obtain this at the beginning of your relationship with the winery or you may find yourself shut out of the very states in which you wish to sell wine. It is a simple letter stating simple intentions, and can be withdrawn by the winery at any time. I stress the latter frequently with new clients. It is not a time-sensitive or legally binding document. It merely states the intention of the winery at that particular moment. If you are resolved to keep the particular brand, you will no doubt hope that it will continue in perpetuity – and it may – but the winery can sleep at night knowing that they can change their minds at any time (subject to any other legal agreement you may have). Two examples of Primary Source letters are below, one an example of limiting both brands and region and the other for U.S. exclusivity for all wines produced by the supplier.

---

(Winery's letterhead)

Letter of Appointment as Importer of <u>Jane Smith Wines</u> into the USA

(date)

(importer name and address)

Dear xxxx:

We are pleased to confirm your appointment as the importer for the following brands produced by Jane Smith Wines exported to the United States of America, commencing 1st August 2022:

Lone Dog Paddock

Wombat Hills

Brett's Estate

This appointment is effective for the following U.S. states:

Washington

Oregon

California

Colorado

Arizona

Should you have any questions regarding this appointment, please do not hesitate to contact the undersigned.

Yours sincerely,

Jane Smith

General Manager

---

Figure 5.2 Example of limited American Source (Appointment) letter

---

(Winery's letterhead)

Letter of Appointment as Sole Importer of <u>Jane Smith Wines</u> into the USA

(date)

(importer name and address)

Dear xxxx:

We are pleased to confirm your appointment as the sole importer for all wines produced by Jane Smith Wines exported to the United States of America, commencing 1$^{st}$ August 2022.

Should you have any questions regarding this appointment, please do not hesitate to contact the undersigned.

Yours sincerely,

Jane Smith

General Manager

Jane Smith Wines, Pty Ltd

Ph: 61 8 8888 8888

---

**Figure 5.3 Example of exclusive American Source (Appointment) Letter**

In the first example, Jane Smith Wines may have already appointed a U.S. importer for the remaining states, or wish to give you a limited number until you demonstrate you can achieve results. In the latter, it is an exclusive appointment for the whole country. Either arrangement can be changed at any time to limit or expand brands or coverage.

# COLA Guidelines and General Information About Labels

Commitments made, wines chosen, it is time now for the process of label application to obtain approval from TTB to import these wines, known as COLA (Certificate of Label Approval).

There are services that provide compliance, and you may choose to hand all matters regarding COLAs and state brand registration and licensing to a service. This is a perfectly acceptable option, particularly if you do not immediately have the time and personnel resources. The process is time-sensitive, and each state has its own requirements, which can appear daunting at first, and delegating is understandable. But in covering COLA issues here, I have provided you with some basics to do this part yourself, or at least food for thought for the future.

Many procedures and requirements have changed, even since the last publication of this book. Some have made the process easier; others are designed to address problematic issues that arise for those submitting COLA applications, which TTB feel the response is to expand, remove or alter the guidelines.

Most, if not all, commercial wine label printers around the world, will have access to, or be intimately familiar with, U.S. label regulations. There are specific facets to this that must be adhered to without deviation but if the printer follows these regulations, they will prepare a label graphic that should be submission-ready for you. If a winery's printer professes to have no knowledge of these requirements, or prepares something that is completely wrong, I would not hesitate to suggest to the winery that they find a printer, perhaps through referral, who is more familiar with the U.S. labeling process. In the long run, it will save you and the winery countless hours of frustration, and no doubt save the winery the expense of reprinting when they discover that the printed label was still incorrect. That is not to say that the experienced printer will not make mistakes — omissions and misconceptions happen all the time — but once you learn what the basics are it is really very easy to review label proposals from your suppliers for compliance. It will save you time, headache and expense.

As an alternative, you can provide your supplier with a template to affix a third label to the bottle, that allows the foreign labels to remain, but provides U.S. compliant information. This only works if the existing labels do not contain prohibited statements, and some do.

Applying for label approval online is the only viable way to go these days. The online option has been available since around 2002. I embraced it as soon as it was available and have never looked back. It is faster and easier to submit online and the turnaround time is far less than paper submissions, so why would anyone still use snail mail. You may as well start your label submissions with the most current methods and systems!

The basics for the mandatory information, directly from TTB, are as follows (italics are mine):

<u>Brand Label</u> *which can be a front or back label depending upon where the mandatory information is in compliance, must contain*:

1. Brand Name

2. Class or Type Designation, *for example, red table wine, e.g. or specific varietal, e.g. Zinfandel*

3. Appellation *if applicable*

<u>Any Label</u> *can be front, back or side, contains*:

1. Bottler's Name and Address

2. Net Contents, *for example 750ml*

3. Sulfite Declaration *used to require specifically "Contains Sulfites" but TTB now accepts "Contains Sulphites"*

4. Alcohol Content *(used to be required on brand label, but has been changed since last publication of book to allow for inclusion on any label)*

5. Health Warning Statement *as set out below:*

**GOVERNMENT WARNING**: (1) According to the Surgeon General, women should not drink alcoholic beverages during pregnancy because of the risk of birth defects.(2) Consumption of alcoholic beverages impairs your ability to drive a car or operate machinery, and may cause health problems. *It must be separate and apart from any other text. In other words, leave at least a one line blank space between this statement and other wording*

6. Importer Details *Imported by… and location (i.e. City, State) - website optional*

There are minimum font sizes for the mandatory information and, dry as this may sound, becoming familiar with these requirements will also enable you to review and approve the printer's proofs like a pro. The following on font sizes i directly from TTB.

<u>Brand Name, Class/Type, Bottler's Name and Address, Net Contents, Sulfite Statement and Appellation</u>:

- At least 2 mm for containers larger than 187 ml
- At least 1 mm for containers 187ml or less

<u>Alcohol content</u>:

- At least 1 mm but not larger than 3 mm for containers of less than 5L

<u>Health Warning Statement</u>:

- Not smaller than 3mm for containers larger than 3 L with a maximum of 12 characters per inch
- Not smaller than 2mm for containers over 237 ml to 3 L with a maximum of

25 characters per inch

- Not smaller than 1 mm for containers of 237 ml or less with a maximum of 40 characters per inch.

I always advise wineries to set out the Government Warning and Imported By…in caps, to avoid any confusion over font size. The label graphics should be submitted to you in separate jpeg attachments, one each for the back and front, and for any other labels that will be on the bottle. There should be no surrounding or extraneous information, such as printer's marks, color notations or approval sign offs on design. Each label must be as it will look when printed and affixed to the bottle. Currently, the file size for each attachment is a limit of 1MB.

Before we go any further, I will stress what I feel is one of the most important aspects of this particular issue: **under no circumstances should you allow the winery to print the label before it is approved,** unless it is an exact duplicate of a previously approved label and the only thing to change is your unique importer details. Even the experienced printer and your careful eye may miss a key element that will be the cause of the label rejection. There are other challenges with submitting online, but you should be able to check your attachments before submission and within a short time it will become second nature. According to TTB:

<u>Top Ten Submitter Corrections for COLAs Online</u>

- The images that were submitted are illegible
- Images(s) were distorted during upload
- Dimensions provided generated a skewed or distorted image on the printable COLA
- Labels must be saved and uploaded as separate image files
- Files are uploaded in wrong area

- Problems with the Government Warning (Health Warning Statement) *they are very strict about the exact wording, punctuation, bold of the actual words* **Government Warning***, but not the text itself*

- Terms are placed in incorrect fields…i.e. "zinfandel" in the fanciful name field *example of fanciful name might be Block 28 Reserve*

- Appellation of origin is missing from application

- You must designate a "brand (Front)" label

- Brand name on application does not match labels

These are examples of reasons for COLAs online to return the application with a status of

"Needs Correction." This notice is given immediately to the submitter via email and noted in the COLAs Online portal next to the ID of the application. It receives priority attention upon resubmission. If all changes are not made when resubmitted, the application will be rejected. Currently, TTB allows 30 days for you to correct an application before it is rejected.

Once rejected, the wine will not be allowed to enter the country until a new submission is made from the beginning with the correct information. This submission must comply with the label on the bottle in the event of a customs inspection, or individual state registrations.

The processing time varies constantly, and is updated daily online, but averages 3-5 days presently, although it can range from 1-30 days. Notification of either "needs correction" or "approved" will be made to you via email.

If you use a consultant to submit your labels, they will presumably be fully conversant with revisions as they occur, and if you decide to do them yourself, there are FAQs on the ttb.gov site that are updated fairly regularly for most situations. Familiarize yourself also with approved appellations and changes in allowed varietal or proprietary names for wines.

Figure 5.4 US Compliant Labels where the "brand label" is the back

Organic wines are a very different animal and organic claims must be correctly stated on the label and accompanied by uploaded documentation that proves it complies with the United States Department of Agriculture (USDA) and its National Organic Program (NOP). This is widely available to wineries in most countries.

To round out general information on this subject, you may also be required to provide a formula, with an application submitted through Formulas Online. This is not required for the average wine, but should you import "other than standard wine": aperitifs, fruit wine, mead, or malt beverages with obscure ingredients, e.g., these will require a formula approval prior to submission for a COLA. There is more on the TTB site, with a list of specific categories.

> **Trade Sample Waiver.** If you are bringing in samples wines, they can only be brought in for one of two reasons:

1. Because you are assessing their potential for the market
2. For a trade show.

To expand on this, as a new supplier you may wish to evaluate wines to include in your portfolio or, as a seasoned importer, you could either be evaluating new wines or styles for your portfolio or taste through a current supplier's new vintages. Under these circumstances, there is no label approval (COLA) for the wine and you may apply for a COLA waiver, allowing the samples to be cleared through customs without a COLA. TTB does make it very easy for you to apply for a waiver, but you must adhere to their requirements.

They will not arbitrarily limit the amount of wine you bring in but none of it may be for sale and it cannot be for personal consumption. If the wine is for a trade show, they will require some documentation.

The section on their website is under International Trade and can be accessed through this link: http://www.ttb.gov/itd/importing_samples.shtml.

There is a template you can download, an example I have included below. The process has changed since both the first and second editions of this book. Originally, it was faxed, then emailed. The letter is still completed and signed but it is now uploaded to the TTB site. One thing that has remained the same is the requirement to provide

US Customs with a COLA waiver for every unaccompanied bottle of wine via air or sea. It is illegal to bring in unaccompanied samples without a COLA waiver (or a COLA). In the (now distant) past, a winery would tell me they had no trouble sending wine over without a COLA waiver, an invoice or FDA approval. Those days are gone. All carriers are aware of the regulations now and will request it from you. If a shipment comes in without one, US Customs will destroy the wine or return it at sender's expense.

Prior to completing the COLA waiver, request a pro forma invoice from the winery so that you can determine exactly what they are sending and in what quantity, and that they have your correct contact details and Federal Basic Permit number. I've encountered mistakes numerous times on these documents. It is not only a difficult concept for wineries outside the country to grasp but for many of them English is not their first language.

COLA Waiver requirements have been in effect since post 9/11, but does not appear to be precipitated by the September 11 terrorist attack. According to TTB, they recognized a need to allow for exemptions of COLAs under certain circumstances, such as for sample evaluation or for a trade show. Despite being part of their requirements for years, I rarely had to provide a waiver until 2010. For several years it was just customary, and it is now mandatory. TTB requires a COLA waiver, without exception, so if your wines are held in US Customs because they require a COLA waiver and you can't produce one, this will likely be returned to sender or destroyed.

> **[LETTERHEAD]**
>
> [DATE]
>
> Director, International Affairs Division
>
> Alcohol and Tobacco Tax and Trade Bureau
>
> 1310 G St. NW, Box 12 Washington, DC 20005
>
> Email: IAD@ttb.gov
>
> To Director, IAD:
>
> We request a waiver from the Certificate of Label Approval (COLA) requirements for a shipment of **[TOTAL# OF BOTTLES/QUANTITY OF PRODUCT]** of [PRODUCT NAME/TYPE] that will be used as samples for [PURPOSE/TRADE SHOW OR EVENT].
>
> Our permit number is [**IMPORTERS PERMIT #**]. The shipment, which will be imported from [**COUNTRY OF ORIGIN**], consists of:
>
> o   [##] bottles of [PRODUCT NAME – LIST INDIVIDUALLY]
>
> o   [##] bottles of [PRODUCT NAME – LIST INDIVIDUALLY]
>
> o   [##] bottles of [PRODUCT NAME – LIST INDIVIDUALLY]
>
> We are aware of the various requirements that apply to imported alcohol beverages. All applicable taxes and duties will be paid on the imported products. Any Country-of-Origin markings will be indicated in English. Each individual container shall bear a label stating "*Sample Only – Not for Sale*" or similar phrase. Likewise, each individual container will bear a label with the government health warning statement mandated by law. If wine, the product will also contain a "Contains Sulfites" label.
>
> We also attest that the products indicated in this letter will be in compliance with the above requirements <u>prior</u> to the product arriving at the U.S. port of entry, and understand that the approval of this waiver is dependent on compliance with these obligations.
>
> If the waiver is granted, please email a copy to the attention of [**CONTACT**] at [**EMAIL**].
>
> Should you have any questions, please contact us at [**PHONE NUMBER**].
>
> Regards,
>
> [SIGNATURE]
>
> _____
>
> [NAME AND TITLE OF AUTHORIZED COMPANY REP.]

## Figure 5.5 COLA Waiver Request Example

TTB's International Affairs Division seems to be a small department and its inhabitants are very friendly and accommodating – a kinder, gentler form of government at work. They used to be able to turn your request around within 24 hours via fax, even sooner if you called and begged. However, since the first edition of this book, the same constraints that most government entities face, namely tighter budgets, fewer employees and greater workload, have afflicted this department and sadly this fast turnaround is no longer true. It now requires whatever they say it is, anywhere from three to thirty days. They will send an acknowledgment email to you once they receive the request. Currently it says this:

> *We aim to review your COLA waiver submission within* **fifteen calendar days.** *There is no need to call or email about the status of your request if it has not yet been fifteen calendar days since you submitted it.*

However, just this week I obtained a COLA waiver on behalf of a client, and I received it within two days, so I suppose it depends entirely on their workload.

I always ask the winery to wait until I have obtained the waiver so that I can notify them to ship the samples. At that time, they should provide you with the carrier and airway bill number to enable you to track the shipment online.

- ➢ **Sample Bottle Requirements.** The winery must also label each and every bottle, per the waiver letter, with the following:

1. Sample Only – Not for Sale
2. Contains Sulfites
3. Mandatory Health Warning (i.e., Government Warning referenced and illustrated in the label section).

Please note that "individual container" in the TTB letter refers to each bottle. If customs chooses to inspect a shipment and these statements are not on the bottles, they will either destroy the goods or return them to the sender – your choice, but your charge too. In addition, the COLA waiver number and type of wine must match the shipment exactly or it will not clear. I once obtained a COLA waiver for nine bottles, and they only sent six, which were now being held by US Customs. I had to obtain a new COLA waiver and cross my fingers that it would be approved before time ran out in custody. I have not found a maximum quantity for sample shipments. As long as you're not trying to bring in fifty cases of one wine, which IAD can rightly assume is ultimately meant for sale. I've submitted, and received approval for, as many as 300 bottles, with sufficient diversity of variety and vintage to satisfy the requirements. I couldn't help thinking of the expense of an air shipment in this instance, but it must have been worth it to the new importer.

Caution each supplier to send wines only in approved shipping containers. I would not have thought it necessary to remind my own suppliers, but I had someone send me a shipment twice that was broken each time before it reached me. I was shocked, because I had never had this happen before and couldn't figure out why. I discovered they were shipping in standard, flimsy wine cartons with thin inserts and minimal cushioning. Shipping companies, such as DHL, FedEx or UPS, are not going to handle your shipments with kid gloves. They will expect that breakable contents are protected according to the degree necessary for rough handling. Boxes and inserts must meet airfreight companies packaging requirements for wine. They should have inner packaging of molded Expanded Polystyrene (EPS) foam, folded corrugated tray, or molded fiber tray. Each packaging component secures the bottles into the center of the shipping container away from the side walls of the shipper. Sturdy outer corrugated containers are required. Personally, I don't like Polystyrene (or Styrofoam) because they are not biodegradable and they're also very bulky to store, which you will eventually have to do for your own domestic shipments.

# My Story

The COLA process is much easier than it used to be, before printers had templates for the U.S. label requirements. But it's not always the mandatory information that presents a problem. Pay attention to statements that can be construed as promoting the consumption of alcohol, even slightly. I once had to remove the phrase *In Vino Veritas* that had been artfully incorporated into the label design, because the translation, *In Wine is Truth,* was deemed to encourage drinking. Another time, the word "lively" had to be removed from the description, because it was a still wine and "lively" connoted a sparkling wine. A beloved family crest can provide an almost insurmountable obstacle, as in this story:

At the beginning of my import journey, I represented a brand whose label proudly bore the family crest, a running fox, beneath which was a Latin inscription in a decorative banner. I submitted my carefully scrutinized label application, duly affixed to a paper form and sent by mail. A few days later, the application was returned to me, without approval and with the words "translate inscription" scrawled across the bottom. I called the winery and discovered the crest had been in the family for approximately 500 years and roughly translated into *Trust, But Beware.* I duly returned the application with the translation and a few more days passed. The mail arrived, I opened the envelope, withdrew the long-awaited form and, to my dismay, there was still no approval. Instead, on the bottom of the form the scrawl, "beware of whom?".

I became increasingly concerned about time frames for labeling and container bookings, and frustrated with the faceless person at ATF (the former TTB) who kept delaying the process. I returned the application, along with a cover letter that outlined in some detail the long and illustrious origins of the family crest, with the explanation, "it has been at least 500 years since this inscription was devised by a long ago ancestor. No one remembers 'whom' anymore".

The label was approved.

## My Client's Story

There are actually issues all the time, since I submit label applications on behalf of clients frequently, but I'll limit it to a few:

➢ A back label that included "CONTAINS: SULFITES" which actually looked fine to me, except that the colon is not allowed in a mandatory statement.
➢ One client who had a series of vineyard-related art and had decided to label *each* bottle in *each* case of the same wine, with different brand label artwork. In other words, a case of 2015 Chardonnay would have twelve different labels, a series of artwork. It was a clever concept, potentially motivating people to collect all twelve in each set, but an absolute nightmare for me. It meant twelve different COLAs for each wine, instead of one! He had six wines, which would have resulted in *seventy-two* label applications. In the end he withdrew the idea.
➢ Many labels (the jpeg graphics that I am sent in anticipation of TTB COLAs) have conflicting mandatory information on the front and back label. For example, front label says 14% alc/vol and the back says 13.5% alc/vol. Or the front label says 2020 vintage and the back label says 2019. Any mandatory information that is in conflict will result in the response: "needing correction".

# CHAPTER 6

# CONTAINERS

Whether you are the corporate executive retiree with a golden parachute looking for an investment or the self-professed wine geek who has scraped together the funds to start the business of your dreams, there is value in learning about ways to maximize your investment. Therefore, as with other subject matters, I will address the subject of containers from a budgetary and common sense perspective. Presumably, whether retiree or wine geek, the idea is to turn a profit from your wine business!

### All You Need to Know and More

## Sizes and Weights

All cargo shipments coming into a U.S. port must also move overland and therefore come under road laws governed by weight restriction established by both federal and local government agencies. There are two sizes for containers, referred to as 20 foot and 40 foot (not feet). While it appears you can cram twice as much into a 40 foot container, this is not actually so. A 20 foot container weight is limited to 39,500 lbs and a 40 foot container to 44,500 lbs. Although there are state variations that allow you to exceed the weight limits, with the use of special equipment to distribute chassis weight more equitably on roads and bridges, it hardly seems worth the effort, cost and risk. The consequences of exceeding the legal limit are fines, rejection of load and potential damage, and having to offload the contents into other transportation.

In addition, Long Beach has its own restrictions, which are currently:

- ❖ 20' (general purpose) in excess of 44,000 cargo weight lbs
- ❖ 20' (reefer) in excess of 41,500 cargo weight lbs
- ❖ 40' (general purpose) in excess of 44,500 cargo weight lbs
- ❖ 40' (reefer) in excess of 41,500 cargo weight lbs
- ❖ 45' in excess of 41,500 cargo weight lbs

Figure 6.1 20-foot container

I have rarely shipped wine in anything other than a 20 foot container. I can always have two containers on the water following one another if I need to, which generally allows for flexibility and staggering of invoice payments. Depending on whether your wines are palletized (on pallets) or stuffed (loaded without pallets), the capacity of a 20 foot container averages 600 to 1100 cases, based on 9 liter cases (12 x 750ml bottles). Particularly in your new brands' introduction stage - your (metaphorical) throw-it-against-the-wall-and-see-what-sticks, find-the-right-distribution-channels stage - it would be wise for you to plan your initial order conservatively, to fit within a 20 foot container.

## Pallets

A pallet, also known as a skid, is a flat, wooden structure used to confine the cases in a (usually) shrink wrapped, stacked configuration with access underneath for a forklift to raise and move the load around with stability. Typically, the average U.S. pallet is deemed to hold 56 cases. In other parts of the world, the pallet load is considered to be anywhere between 50 and 64 cases, a fact to keep in mind when discussing pallets with suppliers. You may both be talking about different amounts when you refer to an order as "five pallets".

When palletizing your order for an ocean freight container, the actual quantity per pallet may depend on load distribution and may not adhere to a generally accepted number of cases or layers. In discussion with people in the U.S. and other countries, keep in mind that each individual has a particular number in mind when referring to a pallet or pallet order.

U.S. Customs and Border Protection, a department of Homeland Security, enacted regulations in 2004, which were enforced in its final form in 2006, to reduce the incidence of transported plant pests into the U.S. As a result of this ruling, all pallets (which come under the heading of Wood Packing Materials or WPM) must be treated and stamped with a mark certifying that the heat treatment or fumigation has been undertaken according to prescribed guidelines. More information can be found on their website www.cbp.gov. The ruling has been in place long enough now that all freight forwarders, agents, ports and shipping companies are familiar with the requirements, but I am a firm believer in acquiring the knowledge you need to oversee, monitor, explain, fix, modify, assist, supervise or whatever the situation calls for in your own business. This is just one of those checklist items that is easy to confirm at the outset and disastrous if it is discovered to have been overlooked at arrival.

## Reefer vs. Dry vs. Blanket vs. ...

I feel I am about to wade into shark infested waters as I embark on this subject, but it is a really critical aspect of not just container shipments, but your overall business and I cannot, in good conscience, ignore it. I am also mindful that, despite any advice or recommendations I might make, this is your business and you have to make decisions with which you feel most comfortable. I will do the best I can to arm you with knowledge and from there you can either choose to follow the most conservative precautions, settle on a hybrid of the choices or take the most cost-effective route and run the risk of temperature damage to the wine. In the latter example, I am not saying you *will* incur wine spoilage, but that the possibility exists.

**Reefers** are refrigerated containers that control the temperature of the interior for the contents of the container, via a generator, for the duration of the voyage. Use of a reefer adds considerable cost to ocean freight but guarantees that the goods will arrive in optimum condition. That said, there is a difference between a reefer and a "working" reefer, the latter meaning that the generator is turned on. A "non-working" reefer is still an improvement over a dry container because it is insulated, but you should understand the difference and what you are paying for. The benefits of a working reefer will be negated if you do not also concern yourself with the conditions during consolidation at port of origin, the temperature of your warehouse upon arrival and the arrangement for reefer trucks during overland transport.

Figure 6.2 Shrink-wrapped Pallets in Partially Loaded Container

The guarantee of temperature integrity is inherent in the use of a working reefer but in the event you wish to confirm the temperature, or for peace of mind, it would be considered prudent to invest in a temperature recorder for either the first or periodic voyages. It is a sealed unit that records the temperature at intervals throughout the trip. The unit is embedded in the shipment and returned to you on unloading by the warehouse. Since the container is sealed at port of loading and remains sealed until it arrives at the warehouse (except in the event of a customs inspection) there can be no tampering with the wine and the temperature recorder en route.

**Insulated** or thermal containers provide insulation on all sides of the box, but no refrigeration unit. This is an option in shoulder season months where temperatures are moderate on both sides of the equator.

**Thermal** blankets can be requested for use from your shipping company to provide insulation for the wine at an affordable cost. These days, most freight forwarders will have their own proprietary version of insulation. Hillebrand calls it a Vin Liner, Albatrans calls it a thermal liner and Giorgio Gori refers to it as a "Gori Liner". In each case, they provide a more secure insulation than just a blanket or insulated box and all charge roughly the same price. It has most often been my protection of choice.

Figure 6.3 Data Logger (Courtesy of MadgeTech)

**Dry** containers are not temperature controlled. They are metal boxes in which the wine is either palletized or stuffed, and temperatures can fluctuate widely during the ocean voyage.

Additionally, you can give stowage instructions to the shipper that stipulates below deck storage, where it will be cooler below the water line, but there is no guarantee that this is always done, nor that it ensures optimum conditions. If you know the ship starts at the port from which your product is loading, you have much more assurance that the container will be below decks because this is where they are going to start loading an empty ship. It could conceivably stop at a couple more ports and continue to take on containers, which will now occupy above-deck space.

If you are weighing options, based on budget, price of wine, type of wine, origin (Europe vs. Southern Hemisphere), which coast the wine will enter and where it will go from there, also factor in time of year. You may consider working reefers in the hottest months and insulated containers or thermal blankets during other times of the year.

Irrespective of your decision, marine insurance is really affordable for temperature-controlled containers, with a deductible of $500 and a limit of $10,000,000, as one example. Insurance, at a slightly higher cost, can also be obtained for insulated or standard containers with insulated blankets. Marine insurance will cover damage during transit, loading and unloading by ship personnel and loss of cargo at port or at sea while under control of the shipping company. Please note, however, that unless the container is a reefer, the wine will *not* be insured against temperature damage.

## CIF vs. FOB

Although you will find that the most common form of payment terms are FOB (Free on Board), it is helpful to be familiar with the term CIF (Cost, Insurance and Freight) in case this option is offered to you by the supplier, and an explanation will allow you see beyond the short term financial benefits to you.

**CIF** can be advantageous in the beginning because the exporter (the winery) arranges and pays for the vessel and insures the freight during the voyage. The winery, or their representative agent, also arranges all shipping details, including selection of the vessel, consolidation and packing of the goods and monitoring of the shipment through their own resources, which could include direct contact with the steamship company or a freight forwarder.

Legal and financial responsibility passes to you, the importer, "at the rail," meaning when it clears the rail during unloading at the destination dock. This allows you to minimize both your initial financial outlay and having to arrange for a container at the early stage when you are unfamiliar with the process, but it comes with its drawbacks. Freight and insurance will ultimately become your responsibility. It is just delayed. Relying on someone else to arrange your shipment means you are not able to monitor it firsthand, do not receive direct notification of any delays or problems and usually end up paying a surcharge for the arrangement. Additionally, the exporter may not find the most competitive shipping company pricing for you. It could be the shipping company or freight forwarder they are accustomed to dealing with. It is all basically out of your hands.

**FOB** means that title for the goods passes to you at the "ship's rail" at the overseas port. In both situations you are responsible for all duty, taxes, customs clearance and overland freight at destination, and in this case you are also responsible for ocean freight and insurance. It allows you to choose your own shipping company, develop your own relationship with a freight forwarder or consolidator, make your own bookings to suit your time constraints or planned arrivals and be informed of any delays or problems en route. You would normally be able to negotiate your own more competitive shipping rates.

**EXW (Ex Works)** is probably the most common pricing term in Europe. It can mean that it is picking up at the winery or vineyard, but it also includes naming the place of pickup. The seller makes the goods available at their named place, which could be the bottling line, storage warehouse or basically anywhere that wine could reasonably be collected. This term places the maximum obligation on the importer and minimum obligations on the supplier because the responsibility for the shipment begins at the place of pickup, rather than at the port or when the shipment has loaded.

There is nothing wrong with this type of arrangement, but since you will be responsible for the costs involved in picking up, this must be added to the importer markups, or accommodated in the purchase price from the supplier.

**Your Own Container (FCL).** Assuming that you have sufficient selections to bring in your own full container, consider the mix of wine, for the initial container at least, on the basis of price points, styles, introductory focus or the brand identity you are establishing and time of year.

Seasonal changes, and new wine placements, take place in spring and fall. There is overlap of course – people still drink red wines in summer and white wines in winter from personal preference or food pairing – but it should be a factor in your planning, as you can well imagine.

Additionally, the *real* selling season for an importer is September and October. It is the best time to launch new brands (as long as you have laid the foundation with the distributor first) and will be the time of year you are likely to sell the most wine – with the exception of unexpectedly high ratings anywhere in the year, but that's for another section. Distributors are buying from you at that time to sell to retailers, who will sell to consumers in the holiday season. So keep this in mind as you go about hunting and gathering your wines to introduce them to the U.S. market.

Arranging your own container is a time-saving and cost-effective alternative, under almost all circumstances compared with an LCL (less than container load). Therefore, although a 20 foot container may hold 1,000 cases as a floor stacking, if you have at approximately 500 cases, it will still be more cost-effective to book a container under your own license, than to deal with an outside consolidation. Although rates may vary considerably from shipper to shipper, freight charges *within each company* are the same for any container you book yourself, no matter how much wine you load. You are paying for the container, not the case count. It is the duty and taxes that vary, and that's dependent on the actual number. It is therefore to your advantage to have as much wine as you can reasonably put in a container, *if you need it*, to decrease the per case freight charge. For example, (using a figure solely for the purpose of this illustration and not to indicate an exact freight rate):

> 500 cases = $2,300 or $4.60 per case
>
> 1,000 cases = $2,300 or $2.30 per case

Clearly you are realizing savings with the 1,000 case example over the 500 case example, but the 500 case example is still less financial outlay, time in transit and aggravation than you will encounter with an LCL arranged through an outside consolidation, which could be three to four times as much. You may wonder how that could be. Five hundred cases is still 500 cases. Is it really that different? Yes, I can assure you it is. Avoid LCL wherever possible, except where necessary at the beginning of your business venture with the understanding that an LCL is not usually a profitable exercise, but often a necessary one.

**Pallets vs. Stuffing.** There is an argument to be made for each, and sometimes a time and place for each. If the wine is palletized, the number of cases will be considerably less, but the wine is organized, often into a particular winery, brand or varietal, that makes it easier to assemble and count at the outset and at the other end. There is also less time spent at the warehouse end, resulting in savings when unloading the product is charged by the hour.

With a stuffed container, considerably more product can be loaded, thereby ensuring that wine you need will make it onto that particular container, reducing the per case freight cost. But whereas you saved money with the palletized unloading, you will spend more on unloading case by case at the warehouse. The wine also has to be loaded into the container in such a way that it does not shift in transit and break. You should only consider this option when you are established and know you can sell the additional wine.

**Consolidation Through Shipping Co. (LCL).** In the case of an LCL, you will be relying on a consolidator – either through a freight forwarder or with the shipping line itself – to put your wine in with any freight destined for almost any location. You don't know where it is loaded, how long it will take to get here, what route it will take (often through China) and how long it will wait in port while arrangements are made for devanning of all the different products. It is can be a three to five week delay, over which you will have no control. Can you afford that kind of time? Remember, the clock is ticking on your investment and the invoice due date. And the longer the wine takes to get to you, the greater the likelihood of missed opportunities, damage and loss.

For this privilege it will cost up to three times as much as the FCL you arranged for yourself with the same weight and number of items. The 500 case example now looks like this:

500 cases = $2,300 or $4.60 per case     FCL

500 cases = $6,000 or $12.00 per case    LCL

## FCL vs. LCL Summary

The more cases you can put into a container the more economical it becomes, but being in control of your own container (after initial foundation) is to your advantage under most circumstances, even when the load is much less.

Exceptions, when the overall consequences or benefits outweigh the expense of an LCL:

- ➢ If you need, e.g., 75-200 cases of wine to supply an order or distributor, because you will lose forward business and have no need of a container for some time. This isn't a large amount, you may realize very little or even no profit, but the good will is worth it.

- ➢ A premium wine is in continual demand and, as it commands a very good price, your margin erosion by the additional cost is sustainable. You have either run out or it is only available in small quantities and it is going to ensure continuity for you with a customer or in the market in general.

- ➢ A wine, also in demand or need (but not necessarily of a particular price point) missed a container because of unforeseeable circumstances – bottle and label delays, mix-up at port, e.g. – and, perhaps because it is mid-summer or just before Christmas, you will not need another container for a number of weeks.

- ➢ There is a special event – wine dinner, trade tasting, consumer tasting, etc. – that you promised this particular wine for and for which publicity has already been generated and there is no FCL container leaving fast enough.

The point is to try to avoid these contingencies as best you can. They will happen – they have happened to me – but prior planning is always advisable, especially in this business.

# Controlled Consolidation (an FCL hybrid)

The other alternative, if you find yourself short of product but do not need an entire container, is to try to coordinate with competitors (other importers buying wine from the same region) who may find themselves in a similar position of needing to bring in a couple of pallets or a few hundred cases. A joint consolidation benefits everyone, either under one Master Bill of Lading and one import license or with each importer taking responsibility for their own charges, billed separately under each individual license and MBL. The latter is slightly more expensive, but ensures that you are not paying for someone else, expecting them to reimburse you, if you do not feel comfortable doing so. This effectively allows each winery to put together a collective FCL, to be offloaded at one destination. Each importer pays their proportionate share of the freight, duty, customs clearance and all charges related to the container. If you can find compatible individuals, it can be a worthwhile collaboration and save each party the LCL surcharges, while maintaining control over your own shipment.

If you decide to have another importer clear a container for you through their customs agent (which means you reimburse them rather than the other way around), you will need to give the importer a letter authorizing them to clear for you. It would look something like this:

> (Superior Wine Company, Inc. letterhead)
>
> (date)
>
> To Whom It May Concern:
>
> Please be advised that Super Duper Wine Importers is authorized to utilize label approvals issued by the Alcohol Tobacco Tax Bureau to Superior Wine Company, Inc. on the following shipment:
>
> (list shipping company and vessel name)
>
> Sincerely,
>
> Eric Johnson

**Figure 6.4 Authorization Letter**

I have done this, with good results, on several occasions. However, I advise knowing something about the importer beforehand, either through developing your own relationship with them or through referral from your warehouse or a trade organization. I suggest you also maintain open communication so that you each know when the container is due to leave and have the goods there in plenty of time or, conversely, that you understand if there are to be any delays, which may impact your sales.

Further to the B/L issue, a freight forwarder is the NVOCC (Non Vessel Operating Company) which issues a House Bill of Lading (HBL) to the shipper. The shipper in the HBL is the exporter or shipper who delivers goods to the freight forwarder. The importer or consignee is the party to whom the cargo has to be delivered by that freight forwarder. After receiving the wine from the supplier, a Master Bill of Lading (MBL) is issued when the freight forwarder re-books the same cargo to main carriers who are vessel owners. Phew!

The terminology can be very confusing to even those of us with many years' experience because it's not something we deal with every day, and for some importers there is probably very little desire to understand the behind-the-scenes workings of the shipping relationship and charges. I find it is not only helpful to acquaint yourself as much as possible with as many aspects of your business, and peripheral connections, and I can guarantee that this knowledge will ultimately save you money.

## Freight Forwarder

You may think that contacting a shipping company directly is the best way to ensure you are getting the best rates and more in control of the transaction. However, the only recommended route is through a freight forwarder. With their specialized expertise, they are able to negotiate rates, determine shipping line schedules, book ships, coordinate shipments for you from multiple suppliers, work with customs brokers, and keep you informed during the consolidation and pre-boarding stages. A good freight forwarder is an arm to your business. You provide them with your purchase order, which apprises them of the exact goods to expect for the shipment. In the case of an LCL, you will also need to obtain pallet measurements and weight from the supplier. The freight forwarder should be proactive in contacting you if they know you want certain wine quickly and they manage to find an earlier booking date, can notify you if a winery's goods will be late, which could delay the entire voyage, or if they are delivered short, not as indicated on your purchase order, or damaged. They are the contact point for the suppliers at the country of origin, which makes it easier for you, a continent away.

Each freight forwarder is the "preferred provider" of a member co-operative. In the case of Hillebrand it is WSSA and with Albatrans it is NASA. In each case, membership is around $100 per annum and will save you in the buying power of the co-operative and will be especially cost-effective for marine insurance.

*UPDATE*: Normally in a revision, I include changes to the wine business environment in the body of the subject at hand. But these times are anything but normal and, although I hope we return to a far less fraught global shipping climate, I have to make it clear that we are currently, and for the foreseeable future, dealing with extraordinary circumstances, primarily as a direct result of COVID.

I receive almost daily newsletters from the major freight forwarders advising me of the current situation regarding ship availability, the costs and forecasting. Today, Hillebrand sent out a comprehensive trade report that sounded, frankly, quite ominous. There were many delay issues affecting almost every port in the world.

For example, despite an increase in volume from Europe to the U.S. of 11.4%, only 14.7% of the vessels were on time. This can mean anything from days to weeks at the present. Hillebrand (now merged with Gori). Void sailings (empty ships) are increasing costs as the volatile global situation with both COVID and the war in Ukraine disrupt routes and ship availability.

China is currently in lockdown for a COVID outbreak and very few ships are leaving their ports, which is helping ease congestion elsewhere. After the initial long-term pandemic response in China, where all manufacturing stopped and the country virtually closed down, production ramped up last year to fulfill worldwide demand for goods. China diverted all the ships for their exports, which meant many ships went to China empty and then flooded ports, last year, which resulted in much of the current chaos. Many other factors, such as worker shortages due to illness and strikes have exacerbated the situation.

Shortages, uncertainty, and rising fuel costs have all culminated in vastly increased freight costs for the importer, which must be incorporated into your current budget (at the time of this writing). You may be thinking this is very gloom and doom and even wondering if you've chosen the wrong career but, as always, my intention is to give you the unvarnished truth. On the other hand, every importer is in the same boat at the moment. All of us are facing the same delays, difficulties and increase in costs. This levels the playing field among suppliers, importers, distributors and retailers.

## Customs Broker

This is an essential resource, and provides a function you cannot perform yourself. Choose a company wisely because you must depend upon them to clear your shipments expeditiously and accurately and – once again - save you time and money in the process.

Typically, customs brokers manage all documentation related to your shipment, including label approvals and winery invoices, provided by you, and B/L, provided by the freight forwarder or shipping company. They track the vessel, pay duty to customs in a timely manner, can arrange for cargo pickup and delivery and, at your discretion, can arrange for an "express" clearance while the vessel is still at sea to minimize the time your cargo spends on the dock before pickup.

Should your container be chosen for a physical, or x-ray customs inspection (rare, but not unheard of, especially with a new importer), the customs broker will also manage and expedite the container removal and pickup in an effort to avoid demurrage charges – fees accruing per day in excess of the "free" days allowed for cargo, currently 7 days.

Port delays are rampant these days on both coasts, due to strikes, terminal closures and increased traffic. It has increased the costs, which have been passed along to the consignee (the importer). With these challenges, it is more critical than ever to have reliable freight forwarder and customs broker contacts who will maintain a vigil over your wine and its disposition.

## My Story

There are times when insurance comes in handy for more than temperature variance.

The first container I ever received (and perhaps for that very reason) was targeted for a customs inspection. It was a "stuffed" container and Customs managed, in the process, to break most of the contents of twenty-two cases of my father's best wine, The Cowra Estate Reserve Chardonnay. The remainder of the twenty-two cases was unsaleable because of stained and ruined labels. I imagine, although was never told, that it occurred when the doors were opened and cases that had shifted during the voyage came tumbling out. But whatever the cause, there was no compensation and no recourse. The wine was finally released, along with a number of soggy cartons filled with shattered glass.

Although it has not happened to me, I have heard of containers going overboard at sea, and shipping collisions resulting in significant damage. Insurance is there in the event of the unexpected, catastrophic event.

## My Client's Story

One client, who has an unrelated thriving business, recently asked me if he could use his own container to ship the wine. Apparently, he was offered an empty container in trade for something in his non-wine business and thought this was an excellent way to save money. I explained to him that the cost of getting the container to the shipping company and the prohibitive expense of shipping this container empty on the outbound voyage would far outweigh any savings he might realize on having his own container.

Another client recently had an x-ray exam of his first shipment. This caused delays at port while the container waited for someone from US Customs to be available, but also resulted in an unanticipated and unbudgeted $750 in additional fees, levied by CBP. These are unrecoverable expenses. X-ray fees can vary from port to port. A physical exam could be even worse. I've never seen one since my own initial container exam, thirty years ago as of this writing. But I am told that this could add another approximately $2,500 to the container budget. At a meeting with a freight forwarder representative, he told me of a furniture company in the U.S. that has its containers examined, at a cost of $3,000, *every single time* they enter a port. This stemmed from the furniture company innocently deciding to ship tea in one of its early containers, because it was light and would be a nice addition to their retail outlets, without going through the proper channels. Since tea is a food product, and subject to FDA approval and other labeling and legal requirements, this was prohibited. As a result, whether from an abundance of caution or out of spite, every single container for the last two or three years has had this physical exam requirement. The takeaway for you is, obviously, don't ship anything in your container that has not been approved and declared.

# CHAPTER 7

# THE NEXT STEPS

You will discover that the wine industry cannot be approached like most other businesses in the corporate world. Although you must create a budget that includes a pricing model for each wine and accounts for markup and margin, there are many variables that become apparent as you start trading. Responding to the demands of the individual distributors, and the industry itself, in a positive and flexible manner is a necessity to survival and to be seen as a savvy player. To sustain a viable business model, you must throw out preconceived notions and rigid corporate paradigms and be prepared to adapt quickly to the changing environment.

## First Container Budgeting

Earlier, I suggested that the first container comprise sufficient wine to sustain your markets for approximately three months. This is often, understandably, a difficult figure to accurately calculate, especially if the wines are brand new to the market, but if you don't make the effort it is more probable that a miscalculation will start eating up your margins. Even if brands were previously established in the U.S., there is no guarantee that they will remain in demand, that sales were not already declining or that the market has not changed since the brand was with someone else, because of a difficult economy, or the varietal or country is over-saturated. The following would be some of the considerations for this introductory time period.

## Pricing

If the wine is priced at the higher end of the market, it is likely to start out slowly. This is before market demand has developed and when the distributor may be reluctant to be the vanguard of the brand's sales. The distributor must also consider their own budgets in committing to a brand that may not provide them with the cash flow or pull-through they envisioned. Because of the higher pricing, they will have more money tied up in these wines than they would in others.

If the wine is priced competitively, or even below its peers, it could conceivably begin selling more rapidly. This is no guarantee but the probability that your customers will buy with less deliberation, and in volume, is greater than for a higher priced wine. The investment on their part is smaller, the risk is reduced and potential for a faster rate of sales turnover, (therefore payment) is more appealing.

## Ratings

Usually, when first introduced, the brand has no U.S. ratings on which to base demand. Other than *Wine Advocate*, commercial wine publications require US-compliant labeling and existing distribution before they will consider a review and rating. This makes new brand introduction slower, and requires more investment in time and money waiting for distributor decisions. Investment in brand building must be part of your budgeting exercise, along with travel to meet with distributors, if necessary, or to work the market later on. It means you must be the driving force behind the wines sales, rather than the ratings either pushing sales or providing a positive impetus, at least in this initial phase.

I don't happen to agree with waiting for a rating before committing to being a winery's importers. Not only is this disrespectful to the winery, forcing them to wait months for your decision and perhaps foregoing an introduction that year in the market, but what happened to relying on one's palate? I am not so naïve as to believe that ratings from the right publications aren't helpful. However, if we all made decisions on wine purchases based solely on the perspective of another palate, then we are dangerously narrowing the flavor profile for an entire market, thereby ignoring and marginalizing the much more important factors of region, terroir, winemaker's signature, vintage variables, etc.

## New brand demand

This may be created through pre-selling (discussed later) or through your own relationships with distributors. It may be the next hot region, still on the upswing, or the opportunity to capitalize on the buzz created in the brand's home country. It could hit just the right note with the distributors you have contacted and to which you have made proposals. But generally, this is a difficult area to gauge and should be approached with caution.

## Old brand demand

If you are fortunate enough to take on a consistently high volume, highly rated, icon brand or household name that has left its current importer, then you will be in a much better position to throw out some of the cautions in the first stages. But as a new, unproven importer, this is unlikely to happen. This type of brand can virtually write its own ticket and will likely have its pick of solid, seasoned veterans of the industry.

A more likely scenario is a brand owner who is unhappy with the sales performance of his or her importer, is losing ground in the U.S. and wants to try someone who they feel will (after proving yourself financially viable) be able to regain the focus that their previous importer has lost. This is still a great opportunity (assuming all positive aspects are aligned) and you can start with a ready-made base of sales and good distributors on which to build the brand back up or to new heights. My counsel to you regarding this situation, from personal experience: last year's sales do not necessarily presage the future, nor are the current list of distributors likely to all stay in place. Brands wax and wane with distributors all the time and this could be their opportunity to bow out of representing this particular one.

## QPR (Quality Price Ratio)

The happy convergence of label, price, quality, perception, style and taste may mean a blast off in sales right from the start, in which case you have done your homework well, but the starting line is usually farther away than you might think, as summarized below.

## Timing

Consider the time it takes for the ship to leave port and make its way over here – generally anywhere from two weeks to a month, (depending upon the point of origin) with unanticipated delays at either port, as well as overland transport to take into consideration. A container trucker to bring the wine to the warehouse, unload and inventory will take an extra two to three days, if they are able to pick it up immediately.

Now, if you have not done any pre-selling, *with order commitments*, you will organize a ground shipment, via UPS, DHL, FedEx or other carrier, of wines from the warehouse (if it is not in driving distance to your office) and start the process of contacting distributors to determine their interest. I advise starting with at least one or two cases of each wine. There may also be publications to submit to, and most of these require two bottles of each submission.

*Some* pre-determination should have been done at this point so that you have at least identified potential distributors, but this may be only a short way down the decision track. In general, it can take several months from expressed interest to an order and this is one of the most important considerations of your budgetary concerns.

# Seasonal Timing

If you have already laid the necessary groundwork – obtained label approval, researched the market, turned targeted potential distributors into solid distributors and pre-sold wine, the optimum months of the year to land a **new** brand, and minimize the time the wine will spend in storage, is early September to October. A launch at this time gets the wine to the retailer for the holiday selling period. Remember, in the pipeline, the winery and importer are at the beginning and the consumer is at the end. The wholesaler and retailer must make their choices and bring wine in well prior to the holiday kickoff.

The first quarter (January to March) is also a favorable launch time for a new brand. At the beginning of the year, distributors will be looking at their holiday sales and how well their brands performed over that holiday time frame. If the brands in their book performed poorly when sales expectations are at their highest, this may be a time to jettison a brand or pull back on commitment, and leaves the door open to new, potentially more exciting, income generating brands to come in and make their mark. More importantly, most groundwork and the pre-sales or commitment should come in the first half of the year, ready for a seasonal launch.

Naturally, if everything you have done results in a convergence of functions that determines a container shipping from port of origin or arriving in the U.S. at another time, then you probably don't want to wait, but the months to try and avoid would be July and August, when heat is of paramount concern and wholesalers are laying low, away for school holidays or waiting for the fall season to begin.

## Incentives

Incentives, in this case provided by the winery, can include:

- free goods – usually cases of the current release in the container
- special bottles such as magnums or jeroboams
- winery marketing paraphernalia
- money
- contests for trips or prizes.

Not all states allow incentives to distributors, salespeople or retailers and we will discuss in more detail later, but some do and this is an opportunity to jumpstart a brand. If a winery is able to offer incentives that can be passed on to the wholesaler, this may also present an opportunity to partner with your distributor or provide ongoing support to periodic promotional efforts by their sales staff.

It generally takes a larger winery to offer incentives beyond free goods and is not considered an essential part of doing business. But a rollout with skillfully integrated incentives can create the excitement, and sense of professionalism, to put the brand introduction into a different category in the wholesaler's minds. It is an element in the decisions you make regarding budgeting for the first containers.

## Pricing the Wine

This is such a subjective area and I want to make it clear from the outset that I am providing guidelines only. Your markups and margins are entirely up to you and should not be dictated by anyone else, but my guidelines have worked for me throughout my many years as an importer and they can provide a springboard from which you may create your own.

In addition to the actual costs and percentage markups, these are other pricing considerations, one or more of which may come into play for your situation:

- maintain a competitive edge in a specific state or nationally
- fit a perception of the wine
- allow for incentive programming
- remain on a relative par with the pricing in the country of origin.

I am constantly asked by wineries to calculate their retail for them in the U.S. They want to know where their wine will sit after they have set their FOB price. They want to know what importers, distributors and retailers are making. They want to know if a point or two in discount will make their wine a better price, or make not much difference at all. The system here is so foreign to the way the rest of the world works that they just want to get a better handle on it any way they can, and one of those ways is to get a feel for where the markups are and what to expect at the other end of the pricing spectrum.

Since the first edition of this book, there has been a bit of an explosion of consultants, webinars, wine law firm specialists and others that have provided some insight or pricing calculations, some of it quite complicated and much too specific. There's nothing wrong with trying to be precise, except that individual state taxes for all fifty states is not something most importers will ever need to know. This presupposes that you will be distributing in each state in which you do business and must become familiar with the taxes, which will not be the case. If you are one of the rare new importers in a position to start buying up wholesale companies in a collection of states, you will no doubt have a legal and compliance team to advise you of your legal obligations. Other than your own state taxes, the others are not your obligation.

Pricing tables that include markups for trucking estimates are also misleading. It gives the impression that the importer is responsible for delivering the wine, and I have had several new clients make that assumption. One even thought it was a good business incentive to offer to deliver the wines. It's not, and would be illegal to deliver over state lines. All orders, unless there is something particularly unusual in your arrangement that must be to your advantage, are picked up by the distributor at your warehouse, with costs incurring to them beyond the warehouse door.

I also received a myriad of false, misleading, incomplete and mystifying information when I first embarked on my importer path, and there was no internet to either clarify the information or further confuse me. Part of the problem lies with the fact that here are fifty states, hundreds of importers, thousands of wholesalers and tens of thousands of retailers – all with their own unique markups and ways of doing business. But you have to be able to start somewhere. And for that purpose, I have included my own simple tables that calculate the price from the winery to the consumer in a generic way that allows you to have a fair idea of where the wine will end up.

Caveat: pricing for you as the importer can vary even more from what I've stated above under the following circumstances, should you choose:

- ♦ Consciously setting small margins for the sake of high-volume turnover or DI (whole container purchases) on specific wines

- ♦ Marking up high end wines (expensive) less than lower priced, higher volume wines, which are marked up at a normal percentage – the markup may be smaller, but the profit could be the same or greater based on price

- State and local taxes (yours and theirs)

- Trucking costs (theirs)

- Government intervention in control states such as, e.g., Ohio, Pennsylvania and Utah (there are currently 18 control states)

- Small wholesalers with higher overhead

- Large wholesalers working on smaller margins

- Large retail chains with narrower margins

- Small, boutique wine stores with higher margins

- Meeting a target retail price

- Building in specific programming (incentive) dollars

I have also included two tables for the Australian dollar to illustrate the changes that have occurred in the past few years, to be aware of what a difference a fluctuation in rates can make to retail price. When I began importing, the FX rate for AUD was around .65. It reached parity (1:1) at the outset of the recession and, as of this writing, has ranged between .68 and .70 for the past year. Fortunately, post-recession, it seems to have stabilized and has not ranged much beyond a tenth of a point or two, making prices attractive and budgets manageable. The Euro is now closer to the USD at 1.01, but had been hovering at 1.1 to 1.2 for a couple of years before this. Global instability has naturally affected economy's currencies. It was much the same during the first writing of this book (I wrote it from 2009 to 2010), due to global economic, making it much more difficult to both preserve a margin and a reasonable retail price. In 2009, AUD FX rate varied from approximately .65 to .91 – an astonishing extreme. In 2009, NZD FX varied from approximately .51 to .74. In 2009, EU FX varied from approximately 1.27 to 1.5.

| Column 1 | Column 2 | Column 3 | Column 4 | Column 5 | Column 6 | Column 7 | Column 8 |
|---|---|---|---|---|---|---|---|
| AUD/btl | 9L case | Price US FX .65 | landed costs at 12.00 | FOB distrib at 1.35 | wholesale at 1.5 | retail mkup at 1.5 | USD/Btl |
| $ 2.50 | $ 30.00 | $ 19.50 | $ 31.50 | $ 42.53 | $ 63.79 | $ 95.68 | $ 7.97 |
| $ 3.00 | $ 36.00 | $ 23.40 | $ 35.40 | $ 47.79 | $ 71.69 | $ 107.53 | $ 8.96 |
| $ 3.50 | $ 42.00 | $ 27.30 | $ 39.30 | $ 53.06 | $ 79.58 | $ 119.37 | $ 9.95 |
| $ 4.00 | $ 48.00 | $ 31.20 | $ 43.20 | $ 58.32 | $ 87.48 | $ 131.22 | $ 10.94 |
| $ 4.50 | $ 54.00 | $ 35.10 | $ 47.10 | $ 63.59 | $ 95.38 | $ 143.07 | $ 11.92 |
| $ 5.00 | $ 60.00 | $ 39.00 | $ 51.00 | $ 68.85 | $ 103.28 | $ 154.91 | $ 12.91 |
| $ 5.50 | $ 66.00 | $ 42.90 | $ 54.90 | $ 74.12 | $ 111.17 | $ 166.76 | $ 13.90 |
| $ 6.00 | $ 72.00 | $ 46.80 | $ 58.80 | $ 79.38 | $ 119.07 | $ 178.61 | $ 14.88 |
| $ 6.50 | $ 78.00 | $ 50.70 | $ 62.70 | $ 84.65 | $ 126.97 | $ 190.45 | $ 15.87 |
| $ 7.00 | $ 84.00 | $ 54.60 | $ 66.60 | $ 89.91 | $ 134.87 | $ 202.30 | $ 16.86 |
| $ 7.50 | $ 90.00 | $ 58.50 | $ 70.50 | $ 95.18 | $ 142.76 | $ 214.14 | $ 17.85 |

| Column 1 | Column 2 | Column 3 | Column 4 | Column 5 | Column 6 | Column 7 | Column 8 |
|---|---|---|---|---|---|---|---|
| AUD/btl | 9L case | Price US FX .90 | landed costs at 12.00 | FOB distrib at 1.35 | wholesale at 1.5 | retail mkup at 1.5 | USD/Btl |
| $ 2.50 | $ 30.00 | $ 27.00 | $ 39.00 | $ 52.65 | $ 78.98 | $ 118.46 | $ 9.87 |
| $ 3.00 | $ 36.00 | $ 32.40 | $ 44.40 | $ 59.94 | $ 89.91 | $ 134.87 | $ 11.24 |
| $ 3.50 | $ 42.00 | $ 37.80 | $ 49.80 | $ 67.23 | $ 100.85 | $ 151.27 | $ 12.61 |
| $ 4.00 | $ 48.00 | $ 43.20 | $ 55.20 | $ 74.52 | $ 111.78 | $ 167.67 | $ 13.97 |
| $ 4.50 | $ 54.00 | $ 48.60 | $ 60.60 | $ 81.81 | $ 122.72 | $ 184.07 | $ 15.34 |
| $ 5.00 | $ 60.00 | $ 54.00 | $ 66.00 | $ 89.10 | $ 133.65 | $ 200.48 | $ 16.71 |
| $ 5.50 | $ 66.00 | $ 59.40 | $ 71.40 | $ 96.39 | $ 144.59 | $ 216.88 | $ 18.07 |
| $ 6.00 | $ 72.00 | $ 64.80 | $ 76.80 | $ 103.68 | $ 155.52 | $ 233.28 | $ 19.44 |
| $ 6.50 | $ 78.00 | $ 70.20 | $ 82.20 | $ 110.97 | $ 166.46 | $ 249.68 | $ 20.81 |
| $ 7.00 | $ 84.00 | $ 75.60 | $ 87.60 | $ 118.26 | $ 177.39 | $ 266.09 | $ 22.17 |
| $ 7.50 | $ 90.00 | $ 81.00 | $ 93.00 | $ 125.55 | $ 188.33 | $ 282.49 | $ 23.54 |

| Column 1 | Column 2 | Column 3 | Column 4 | Column 5 | Column 6 | Column 7 | Column 8 |
|---|---|---|---|---|---|---|---|
| EU/btl | 9L case | Price US FX 1.2 | landed costs at 12.00 | FOB distrib at 1.35 | wholesale at 1.5 | retail mkup at 1.5 | USD/Btl |
| € 2.50 | € 30.00 | $ 36.00 | $ 48.00 | $ 64.80 | $ 97.20 | $ 145.80 | $ 12.15 |
| € 3.00 | € 36.00 | $ 32.40 | $ 44.40 | $ 59.94 | $ 89.91 | $ 134.87 | $ 11.24 |
| € 3.50 | € 42.00 | $ 37.80 | $ 49.80 | $ 67.23 | $ 100.85 | $ 151.27 | $ 12.61 |
| € 4.00 | € 48.00 | $ 43.20 | $ 55.20 | $ 74.52 | $ 111.78 | $ 167.67 | $ 13.97 |
| € 4.50 | € 54.00 | $ 48.60 | $ 60.60 | $ 81.81 | $ 122.72 | $ 184.07 | $ 15.34 |
| € 5.00 | € 60.00 | $ 54.00 | $ 66.00 | $ 89.10 | $ 133.65 | $ 200.48 | $ 16.71 |
| € 5.50 | € 66.00 | $ 59.40 | $ 71.40 | $ 96.39 | $ 144.59 | $ 216.88 | $ 18.07 |
| € 6.00 | € 72.00 | $ 64.80 | $ 76.80 | $ 103.68 | $ 155.52 | $ 233.28 | $ 19.44 |
| € 6.50 | € 78.00 | $ 70.20 | $ 82.20 | $ 110.97 | $ 166.46 | $ 249.68 | $ 20.81 |
| € 7.00 | € 84.00 | $ 75.60 | $ 87.60 | $ 118.26 | $ 177.39 | $ 266.09 | $ 22.17 |
| € 7.50 | € 90.00 | $ 81.00 | $ 93.00 | $ 125.55 | $ 188.33 | $ 282.49 | $ 23.54 |

Figure 7.1 Pricing Tables for Australia and Europe

I have used Australian dollars and Euros in the above tables for the purpose of comparison. These tables can obviously apply to any other currency, such as Chilean or Argentine Peso or South African Rand. The table functions are the same; only the exchange rate changes.

Again, I have used very generic markups in each area of the table for ease of arriving at a figure quickly under any circumstance. This is not for the purpose of stipulating a wholesale figure to the distributor, nor dictating a retail price that this wine must sit at on the shelves. *It is for you to set your own markup, which you **can** control, and have a fair idea of where it will lead based on the markups which your customers control.* The table is broad and simple, but does the job without all the manipulations and calculations you could spend countless hours on, time better spent in sourcing, marketing and selling wine and running your business.

## Columns 1 and 2 (Bottle and 12/750ml case)

Using the original FOB from the winery, which will include getting the boxed, palletized wine to the port of departure, Column 1 shows the bottle price for a 750ml bottle and Column 2 shows the same price for 12 750ml bottles in a case (a total of 9 liters). At this stage it is in the currency of the originating country, assuming they are not quoting in US dollars.

Calculations will need to include a further expense for EXW, if that is your arrangement with your producer. In other words, if you are paying for product to be picked up at the winery or vineyard and taken to the port of origin.

## Column 3 (USD per case)

In each template, I have used the currency indicated and multiplied the original currency by the indicated exchange rate to arrive at the USD, e.g. $42.00 x .60 = $27.30.

## Column 4 (Landed costs)

I have added $12.00 USD to account for ocean freight, taxes, duty, associated container charges, overland freight and delivery to the warehouse. This is a baseline for a container with an insulated liner with average ABV (alcohol by volume) wines. Reefers, distilled spirits and sparkling will increase the costs. It is an arbitrary figure for this exercise but not overstating the costs under *normal* circumstances. Unfortunately, in these unparalleled times, it has doubled or tripled due to container shortages and the global shipping factors I have already laid out previously, but I am using the $12 laid-in cost for this exercise as a foundation for more stable times. Using a formula of your own in your excel spreadsheets you can manipulate this to suit the circumstances. Please note: this is for FCL. Whatever the market conditions, it will always be considerably higher for LCL. You may choose a baseline landed cost that is specific to your region and use that instead. Once you receive a quote from a freight forwarder, you can change this figure to allow for your own origin, destination and related costs.

Again, I have seen tables online that break out the landed costs in very specific items, down to pennies, but I just haven't found this to be necessary for my own purposes, especially without a large staff. I once had a bookkeeper on payroll that was costing me far more than she might have saved in calculating exact costs. Gathering this information on specific clearances at the beginning, utilizing the billings from the customs broker, will help establish a reasonable cost and preclude surprises. Be particularly aware of whether you have a majority of sparkling wines, fortified or >14% alcohol. All of these can increase the duty considerably. From the foundation point, establish one figure for subsequent shipments. Checking invoices periodically will determine if you remain on track but using a different figure for every single shipment and every single brand is time consuming and not worth, in my opinion, the additional expense of your time and effort for the return.

## Column 5 (Importer markup FOB)

This assumes a markup of 35% for the importer. Again, you may configure it another way, and in fact some importers use 30% and make a good living on large volume, some may use 40% to allow for incentives. You are starting out with little volume and high overhead and will find this margin is eaten up quickly. However, I would caution you to be careful about getting greedy. The wine is worth or perceived to be worth something definable to the individual making the purchase. In addition to this rather nebulous rationale, there is plenty of opportunity for the distributor, retailer or consumer to use the internet to research its cost in its country of origin. Exchange rate notwithstanding, there is certain to be pushback if your end point – the retail – is too high.

You may decide, as an example, that because the higher priced wines produce a higher profit you will charge a lower percentage for those and 35% for the rest of the portfolio. You may decide to aim for a specific retail for the lower priced wines and cut the margin to reach that all important figure on the shelf. It is up to you, and I won't belabor it. Consider what you have invested in the wine and what you intend to invest in travel, marketing, discounts for volume and free goods.

## Column 6 (Distributor markup)

Wholesaler and retailer markups enter a very grey area on any importer's spreadsheet. You can predetermine your own markup, and this is your prerogative. You cannot dictate someone else's except in rare situations, which we can get into later. I have used an arbitrary figure of 50% for the distributor markup (this has increased from 45% in the last book due to distributor consolidation and markup creep). You will drive yourself mad if you start looking at every state's taxes, likely freight charges and other expenses that go to make up what is known as 'laid in costs.' A distributor may only mark up 33%, but by the time you add in the laid in costs, along with increased fuel costs, you have arrived at a point that is a 50% increase from the price of the wine they purchased from you.

## Column 7 and 8 (Retail price per case and bottle)

This retail price now allows for a 50% markup. As with Column 6, I used 45% as the retail markup in the original book, but times have changed. The same variables as for wholesaler apply for the retailer; he has laid in costs of his own and the markup might actually only be 25%. On the other hand, at smaller, fine wine stores in high rent areas, the markup could be 60%, *after* the laid in costs. Using 50% for both generally gets the price to an average national retail.

It's only an exercise, but under ordinary circumstances it is a pretty realistic one. If you are particularly concerned with a magic retail number, < $10 or <$20, e.g., or achieving realistic glass pours, you may wish to hone your numbers further, speak to the winery about a bit of leeway, or see what your distributor may offer in terms of suggestions or participation in reaching that target number.

Most stores still price their wines with a .99 remainder - $7.99, $9.99, $19.99, etc. The spreadsheets reflect the raw numbers reached by the calculations, but a retailer will usually take it to the next available .99. In the first sheet, $8.80 becomes $8.99 and $9.22 would most likely become $9.99, rather than the closer $8.99, because the margin is higher and, as long as the wine is under $10, there is not a great deal of difference between $8.99 and $9.99, but it could still go either way. If the retailer prices a wine at the upper end it also enables them to offer a case discount or other promotional opportunity.

There are additional exceptions to these calculations. In Ohio, e.g., you can actually figure out quite accurately how the wine will sit at retail because the State of Ohio sets its pricing and those who do business there must follow. In many states, being at $24.99 or $26.99 makes little difference to the ability to sell the wine. In Ohio, it is far better to price at $19.99 and $29.99 than somewhere in between. Their matrix looks like this:

| | |
|---|---|
| $174.00 | Wholesale FOB |
| $   6.00 | laid in costs (tax, freight) |
| $180.00 | total |
| $360.00 | case/retail by doubling the laid in wholesale |
| $  29.99 | bottle/retail |

Or, if you look at Costco: at the time of writing, their markup in the fine wine bins is 14%. They also expect, as well they should based on the volume and exposure they offer, that the distributor's price is the leanest it can be. This could mean a 10% discount from the distributor, based on a customary across the board pallet discount to their customers, or it can mean a price the distributor arrives at to give them the most competitive advantage with this buyer. My experience with Costco is that they expect honesty in pricing and the best deal you can offer, but nothing beyond what you will offer another retailer for similar volume.

You will note, this low markup changes the retail dramatically. It will take a $21.99 wine down to $16.99 in most states and in the Ohio scenario it will mean the difference between $29.99 and $16.99!

What is readily apparent from the spreadsheets is that even a small change in exchange rate creates quite a different pricing scenario. Once you look at the Euro FX rate, the difference is marked and takes it from one pricing level to a completely different one. This must all be taken into consideration when setting your own prices. Build sufficient room in the price to allow, as much as possible, for the following factors:

- exchange rate fluctuations

- promotions – incentives, programming, contests, rewards

- sample usage – salespeople, publications, spoilage

- overhead – whatever your own situation dictates, including travel and personnel

In addition, consider where you want the wine to "sit" as a price point on the shelf or how well it might fit a glass pour in a restaurant.

*SUMMARY*—These stories are told to illustrate the advantage of relying on your palate, your intuition, your research and your own circumstances in making decisions. These are things to weigh in your own career, whether you think you already have the best wines or insufficient gravitas, whether sales of an established brand were blockbuster or lackluster. These may influence your decision in a way that prevents you from seeing a clear picture. The new wine could turn out to be better than the best wine you currently have or a dismal failure. Previous sales offer some indication of the immediate future but are no barometer for the long term success of the brand.

# My Story

I can give you two very good examples of wine selection that did *not* rely on two of the criteria that many new and seasoned importers use to determine a brand's value: ratings and history. In both cases, I relied on my own palate and intuition, an approach that was all too lacking in our industry in those days. Until relatively recently, there was too much reliance on numbers as a criteria and a guaranteed history of sales on which to base future sales. I am not saying that either is not beneficial – clearly they are. But to build one's own portfolio on those criteria alone is to miss out on golden opportunities.

A few years ago, a competitor approached me to see if I was interested in taking on a brand he was giving up. He was a friend of mine and I knew he had the best of intentions. I had lost a couple of strong brands in the implosion of the greedy brand owner's business I alluded to earlier, and this importer had a conflict. He represented two brands from the same area and one, a stronger and more reliable seller at the time, was applying some pressure to focus on their brand.

I looked at the brand. It had a great 'story' of family-owned vineyards in a renowned area and some interesting wines. The family was financially secure and was poised to increase volume. The wines themselves were not particularly strong, the ratings were mediocre at best, but they had potential. The young, energetic winemaker talked enthusiastically of his plans for the brand and assured me that the wines were only going to get better – more fruit-forward, more redolent of the character and style of the area. He also talked of what he wanted to do with some of the older plantings on the vigneron's land.

Quite frankly, if I had already possessed my own stable of stars I might not have taken on this brand but in seeing the holes in my own portfolio and the potential of this brand, I decided it was a worthwhile opportunity. It turned out to be the best decision I ever made.

The quality did go from strength to strength and, although the old distributors had fallen away and I could not rely on them for a distribution base, sales increased, and I added more selections to the range. The older plantings turned out to be arguably the oldest Shiraz vines in the world and although the yield from these vines was miniscule, it added cachet to the brand.

In two short vintages, one of the wines was rated higher than any wine *of its price point ever* in *Wine Spectator*. There was a feeding frenzy for this vintage and the other varietals and blends were drawn along with it. Sales skyrocketed and exposure for the portfolio was greatly increased. It has twice made the Top 100 Wines of the Year in *Wine Spectator*.

In the next story, the winemaker, a good friend of mine, formed his own brand with partners and produced one, small production, unusual cuvée to launch in the States. He said I could have 200 six packs in the first year. I loved the wine, the label, the unusual blend, the price point and, just as importantly to me, the opportunity to work with these fine people. It was also a modest beginning and did not require a huge financial outlay from me.

I launched the brand without any ratings or reviews and achieved some broad market distribution. In a few months, the wine gained a couple of respectable ratings in two publications, but in today's market if it doesn't break the 90 point barrier it does not contribute to the wine's success. I continued to sell the wine based solely on the interest of the customers, my enthusiasm in presenting it and the story behind 'the little brand that could.' I asked for more allocation and ended up selling 1200 six packs that first year – easily three-quarters of their production - all without resounding national reviews. I also credit others with thinking outside the box in making their buying decisions and contributing to the success of this wine's national sales.

And finally, a story of when I didn't just ignore my gut instinct, I failed to even check in with it. In the first two examples, all went happily right because it was a reasonable risk based on the evidence of my palate, coupled with attractive pricing. In those days, at least, before the economy went to hell in a hand basket, you could rely on finding markets for solid, well-priced wines. I came across an individual who was well connected to Hollywood, a lovely man with an equally engaging wife, both film directors and producers. Their story was unique and intriguing and I felt sure I could rely on the couple's connections to sell the wine, at least in California. In addition, they had retained a respected vineyard consultant to plant their beautiful property and a recognized, if pricey, winemaker to make the wines. The downside? The wines were from esoteric varieties and expensive and, quite frankly, I wasn't that crazy about them. I overrode red flags in my zeal to represent a brand that appeared to be courted by others, something I felt would sell on reputation and connections alone, and my ego got in the way.

Needless to say, the wines were not a success. I believe if they had been priced much more realistically, they could have stood a chance. There were LA restaurants that clearly wanted to make that connection for the prestigious brand owners but balked every time at the price. In the end, this was a valuable lesson about not allowing emotion to override practicality.

## My Client's Story

A short story on timing might make a difference for you too. A malt beverage client was bringing in really interesting new beers from Italy with a container order pre-sold to a distributor, ready to be picked up as soon as it arrived. However, the brewery took so long to provide US compliant labels that the importer missed critical timing for the distributor's needs and the order was cut in half. Producers in other countries can be particularly laid-back about responding to requests or they just don't think of it as that essential to the process. Especially with increased competition in the U.S., timing really can be everything.

# CHAPTER 8

# IT'S ON THE WATER – MAXIMIZE YOUR WAITING TIME

If your terms with the winery start at bill of lading, then the clock is ticking as soon as the ship leaves the dock in the port of origin. It is to your advantage to begin making good use of your time while waiting for the shipment by making a start on the many tasks ahead of you, both in terms of organization and sales.

## Winery Marketing Materials

At this stage, we will operate on the assumption that the wines are brand new and you have no U.S. ratings. As I have stated before, I don't believe this is a detriment to your sales at all. Most people do not wait for a *Wine Advocate* rating before they commit to a wine. The release timing for publications these days seems to be counterintuitive to this approach anyway. For example, the Australian issue, originally slated for an October release in time for holiday buying, was last released in February. Ratings are a boon, there is no doubt, and quite possibly an essential tool in most U.S.

markets but remember, in the beginning you selected the wines for your portfolio based on criteria *other* than a U.S. rating. Now you must do the legwork to ensure the wines' successful release without a rating net.

Most winery owners will point proudly to the trophy they were awarded at the local wine show, the five stars they garnered in a foreign publication, accolades they received from the hometown wine stores. And of course, they should be proud. These are barometers of the wines' desirability and worth on a national level; they mean absolutely nothing to the U.S. industry professional or consumer.

There are always exceptions to every rule. If the gold medal is from a show that has international recognition, the rating is in a publication such as Decanter (Great Britain's most significant wine magazine and widely available in the U.S.), James Halliday's Wine Companion or Michael Cooper's Buyer's Guide or the recommendation from Master of Wine and renowned writer, Jancis Robinson, then the rules are slightly different. Sadly, these ratings don't ultimately replace the U.S. ratings, but they are a providential boost to the wine in the early days, a reasonable precursor of how well it will do when it does appear in a U.S. publication and an immediate marketing tool.

In the meantime, what does the winery have? Brochures? Background on the winery? Tasting notes? Lists of medals, awards and favorable reviews? Photos? All of these can be utilized in the quest for sales. These are just fine in PDF format on email to you, or shared in a Drive folder.

**Brochures and background materials** can speak of the professionalism of the winery, the history – or perhaps just 'story' – behind the vineyard operation, the credentials of the winemaker, the open faces of the family. By themselves, these aspects will not sell the wine. Together with the combination of packaging, style, price and a developed rapport with you, they will begin to build a foundation for the distributor and a desire to get behind the brand.

**Tasting notes** are essential to your operation. Ideally, the brand owner will send you a professional looking press kit, complete with bottle shot and good technical information in PDF to include on your website, and for emailing to potential customers. But I've also had tasting notes emailed to me in garbled, run-on, unformatted, plain text; I've had them dictated to me as a few random thoughts from the top of a tractor in a foggy pasture early in the morning, leaving me to decipher and turn into a professional document. If they are not already in a tasting note/tech sheet format, you must put together something you can send to your potential customers or use in a tasting for reference.

Winemakers are as individual as people are in any profession and they tend to compose notes in individual ways, sometimes as bare technical data and sometimes as a fluffy PR piece that would be interesting to a consumer at cellar door but virtually useless to someone in the field. Technical data, tasting notes and viticulture and vinification should ideally be kept to one sheet. Whatever else you learn about the vineyard, through observation, education and additional notes, can be stored for your own tastings and presentations.

I find the following details to be helpful, for which I have included one type of example for each. This is an example only. There are many other ways that the more subjective areas can be characterized and described and much of the information would be lumped together in sections:

1. Synopsis of conditions for that vintage, including anything that made it particularly difficult or particularly favorable.

   The climate is characterised by hot summer days and relatively cool nights with diurnal ranges of up to 26 degrees Celsius. The 2022 season was an exceptional vintage, long and warm with cool nights, which is reflected in the wine. The summer/autumn rainfall was low.

2. How grapes were picked (and sometimes when).

> Grapes were harvested by hand. Each clone of fruit was harvested separately and kept separate at all stages of vinification. The fruit was de-stemmed, with some batches having a percentage of whole clusters retained.

3. Yield.

> The vineyard is trellised on a Geneva double curtain and spur pruned to 10 shoots per metre. It is extensively thinned to 6 tonnes per hectare.

4. Varietal, including percentages of blended grapes, no matter how small – the purpose being to identify what is in the wine for your customer, not to comply with a legal requirement.

> Cabernet Sauvignon 72%, merlot 23% petit verdot 5%.

5. Where grown (estate, sourced, steep slope, soil, etc.).

> Soils are free-draining river gravels.

6. Fermentation process.

> The must then underwent 3-5 days of pre-ferment maceration after which it was warmed to 17 degrees and inoculated for fermentation. Most batches were pressed off at dryness while some were left on skins for 7-8 days.

7. Aging, including type of oak if oak aged.

   14 months in seasoned French oak.

8. Other details of interest, such as whether the wine was fined and filtered, whether the grapes were organically or biodynamically grown, etc.

   Sourced from 90 year old bush-grown vines in the northeast of the valley.

   All fruit was organically grown on the estate and certified by Certified Organic Farmers.

9. Description of wine characteristics such as color, weight, flavors, finish. This is a very subjective area that becomes a bow to the winemaker's own style, which can be short and succinct or flowery overstatement.

   Color:         Intense garnet

   Aroma:   A very desirable cabernet which doffs its cap to the great wines of Bordeaux. Earthy and complex, it oozes ripe blackberries and black cherry fruit. Developed cigar box character and vanillin oak mingle pleasantly with nuances of cloves and star anise.

   Palate:   A stylish palate that offers loads of ripe fruit, but avoids jamminess. It has terrific flavor persistence, complexity, fine elegant texture and oak integration

10. Technical data, such as that which relates to a particular wine.

| | |
|---|---|
| Sulphur dioxide at bottling - Total (ppm) | 42 |
| pH | 3.40 |
| Acid (g/L) | 6.80 |
| C6 Sugars (g/L) | 0 |
| Alcohol (%) | 13.9 |

11. If appropriate, i.e., of a higher standard, a SUMMARY of medals, awards and trophies.

> Gold Medal – Sydney International Wine Competition
>
> Decanter – Top 100 Wines of 2021
>
> Silver Medal – Royal Melbourne Wine Show
>
> Five Stars – James Halliday

12. Food pairing suggestions, which are at the discretion of the winemaker – not essential by any means, but often an interesting – and unusual! – guide.

> Try this with aged beef and a reduced red wine sauce. However, we have been known to drink it with garfish, salads and paella and makes for a sensational celebration regardless of a meal!

This is a lengthy list, but as you can see, some aspects can be handled in a word or number. Ultimately, the more comprehensive the information is, the better prepared you are to discuss the wines in an informed and knowledgeable fashion. You can also develop your own standardized template in which you can insert the appropriate material in each instance, whatever the brand:

- **The Winery** — Background.
- **The Region** — The area in which the vineyard or growing area is situated.
- **The Year** — Something about that particular vintage.
- **The Fruit** — Not just which varieties, but something more about them.
- **The Winemaking**— Details.
- **The Juice** —Nose details. Palate details. Technical details.

I also include a bottle shot or label graphic. A tasting note/tech sheet can be in many different styles, but style is irrelevant (beyond being neat and clear) as long as it includes much or all of the essential information. You can find other examples in the "trade" section of many winery or importer websites.

## Setting up a Website

Whether you are a webmaster or have only used your computer skills to navigate your way around the internet, a website is an essential tool for an importer. I'm still surprised, in 2022, to Google an importer and find no website. Budgetary constraints – or not - will dictate the scope of your site, but if you have the time, inclination and a limited budget, it is extremely easy to put together a credible and useful site utilizing the templates of companies such as Network Solutions at www.networksolutions.com, Word Press, www.wordpress.com or Wix at www.wix.com as just some examples. Your website can look customized, informative and appealing, with very little expense. Check out reviews and compare website hosting online.

# POWELL & SON

## BAROSSA

## 2019 Marsanne

*The marsanne provides aromas of ripe stone fruits, honeysuckle and hawthorn flower with nuances of toasted butter and flint.*

*In the mouth the wine is rich but restrained. The texture is honeyed and round, but the acid backbone lifts the wine and keeps it liveliness.*

*200 dozen produced*

Varietal: 100% Marsanne
Region: Barossa Valley
Districts: Kalimna
Altitude: 280 metres
Soil: White sand on yellow clay
Vines: 20+ years old
Harvest: 26th February
TA: 4.7 g/l
Alcohol: 14%

Vinification:

The grape parcels are hand-picked and whole bunch pressed, then the Marsanne is fermented in 50% new and 50% old French Oak barrels. Following 6 months of barrel maturation on lees the Marsanne racked off to tank. The wine is then cold stabilised and sent to bottle.

Drink now or over the next 10 years. Serve chilled. Best with crab or lobster, chicken and also a great accompaniment with spicy food.

Figure 8.1 Tasting note/tech sheet Example

The work you put into setting up a website will be offset by the following benefits:

- Credibility— a website says you have some stability and shows clients and customers the wines you carry.

- You can include a mission statement that clearly states your objectives and philosophy, which encourages prospective wineries to consider your representation.

- Trade tools for your distributors and their salespeople. This is a lifesaver when salespeople are looking for assistance in their sales endeavors, and provides information for their own marketing materials. It often saves them from calling you to send or email the information, or gives them last minute material to download and print for an event.

- News and updated reviews and ratings can give distributors the edge in selling and alert them to new vintages or exciting new brand arrivals, or when items are sold out or in limited supply.

Although the website should be interesting and welcoming, my suggestion is not to become too ambitious with graphics, large file sizes or audio. You want a site that is easy and quick to load, and doesn't require too many maneuvers to navigate away from scenes and audio intros, and in which each area or page can be accessed immediately.

## Bookkeeping, Invoicing, Forms and Inventory Management

Setting up your general ledger and chart of accounts for tracking financial activity should be undertaken in the early stages of your business establishment, once you have decided what type of legal entity you are going to be. It can, and often should, be handled by an outside service, depending upon your level of expertise and that of office employees, if any. The Small Business Administration (www.sba.org) is a wonderful resource for small businesses, and the experienced retired professionals at SCORE (www.score.org) can offer advice and direction from their real-world experience and qualifications. The definition on their site is:

*"SCORE is a nonprofit association dedicated to educating entrepreneurs and helping small businesses start, grow, and succeed nationwide. SCORE is a resource partner with the U.S. Small Business Administration (SBA)*

In addition to mentoring, advice and training, SCORE offers inexpensive workshops and webinars on a regular basis on financial statements, setting up a small business, QuickBooks and many other related subjects. They are also a resource for SBA loan applications. Unfortunately, a successful loan application will be unlikely when you are a new, inexperienced importer without appreciable assets or history. Applying for a SBA loan may be useful later as growth investment, if needed.

Purchase orders, invoices, statements, accounts receivable, inventory management, sales history, invoice ageing – all very important tools once your business is established - can easily be linked to the financial side through a program like QuickBooks Premier: Manufacturing and Wholesale Edition, from Intuit. (www.intuit.com) It is a comprehensive program that covers all aspects of conducting business for importers and distributors. It is not designed purely for this field, in fact it is a generic program for a myriad of businesses, but it will ably fill all your requirements. There are programs more suited to winery operations where, in addition to distribution of their product, the winery also has to keep track of vineyard operations, harvest, production, etc. However, in my view, that type of program will be more than you need for your purposes. All QuickBooks programs are available as a product to load onto your computer, or can be set up online to allow others in your company to access the program across the country or across the world, with your permission and password.

Set up can be a steep learning curve and I urge you to begin as soon as possible. The earlier you start capturing information, the less catch up you have to do by inputting items that have already been processed and stored elsewhere. An accounting program like QuickBooks will soon become an invaluable and straightforward tool for access to the types of reports you need to run your business and manage your customers and vendors.

Purchase order quantities to the vineyard can be used to set up inventory. At this stage in the process, your entries will be inventory in transit, which will then easily convert to inventory received, upon arrival. Tracking inventory in QuickBooks is optional, in my opinion. It is easy to forget to do it and can be an aspect that is cumbersome to track consistently. It will require diligent attention to recording every movement of a case or bottle and mistakes may take a while to become apparent and recover. If you have multiple locations, will be storing all product yourself or have a background in this level of organization and order, then tracking inventory may work well for you. It will allow you to know immediately when a product is low or insufficient to supply a particular order. On the other hand, reputable, commercial warehousing companies offer real time product information on line and data such as item inventory and open and shipped orders can be accessed daily or as often as you like.

At whatever stage you are setting up your books, you will want to include a customized template for the forms you will be using. There is very little in this arena that is as important as the invoice – the means by which you will bill and collect monies owed. A company invoice should have preprinted boxes or line items for the following information:

- Company name and contact details
- Pick up date
- Purchase order number (assigned by your customer, the distributor)

- Invoice number (establish a working system to track easily – could be dated, e.g., 21-0001, numbered, e.g., sequentially starting with 0001, or by state, e.g. CA-0001. It doesn't matter, as long as it is something that makes sense to you )

- Ship to

- Bill to

- Terms

- FOB point

- Due Date

- Item

- Description

- Quantity

- Rate (cost per case)

- Total per item quantity

- Total owed on invoice

**Optional inclusions are:**

- A preprinted message to your customer thanking them for the order or specific directive

- A preprinted statement as to how past due bills will be handled, i.e. interest or penalty

♦ Sufficient room for messages that apply only to that invoice, e.g., "short 4 cases of '20 cabernet sauvignon – will ship with next order."

Several other examples of invoices can be found in QuickBooks and modified to cover the above items and any others you may need.

# Warehouse and Customs Broker Notification and Arrangements

## Warehouse notification

With all the warehouse review, selection and licensing in place, you will have met and spoken with the warehouse personnel sufficiently to establish the start of another important relationship. Treating them with courtesy and consideration from the outset will make life a great deal easier when you run into problems, inventory mistakes and mismanaged shipments. These people will go above and beyond for you if they feel you respect what they do.

Notifying them of an impending shipment arrival is not only courteous, it saves you and them considerable time in scheduling and avoiding potential delays in receiving the goods. Individual entities can tell you of their own requirements, but at the least you should send them a list of each item, including brand, varietal/blend, size of individual container, the number of bottles per box and an ID number, preferably of your own choosing. This is what will be used to identify your wines in inventory at the warehouse, for purchase orders, shipments, and so on. The first letters will be your own company. In this example, I used BL, for Bluestone.

| | | |
|---|---|---|
| Cassowary 2021 Cabernet/Merlot 12/750ml | 20 cases | BLCCM21 |
| Billy Bob 2022 Botrytis Semillon 6/375ml | 10 cases | BLBBBS22 |

This ensures that the warehouse easily identifies the item and counts and segregates appropriately. It also helps to avoid mistakes, such as assuming that the entire pallet is one wine simply because the outside cases all look the same. Giving the warehouse a heads up also allows them to plan the shipment's arrival and put the delivery in a queue. Some warehouses will have their own notification form and require that you complete it online or email it to them.

## Overland Container Transport

This is also the time to consider what trucking company you will use to transport the container from port to warehouse. It has to be a trucking company that specializes in this type of transport, rather than small truckloads or local pickup and deliveries. Warehouses often either have their own logistical arm or can recommend a carrier, as can customs brokers. As with everything else, do your due diligence to compare costs and references. Give the trucking company a chance with a couple of containers to see if they are communicative, deliver on time and follow up diligently. If you see a pattern of disinterest or chronic delays, move on quickly to someone else.

This is where I stopped with container transport advice in the first edition but so much has changed since then in terms of ports and carriage charges. Port congestion, strikes, terminal closures, and modifications in shipping schedules have all given rise to uncertainty in delivery dates and times. This is why I recommend getting a quote from the freight forwarder for a "door move", one that includes picking up the container once it is released and taking it to the warehouse destination you designate. There will still be some variables, such as additional waiting time and fuel surcharge, but it should be a competitive rate and the freight forwarder will be motivated to pick up and deliver the container as quickly as possible to avoid demurrage charges (fees incurred once the container exceeds its free days in port). This is an aspect of your business where you could benefit from getting competitive quotes, but bearing in mind that each shipment may be different.

## Customs Clearance

By now you have the necessary COLAs, invoices, shipping documents and bills of lading to submit electronically to your customs broker for them to begin the clearing process while the container is on the water. Customs brokers will now do this with an electronic *express clearance,* instead of the old method of requiring original documents. This allows a pre-clearance of goods before arrival through U.S. Customs and potentially decreasing waiting time at dock. If the customs broker encounters any problems with documents or the information you have provided, there is presumably plenty of time to rectify the issue before the ship docks.

By contracting for your own FCL, where you control the Master Bill, you have the most control over this stage of the process through clearance and transit to warehouse. Through express clearance, booking a trucking company and alerting the warehouse ahead of time, you have streamlined the process, cutting days off the schedule, and potentially shaving weeks off the time it would take with an LCL container. Keep in mind that I am aware you may not need an FCL yet and not encouraging you to purchase more wine than you need, but only pointing out the difference.

## Pre-Selling

This is an optional, but potentially important, early task if you have the necessary wines and connections. The winery may elect to airfreight wine ahead of the container for you to use to interest potential distributors and jump start the order process. Air freight is a fairly expensive proposition, however, and may not be feasible, or the winery may be reluctant to continue to eat into their margin. In later containers, new release wines can be put in the container along with your order and save the winery the expense of an air shipment. You will be paying for the freight on the samples in the container, as opposed to the winery paying for the air freight, but the cost is negligible and you will most likely receive far more in the monetary value of samples with your ocean freight than you would have had they been sent via air.

If you have identified, or worked with, a viable distributor who expresses interest, knows the pricing and has some idea of the style and type of wine, then this is most likely an excellent time to put those samples to good use. If you are simply contacting distributors randomly or without thorough vetting, the samples may be wasted. Most wholesalers don't have the time or inclination to tell an importer to send them product they have no intention of representing but the idly curious may do so. And even worse, the less scrupulous companies may do so simply to drink free wine. It happened to me, twice, with the same distributor. Always willing to give someone the benefit of the doubt, I sent more samples when they indicated the first set was lost. This was before tracking was available online. These days there is every opportunity to track your product to ensure it hasn't gone astray and when it was delivered.

We'll get into the distributor search process more in the later section of the book, which will apply both in pre-selling and finding long-term distribution. It's all the same as far as you are concerned. You are not looking for a one-time sale; you are looking for a working relationship.

## Submitting to Publications

Depending upon the number of samples you receive ahead of time, if any, this is an excellent time to submit to national publications. Each publication will require two bottles of each submitted wine. Submission requirements, including individual forms that must be completed according to the publication's specifications, will be available online at each website. You should also call and request to be put on email notifications of these major publications and online review vehicles:

* *Wine Spectator*
* *Wine Enthusiast*
* *Wine & Spirits*

Figure 8.2 Wine Spectator Website

They will generally notify you of the tasting deadlines for each country or specialty editions: reds, whites, pinots of the Northwest, blends of the Barossa, whites of Chile, e.g. Each publication will advise whether they want tasting notes, suggested retail pricing, production or number of cases imported, or if an extensive history is helpful, along with viticultural practices and winemaker's notes.

Vinous is another review vehicle that has emerged since I stopped large scale importing my own products, so I have limited familiarity with it, but with regard to the well-respected principals involved it is undoubtedly worthwhile. It is a collaboration between Antonia Galloni, a former senior wine critic with *Wine*

*Advocate,* and Stephen Tanzer's *International Wine Cellar.* They bring together other top wine critics under their banner in an online format that includes an interactive environment. It operates on a subscription basis for daily reviews, articles and updates.

If you have limited samples, my suggestion is to submit to *Wine Spectator* first. I say this without bias, as it is the most widely read, visible consumer wine publication if you are choosing only one publication for review at this time. It will also be a review that retailers will give the nod to for an estimation of quality and a worthwhile addition to a shelf talker, the ubiquitous cards that front the bottle in a retail wine store.

Since the first edition, submission practices have changed quite dramatically. In the case of *Wine Spectator,* they no longer accept unsolicited samples as a result of the ever-increasing hordes of samples they were receiving and had no time to review.

According to their site:

*Wine Spectator reviews more than 16,000 wines each year. All new releases are reviewed in blind tastings in flights with their peers.*

*Our goal is to review wines that are important and available to our readers. In most cases, we review only wines that are distributed in major markets in the United States.*

*The task of managing these tastings occupies a staff of tasting coordinators based in Wine Spectator offices in New York and Napa. Each office is responsible for specific wine regions.*

*All samples must have U.S. Alcohol and Tobacco Tax and Trade Bureau (TTB)-approved front and back labels on them. We will not accept wines with unfinished labels.*

*Wine Spectator* also advises that wines that are sent without the supplemental information they require will not be tasted.

*Wine Enthusiast* is accorded noteworthy status in some circles and others find it too lenient in its scores. *Wine & Spirits* would possibly be the least weighted of the three publications in general, I would say, although it is also widely available in stores and, as far as I am concerned, provides a credible opportunity for great scores (if applicable) that make a nice quote and look good on shelf talkers.

You will undoubtedly find many and varied opinions regarding the significance of each publication's rating and the reviewer - "oh, she only likes cool climate wines" or "he's a Bordeaux fanatic". But you can find value in submitting to these publications as a start and to build up name recognition. It is, after all, free, other than for the cost of the wine and shipping.

There are many other to submit to, most notably The *Wine Advocate*. To many wine savvy collectors, it has enjoyed iconic status that is, or was, unequaled in the wine world and they will buy only on its recommendation. The publication was once a scholarly looking periodical that accepted no advertising, available only via subscription. It is now exclusively online.

Robert Parker used to be the final arbiter of reviews of all countries, but long turned over regions to others — very fine, educated, and experienced wine experts. This has accomplished three things: 1) opened up the tastings to more wines and a broader base of each country or region, 2) broadened the range of reviewer palates, and 3) given the devotees a "wait and see" attitude about the future of its iconic status and whether, without Robert Parker's personal endorsement of each and every wine, the rating has the same impact and prestige. To some extent in the short term, the changes have diluted the value of the rating. In 2012, Robert Parker sold a major stake in the company and later that year stepped down as CEO, turning over the reins to Lisa Perotti-Brown, MW, the Southern Hemisphere reviewer based in Asia. The company has also moved content completely online and continues revamping its website and review guidelines.

Much has also changed with wine submissions with this publication. I used to go to the *Wine Advocate* home office town in Maryland to meet with the Australian wines reviewer over a leisurely lunch. Reviewers are scattered all over the world now.

157

The country of origin of the wines will determine where they are sent, if requested, although this has nothing to do with the actual location of the reviewer. At time of writing, the South African reviewer is in London, the Greek reviewer is in Philadelphia, the Australian reviewer is in Singapore.

Today, all interested wineries/producers must first go the website and upload details of the wine's origins, including vine age, soil conditions, yields and much more. Information on specific labels you wish to be considered is next, and most recently the publications require label images. It is from this database that the reviewers will select the wines they want to taste:

According to the *Wine Advocate* website instructions:

*[WA] accepts requests to submit wine samples for taste evaluation and rating in conjunction with the scheduled reports published in the Wine Advocate's Editorial Calendar. For each report, Wine Advocate Reviewers will select wines to review from the Wine Advocate's Producer database and invite the selected wineries to submit samples directly for tasting.*

*We do not accept unsolicited samples for review and do not accept wine samples that are unrelated to scheduled reports.*

At their discretion, a taster/reviewer will elect to go to the cellar door of the winery to taste on site.

*Wine Enthusiast* will still accept unsolicited samples as long as you follow all instructions on their website and their forms accompany the wines, completed as instructed. Any wines without the completed form will not be considered for review. *Wine Enthusiast* also have an extensive FAQ on their site, which should clarify most issues. They do not accept any wines that are not currently imported into the U.S. If your wines have U.S. approved labels and have arrived just ahead of the first container, they qualify as "currently imported".

*Wine and Spirits* also accepts unsolicited samples, but asks *"that you submit samples according to our editorial tasting calendar and send only wines that fall into the categories listed under each issue"*.

For most publications, expect to wait four to six months for a review to appear. This is why it is helpful to be able to shorten your wait by submitting before the wine has reached the U.S. shore and taking notice of the publication's issues that relate specifically to your category.

In the case of *Wine Spectator* and *Wine Advocate*, an online subscription, in addition to or instead of a magazine subscription, is advisable. This will allow you to receive advance notification of issues and you can easily check reviews and ratings. From *Wine Spectator*, you will receive advance notice of issues and "insider" reviews. It is advisable to periodically search for ratings for your wines in the event they have listed a "web only" review. This is not as helpful as having it in the print publication because of the lack of consumer exposure but if it is a high rating, it is just as valuable to you, enabling you to use it on a shelf talker and as a PR tool with distributors and retailers.

Signing up as an importer with *Wine Enthusiast* (with or without a subscription) will entitle you to receive an emailed Advance Buying Guide – Wine, Spirit and Beer Reviews, free of charge, approximately two months before publication.

Once you submit samples with the appropriate invitation and forms, be sure to track your package to verify it is received. If you have determined it was received and still have not seen anything in six months, I suggest a call. You will not be given much in the way of specific information but can certainly be advised as to the physical status of your shipment, such as whether it has been reviewed and the review is expected to be in an upcoming issue, or you will learn if the shipment has somehow been misplaced. This is rare, but has happened to me. They will never give you a rating over the phone.

In the event of a high rating, you will be aware of the status of your wine without enquiring because *Wine Spectator* will call you to request a label to include with the review (free of charge) and *Wine Enthusiast* and *Wine & Spirits* will alert you via email to the rating and whether you wish to submit a label (for an advertising fee) as an accompaniment to your review.

Some people believe that a good rating in *Wine Enthusiast* and *Wine & Spirits* is dependent on this advertising supplement, but I have rarely exercised this option and still received some very high reviews. They notify you of the rating prior to their solicitation for a label fee. Others will say that *Wine Spectator* gives favor to the big advertisers in their publication, but I have also had some very high ratings in this magazine and never advertised. I think the personal palate bias that is inescapable in any taster's review of a wine has more to do with the rating variable than anything else. Certainly, a wine is either well-made or deficient, and true to its variety, its heritage and expectations of the vintage or not, but after that, there has to be, even in some indefinable, unconscious way, a tendency to rate higher or lower because the wine fits, or does not, the style the reviewer enjoys most. So be it. It's an imperfect system but it is so heavily relied upon that we must, for the time being, incorporate it into our marketing plans and rejoice when we receive an exalted rating.

Conversely, when the rating is poor in one publication or, these days, a rating below 90 out of 100 points, we can elect not to use it in our PR efforts or pick out a choice phrase or two to quote. It will usually be forgotten and perhaps another publication will be more positive. It becomes a game at times but occasionally we're firing on all cylinders in all publications and the consensus among our potential customers is overwhelmingly favorable. In that case, we're on the way towards building a highly sought-after brand.

There are several other media channels and review sites that have been around a long time, but these days the urgency for a publication review, in print or online, has diminished significantly. There is still some value in any promotion and marketing by independent sources, but it will depend upon your wine's styles, its origins and appeal as to what else you may pursue to garner some attention.

Individual blogs have risen as very helpful and relevant to wine brands. The best of them have wide readership and a professional approach and their recommendations are well regarded. There are many I could recommend but there are always new ones, so my best suggestion at this point is to simply do an internet search.

As the most influential buying generation these days, millennials cannot be underestimated as a resource. Peer review on social media are especially important to them and they have a tendency to eschew traditional ratings and review processes.

*SUMMARY* — Take advantage of this time between purchase order and arrival to approach tasks in a cost-effective, efficient, and well-organized way and keep building that solid foundation from which you construct a successful wine business. Don't cut corners and don't wing it during this time. There is too much to do and too many areas in which you can run afoul of authorities or create unnecessary backtracking and delays for yourself. You may think of this period as the last opportunity to take a break before you really have to get down to work, but it is really the perfect time to get these important responsibilities out of the way before turning your attention to the real business of selling.

# PART III

# CHAPTER 9

# DISTRIBUTION – THE FIRST STAGES

Your goal is to find the finest candidate to represent your wine at the next level (that second tier on the three tier system), with the greatest chance for long term success. It is not something to plunge into lightly, desperately or with a laissez-faire attitude. As with most things in life, there are no short cuts. You either go for immediate gratification (a quick sale that could be the only one you get) or take a well-researched approach that sets the stage for an enduring, mutually beneficial relationship.

## Narrowing the Search for the Right Distributor

Now, I'm not suggesting that, despite all your efforts, each and every distributor choice is right forever. Some are right for where you are at that particular time and some are right only as long as they remain the type of company they were when you found them. Some get too big, some struggle to pay the bills, management changes, focus realigns. These are the inevitable evolutionary journeys businesses take. But if you don't at least do your homework at the beginning, you may not only be doomed to failure, but at best you will spend more time playing catch-up, making allowances for their shortcomings and giving them second, third and fourth chances while the months tick by. So what should you look for?

- A company with the same general business philosophy as yours
- A financially sound business
- Terms that are reasonable – i.e. 30-60 days, which they stick to (preferably 30 days, but there are exceptions we will get into later)
- One that covers the geographical area you are looking for – whether that is three adjoining states or only one county in one state
- Management that communicates well and is accessible
- A company that has a plan to invest in your brand(s) and is willing to take a position across the board, instead of cherry-picking
- Not necessarily a company that will take *all* your brands, if you have taken on more than three or four, but one that is willing to look at representing a healthy segment of your portfolio
- A company that fits what you represent – e.g., small, organically farmed, biodynamic, estate grown, or obscure French chateaux – and has the skill and expertise to represent the wines appropriately
- Focused management and salespeople
- A portfolio that may include some of the country or region you represent, but is not saturated
- A company not so large that you, presumably the small, new importer, don't get lost amid the demands and quotas forced upon them by the big brands.

How do you find these paragons of virtue, these business soulmates? If you are coming from some other sector of the wine industry, you should definitely take advantage of the connections, relationships and acquaintances you have made and mine them for information and assistance. These particular individuals or companies may not be what you seek but, like six degrees of separation, may know someone who knows someone who is. This may start the chain of referrals to an obscure distributor or someone who may just be looking for what you represent. Very often, as in a job search, you call your acquaintance Jill who happens not to have an opening. She refers you to Joe at ABC Wine Distribution and when you call Joe, you mention Jill's name and this immediately opens the door to a conversation, which may not find you a job but takes you to Bob…and so it goes.

Having prior experience working for an importer, distributor or retailer gives you specialized knowledge and some advantage in the search. It also shows you who you would *not* want to be in partnership with.

> **As a retail** employee, did one wholesale company stand out as having a series of lazy salespeople who didn't last long, rarely came by and when they did, begged you for a sale because they needed to meet a quota? Did the salesperson seem ill-prepared or lacking in knowledge?

> **As a distributor** sales rep yourself, your inside knowledge of the company you worked for may have made you aware of how they sloughed off their importer supplier or gave too many excuses as to why they hadn't sold through a vintage, when in reality the wine was collecting dust in the warehouse. Did the company discourage giving sales reps samples or were stingy with allowances, making it difficult for the rep to do an effective job?

> **As an importer**'s employee, you knew distributors firsthand and while there may be some type of non-compete in place to preclude you doing business with this importer's customers, the experience you had with these companies demonstrates what to look for in partnering with your own distributor.

For the new importer, armed with the tools and guidelines from this book but who may not have been in the field before, the starting search is much like it will be further down the line. Some of the methods I myself have employed are these:

Google wineries you respect, whose wines you enjoy, are of high quality and may be from a similar region (thereby ensuring a distributor's familiarity with this region). It may simply have been a brand on your radar for some time that you know, by seeing more and more of their wines on the shelves, has grown quickly. Many of these wineries will list distributors in different states. Print out this list or copy down the ones you wish to start with.

Start looking for trends among the distributor names. Is there crossover? This may indicate a discerning wholesaler, or it may indicate a full portfolio, but it's a point of reference.

Discard, for now, the behemoth wholesale houses. I do not mean to disparage them - and don't we all wish for their degree of success - just as I would not denigrate Two Buck Chuck or Yellow Tail. Who among us would not want the income produced from their volume? However, they are unlikely to be receptive to a new, unseasoned importer and you may well spend valuable time spinning your wheels waiting for callbacks, responses to samples shipped for evaluation, etc. They have their own compelling obligations, and they are legion: the brands to whom they owe their size, and their success and will always come first.

Unfortunately, recent years have seen the further consolidation and buying up of distributors, resulting in a number of huge, national distribution chains. The reason for the consolidation and acquisitions is because there must be a brick and mortar, fully licensed and operational business in each state in which a company distributes. A wholesaler cannot simply buy wines for their Ohio operation and ship across to Michigan, Illinois and Indiana, for example. The most current acquisitions have seen the absorption of the best of the smaller operations with which I was familiar. However, as with all market economics, small operations emerge to fill the void. As a result, you'll find new distributors, often with experienced principals, looking to add to their portfolio. A good example of this just came to my attention when the long-term management team of a California importer/distributor formed their own company. They are already a known quantity in the industry and have an impressive lineup of foundational wineries. As a principal of this company said,

*We felt there was a niche in the marketplace for a distributor with a strategic portfolio that allows the sales reps to provide the focus desired by our suppliers. Our sales reps have a passion for wine, and are skilled at pairing the right wine with the right customer.*

Now look with a discriminating eye at the distributors' websites from your list.

- How professional, updated and friendly is the website?
- What other brands do they represent? (Google to check them out as well)
- How big is the portfolio?
- What other importers' portfolios do they represent?
- How well does the portfolio fit your own style, brands, regions?
- What is their mission statement and how well does it reflect yours?

Another approach is to contact fine wine stores, well known retailers or retailers you have researched that carry wines of the type/style/price point/region you feel is reflected in your own wines. Ask them which distributor *they* like dealing with. I've done this on many occasions when a retailer has emailed me looking for one of my wines and I haven't had distribution in their state. I will respond that I would love to supply them with the particular wine, but unfortunately it is not available in their state, and do they have a recommendation? In almost all cases, the person has responded with at least one suggestion, and sometimes several, including reasons for their recommendations.

These are all simple strategies, but give you far more information than if you were to conduct a random search, look up companies in an industry reference book, or just wonder how on earth you begin.

The next step is to call one of these targeted companies and find out who makes decisions regarding new wine purchases, if the website has not indicated a clear contact. Unless you're engaged in the "Jill gave me your name" process, this is very much cold calling at this stage and can be daunting, frustrating and unfulfilling. But in anticipation of speaking with someone, have a prepared 'elevator pitch' ready to grab their attention. Avoid embellishment and stick to relevant points of difference in your portfolio and how this will help theirs. Try to personalize it. Show them you've sought them out for a reason. If applicable, tell them that such-and-such retail store recommended them. Let them know you really like their mission statement or the quality of the wines in their portfolio. Do they carry wines of your region? If so, let them know why yours would be a good fit. If not, this is an opportunity to see if they might like to fill a void. Let them see a glimpse of your personality, your expertise in the area, a reason that they might want to initiate a new relationship. Don't keep them on the phone forever; refine your pitch so that it is friendly, informational, engaging and succinct. This is a sales pitch and you only have one chance to make a good first impression. Avoid leaving a message on voice mail. You are a stranger calling and are now a disembodied voice. The point is to make a connection and set the stage for further communication. Having a one-sided conversation on voicemail makes this difficult and very often a waste of time for you and them.

If you are not able to reach the purchaser/principal when you call, my suggestion is to call back at least once. Speaking with someone is far easier if they are not required to return your call. Many will, and they do so with pride, irrespective of their response or particular wine needs. They know that what you are doing is difficult and put themselves in your shoes. I respect that immensely. I think it's also indicative of the quality of the individual. However, people are also out of the country, very busy, working with a deadline, not given the message or sick. So if you do leave a voice mail message, persevere a bit and see where it goes. Be systematic in your line of attack. Don't call too soon, or let too much time elapse.

Whether you use Onenote, Google Notes, Evernote or something else, make sure you create a record of your calls and follow up. Perhaps because it's worked for me and I've been using it for so long, I still rely heavily on the Tasks component of Microsoft Outlook to record my calls, emails and general activity, especially as it relates to sales efforts. It allows me to schedule reminders to myself and I can make basic notes. But there really are better apps out there now and if you're just getting started, you might as well get started with the latest and most efficient.

Whatever you use, please use something. You would be surprised at how quickly time goes by or how easily you can forget whether it was this or that company you called and the result. I have kept notes on my contacts for years, including a folder labeled *Inactive Potentials* for those I have contacted in the past and it led nowhere or with whom I had a negative experience (e.g. sent them copious samples and no one responded to numerous follow up calls). You may find you can resurrect one or more of these because circumstances have changed or sufficient time has elapsed or you want to be reminded not to contact them again. In any event, it's helpful to have the records as a reference point.

## Following the Distribution Trail

When you do elicit an expression of interest, this will most likely be in the form of a request for an emailed FOB price list, if you didn't include it the first time or they are responding to a phone call from you. No one requests snail mail press kits anymore so don't waste time preparing them. You can include any POS materials with samples or during a visit with the distributor. In the meantime, be prepared to submit a professional, well-organized and informative attachment. Do not bombard the recipient's email box with huge files or multiple attachments. If not included on your FOB, send one or two additional attachments to show a label or particularly impressive press from credible sources. "*Wine of the Year!*", "*Highly Recommended*", "*94 points…Editor's Choice*" type of thing. But try, if possible, to include pertinent details on your FOB and avoid the additional attachments.

Refer the potential customer to your website for more information, which will demonstrate how informational and helpful this site will be for them as your new distributor. Be brief in the body of the email and personable. Emphasize a willingness to be a collaborative partner because they need to know that you understand this process.

And then wait. Until several days have elapsed and then you may email them with a polite "Just checking to make sure my FOB came through on your email" or "You may not have had a chance to look at my FOB but wondering if you have any questions". Many times, the recipient will tell you they had meant to, and glad you reminded them, or he or she intended to find the time to go over the list with the sales manager and to email them again on Friday. Other times, it is not on their radar or they are putting out unexpected fires. This is not the time to be annoyingly persistent. This will signal to the potential customer that you will be even more annoyingly persistent when they become your actual distribution partner.

There is no realistic short cut through this process, unless you happen to have a brand that has already demonstrated it is eminently desirable or has achieved national recognition for a spectacular rating in a major publication. Then they'll cold call *you*.

Some time has passed, weeks, months, years…it all starts to run together after a while and finally the distributor requests samples. Hallelujah! Now we're making progress. Not so fast. Yes, this is a good sign, a very good sign. As I've pointed out, most distributors, and certainly any reputable, honorable ones, will not request samples if they do not intend to give serious consideration to your portfolio. However, it is another stage of the journey and the destination is not yet in sight.

Consider which items you will send in response to the request. Unless they have specified, after reviewing your list, exactly which wines they wish to preview, make a one case (12 bottle) selection based on what will be most representative of your portfolio. You may only have 8 wines at this stage, so send them all 8. They all need homes. But if you have 40 wines spread over 8 brands, consider your choices carefully. Don't make the mistake of sending all top-end to impress them. They want to see a cross-section of each brand, something indicative of the style and quality of the brand overall. They will want answers to the same criteria questions you posed to yourself at the outset regarding QPR, packaging, etc. Don't send all reds just because you think they will be weightier and more serious unless the distributor specifically makes the request. Send a balance of reds and whites, again to show the versatility of your portfolio.

If you have more of an idea of their needs from conversation, this will influence your sample selection. In terms of South America, they may be more interested in Chile than Argentina, e.g., certain price points, restaurant wines, cooler climate, and so on. Pay attention, respond accordingly and they will appreciate it.

More waiting is bound to ensue. They say they must find the time for a sales meeting to gather the team together in a democratic process. As I've been told on several occasions, "they are the ones who must go out and sell the wines; therefore, I need them on board from the outset". That's not how behemoth distributors operate, of course, but then you're trying hard to find a more compatible, friendlier match and one in which you will presumably receive some attention after the initial sale.

Figure 9.1 Brand Lineup Ready for Tasting

They may have more wines in the office to taste through than they at first envisioned and want to do them all justice. There can be any number of reasons why this will again become a somewhat protracted process. Which is why you always want to start the distributor search as early as possible and pre-selling while the container is on the water is one way to do that. Make sure you have a system of checking and following up at each stage. It is the only way you are going to ensure that it doesn't get away from you and turn into months instead of weeks. Just remember that it will all take much longer than you anticipated and be prepared.

The value of holding inventory in a *recognized* warehouse will become apparent as you are about to receive your first order from this customer, and they ask where the order can be picked up. The relief at knowing they don't have to make special arrangements and incur additional expense is almost palpable over the phone. It is a warehouse they go to frequently and can add your order to existing orders, or their trucking company can incorporate it into their regular routine.

# What a Distributor Looks For – Are You on the Same Page

There is no magical answer to this question. It always goes back to what your expectations are and what the distributor is willing to deliver. It can vary from individual to individual and change with circumstances but whatever it is, the key to a harmonious relationship is clearly communicated objectives and aspirations. Don't be desperate. This is too important. Don't hope – like entering a marriage – that you can "change" that individual in the future. Whatever they are now, is what they are likely to manifest towards you as you proceed.

On occasion, you will find a distributor who is only interested in "cherry picking" your line-up, i.e. taking only the very best item of a brand or only one brand from your portfolio, because that's the one with the eye-catching ratings. This should not only be discouraged but avoided, unless it is a wine in good supply and suits your program. It is understandable that you would want to secure distribution with a live body now that you have one but remember this is a long term proposition. Is the distributor who ordered the one 95 rated wine in your portfolio going to drop you the following year when the rating for that one wine drops?

The wholesaler you choose, who in turn chooses you, should be making a reasonable effort to invest in your wines across the board. It demonstrates fair play and a willingness to look at a long term plan. This does not necessarily mean they should order a comparable amount of each wine, but a good faith effort is required. They may be surprised at the result and continue to purchase more and more of the other wines, especially when the highly rated one has been allocated and quickly sold out. During a recession, some additional flexibility may be needed on your part to establish business and weather a challenging economy but in general this is good advice to follow.

Does this distributor rely heavily on restaurant placements? Is this a good thing because your wines are esoteric, require hand-selling and tend to be far better when paired with food? Or do they have supermarket or chain store relationships, which better suits your lower priced, daily quaffing wines that need to be sold in volume to make your margins more attractive? Their focus and their experience are important components on the decision-making path.

## Vetting the Distributor

The distributor's interest really only becomes clear, and evidence emerges, when they indicate a desire to place an order. Until that point, they may like the wines, be only marginally interested, not have room now but could have in future or they are just looking at annual projections to see if they can incorporate your wines into their budget. Before this order, especially with a newish distributor, but after an expression of substantial interest, consider asking them if they would fill out a credit application and provide references. These references should include a couple of their vendors but more importantly, their other winery customers. Of course, they are going to give you their best customers, but the information you glean from this winery's answers will allow you to determine whether it is a reasonable risk.

- How long have they been supplying the distributor?
- How frequent are the orders?
- What is the size of the orders?
- What terms do they have with this winery?
- How well do they adhere to these terms?
- Are there any other issues they have with the distributor that could be helpful to know?

You would be surprised at what people will tell you.

Don't make the application so onerous that you deter them from completing it at all but make it sufficiently thorough to establish your professionalism.

Include a statement regarding your terms and interest penalty, if any, on unpaid balances. The industry, as a whole, used to be very much a handshake business and contracts between importer and distributor were rare. However, since the first edition, I would say that contracts, or at least a basic written agreement, while still unusual with small distributors, is more common with larger ones. If a wholesaler is brand new and has no previous credit history or references, I suggest to at base your decision on some information, such as banking references and/or prior business history. You could also ask for a deposit with the balance strictly in 30 days. All of these options will depend upon the circumstances you are faced with and to what degree you can realistically feel comfortable with the arrangement. Do not fall prey to the idea that no one else will want your wines and you had better take this opportunity – sort of like marrying someone because you think no one else will have you, only to endure an inevitably messy and expensive divorce down the track.

```
CREDIT APPLICATION

Date:

Business name:                          License:

Trade name (if different):

Address:                                City:

State:                                  Zip:

Telephone:                              Owner/President:[name]

How long in business:                   Credit rating:

Trade references in the wine industry (names and addresses):

1.

2.

3.

Bank references (include account numbers & addresses):

The undersigned authorizes an inquiry as to the credit information of the business. I certify the above information to be true.

_____

Name/Position
```

Figure 9.2 Credit Application

# Partnering with Your Distributor

The early preparation ensures your distributor is everything you want them to be – or at least as close as you can get – and you have protected yourself. But once you have made the decision and the stage is set for distribution with this company, make sure you keep your brands at the forefront of their thinking. Be a proactive partner by letting them know:

- how you would like to launch the brand(s)

- what you are willing or able to do in terms of marketing, support and incentives

- what wines are available or what is available among your brands in general

- if there is an allocation of limited production wines.

Discuss early expectations and give them some extra time to introduce wines that may be unknown, at least to them, and solicit their suggestions and objectives. In short, let them know this is a combined effort. You do expect them to put effort into selling the wines once they have brought them in but they are not alone in this effort. You are there to support them every step of the way.

# States in General

Every state is completely different in their requirements and these have changed dramatically since the advent and evolution of the internet. Each state also has different names for what they require, so this takes time to recognize as well. It could be called a broker license, a Certificate of Compliance, brand registration, Primary Source Appointment, Out of State Manufacturer/Supplier, Non-Resident Seller's Permit and others. They may require a surety bond, obtained from a surety bond company, or a Certificate of Good Standing from your state. If you are not a US citizen the state may require a criminal background check.

Unfortunately, there is no widespread rule for all states. Researching each one is unavoidable. I still do it today for my clients. Often I find the answer on the relevant state site, as some lay out the licensing requirements and forms in one comprehensive section. But it is often much more complicated than that and may require a phone call. Sometimes, it absolutely requires a phone call, such as in the case of Rhode Island. This state has very simple out of state licensing regulations but requires that you call and get an ID number before you can apply for brand registrations.

Most states require monthly reports by a designated date. This is something to be taken very seriously. In all instances, they will eventually contact you in the event you fall delinquent. In some circumstances, there are penalties and interest. Georgia, for example, charges $50 for every single month you are late with a report.

# Franchise States

The appointment of a wholesaler becomes especially critical when applied to a "franchise" state. This definition, for purposes of the wine industry, refers to the inexplicable and over-reaching protection afforded the wholesalers in certain states. It has nothing to do with the concept of franchise as most of us know it. It does not mean the appointment of a licensed entity to sell recognized goods and services in a cookie cutter format, such as McDonalds or Starbucks. It defines the relationship between supplier (you) and the wholesaler in that particular state as being heavily weighted on the wholesaler's side. Although laws vary in each franchise state, essentially you are not permitted to change distributors, even if you want to, even if the wholesaler has not paid its bills or ordered sufficiently from you to make doing business with them worthwhile.

The repeal of Prohibition in 1935 led to laws being enacted for the protection of each state, depending on the strength and will of the state's legislature and the lobbying efforts of its liquor distributors. At one time, this may have afforded the tiny wholesaler protection from the large distributor but today all it seems to do is afford the unscrupulous wholesaler protection from you, the supplier.

It is important to know which states are franchise states at the time you go into business, but also be aware that this may change from time to time depending on the challenges that are taking place from the local courts to the Supreme Court level. If in doubt, check with the appropriate licensing board at the time you consider your foray into that state. I am not trying to discourage you from entering into franchise state distribution, as one client recently thought I intended in the first edition of this book. But it can be fraught with particular challenges that I do want to make clear. There should be no doubt about the status of the law regarding your ability to withdraw your product in the event that the wholesaler does not perform adequately or appropriately on your behalf.

It is important to have a frank discussion with a franchise state distributor before entering into business with them. What are their policies regarding termination of a brand? Of course, what they state to you now may change as time elapses and relationships metamorphose into something less positive than the optimistic, friendly days of the inception. But their stated intentions may raise a red flag or gut reaction from you or go a long way towards assuaging your concerns. They may have been in business for many years and encountered sufficient termination situations to handle them all with fitting resolution. After all, if I were to put it in a more cynical light, how many brands can a wholesaler hold hostage before the wine world (a most intimate place at times) gets wind of it and steers clear.

In most instances, the supplier can terminate the relationship "with cause," a criteria that also differs from state to state but usually encompasses issues of gross under-performance or non-payment. A contract between you and the wholesaler, spelling out your rights and termination intentions, will not protect you if it is conflict with the franchise laws of that state so, although I would not discourage a contract, it might be more advisable to specify and document reasonable performance levels and the results. We go into every relationship with the hope of a long and wildly successful journey – or should – but this does not mean we should enter into it with our eyes closed.

## Control States

This term refers to a state that has the monopoly over the sale of alcohol, again as a result of the repeal of Prohibition. As of this writing, there are 18 control states and one county in Maryland. Utah and Pennsylvania, e.g., are the sole purchasers of alcohol and operate state run stores. In fact, Utah has one individual who decides the wine choices of an entire state. Pennsylvania makes these decisions through a board. Other states may license retailers, or elected to control sales in certain counties. The important point to take away from this section is to be aware of the existence of control states and each one is approached from a different perspective than that of the thirty-two states that are equally regulated but provide less monopolization of the sale of alcohol.

The Utah Department of Alcoholic Beverage Services states:

*The purpose of control is to make liquor available to those adults who choose to drink responsibly - but not to promote the sale of liquor. By keeping liquor out of the private marketplace, no economic incentives are created to maximize sales, open more liquor stores or sell to underage persons. Instead, all policy incentives to promote moderation and to enforce existing liquor laws is (sic) enhanced.*

Unlike franchise states, there is no monopoly of a single brand by an independent wholesaler but the degree to which the state adheres to the control model dictates to whom you can sell. In some states, including Utah, Wyoming and Mississippi, it is almost essential to appoint a broker who understands the presentation times and has a relationship with the State's purchaser(s). The states in which you elect to utilize a broker does not necessarily indicate to what extent alcohol sales are "controlled" by the state. In Pennsylvania, an example of a pure control store model, a wholesaler may sell to restaurants and most wholesalers have experience making presentations directly to the Board. In many control states, you may approach and sell to a distributor in the same manner you would to a distributor in a non-control state.

State websites are often an invaluable resource, although there is no standard across the internet and some are clearly more helpful than others. Always call the state board to determine their exact requirements even if it is a well-documented site. This advice is offered to further your quest for distribution in any state. It can be a lengthy process to obtain a license and it is far better to have all paperwork completed when the office receives your submission. In the case of control states, it is easy to determine which those are, as indicated on the TTB site.

## Territory Assignments and Restrictions

Certain states, such as Ohio, Tennessee and Georgia (using only a few examples) require territory designations from you to the distributor. Are you going to allow your distributor access to the entire state or only one segment? Are they capable of covering the entire state?

When you see the confusing array of counties, none of which you recognize, the temptation is great to just let the distributor have the whole state. In the case of franchise states, this is not a decision to be taken lightly and may well be a mistake. Wholesalers may tell you that they "plan on expanding" or "will be putting a salesperson in that area soon" and would like you to designate the entire state in the brand registration or state license application. Find out when this is likely to happen and what steps they have taken to set this in motion and weigh the answers.

In Ohio, for example, it is quite common to have several distributors in different quadrants of the state. There is even a place on Ohio's territory designation form to select a *partial* county. Fragmenting sales areas is not likely to incur an objection from your prospective wholesaler unless they really do cover the entire state through a cohesive network of delivery sites and personnel.

It is in your best interests to determine what area the wholesaler is legitimately able to service and be specific in your territory designation. In the case of Georgia, as a prime example, limiting territory can mitigate the damage in the event of a poorly performing wholesaler.

## Brokers

Whether to use brokers can be a controversial issue in many states. A sore subject for some, a necessity for others. First of all, it should be understood that most brokers charge a 10% commission for their services, to be paid after the invoice funds are remitted to you, the importer. Occasionally, they charge a higher percentage or a retainer but I'd really want to know why and what they intend to do with it and it had better be worth it. It adds yet another layer to your pricing, making it a *four* tier system instead of the already burdensome three, or cuts 10% from your margin. So, irrespective of what they charge, be aware of **why** you need them, **where** you need them, **who** they should be and **what** they can do.

For these purposes, I'm talking about regional or state brokers, rather than local brokers who support your efforts as a distributor in your own state, but we'll get into that later.

**Why** – because you can't be everywhere and do everything, because you may be a small, undercapitalized start-up who cannot expend funds in putting sales managers on in various regions or any sales personnel at all – which is not unusual. A broker can be your independent salesperson in that region or state and be well worth their commission. It is up to you (in non-control states, e.g.) to decide whether you can afford the additional tier in your pricing model or whether you should absorb the difference.

**Where** - in control states they can be invaluable, and actually a necessity. They know the players, when a particular country's wines are scheduled to come up on the

State's calendar and understand what the buyer may be looking for, how to monitor sales in specialty stores, manage reorders and generally perform functions that you are unable to do yourself. In highly competitive non-control states, having a broker can mean the difference between securing a great distributor or no distributor at all.

**Who** – a broker is only as good as their sales. If they don't sell, neither of you make money. Taking on wines they put no effort into makes no sense, yet does happen. A broker should have a proven track record, have a reasonable, but not enormous, portfolio of their own and be a full-time, energetic proponent of your wines. Someone with extensive experience will have the ear of a distributor in any state in which they operate - perhaps even a strong, warm relationship - and will endeavor to present your wines, follow up, monitor and market successfully. This is not to say a new broker cannot do well but connections and prior experience do have a bearing on the success of their approach and the ability to secure distribution.

**What** – the right broker can actually save you money, despite their commission, by limiting the quantity of samples going out to prospective customers, lessening the number of visits you need to make to the market and working with the distributor's salespeople to keep your brands at the forefront of their attention.

Initially, they can vet distributors for you in areas with which you are unfamiliar, get the attention of those who may not be willing to respond to you – in their mind, "yet another new importer." Most distributors would very much like to deal with only so many suppliers, or portfolios, much like a retailer who would rather contain the number of distributors they deal with and have to see every week. For a wholesaler, this can mean that they would rather transact business with a known quantity, in the form of a broker, rather than take on the unknown quantity, in the form of you.

The right broker will also be honest with you about the assessment of your wines by the various distributors or retailers (as opposed to the way these same entities invariably share less transparently with you), have an ear to the ground for which wines are likely to be in demand and be poised to recommend a switch if they see a negative trend in the current wholesale house.

***SUMMARY***—It absolutely comes down to avoiding the short cuts, whether you are dealing with distributors, franchise states, control states or brokers. The consequences can be anything from a costly inconvenience to a long, time-wasting, money-draining delay. In the case of a franchise state: a catastrophic mistake that requires an expensive buy-out or a requisite two year absence from the state. Brokers don't replace the need to do your own homework, evaluate the prospective customer yourself and establish your own relationships, but they can, under the right circumstances, be an invaluable arm to your business and allow you to focus your attention on more pressing tasks or regions. Just don't forget chemistry. The relationship can enhance your life or make it a living hell.

# My Story

Most of my early stories in the search for meaningful distribution originate from inexperience and naïveté. For example, I continued to send samples to one particular prospect who kept promising to look at them, or could he see some of the other wines, or now that that vintage has changed could he see that. I would call him back, call him back, call him back…all to no avail. It was a classic carrot in front of the horse. If I just kept trotting along, keeping the promise of sales in sight, and continued to respond with whatever he needed, I would have distribution. I should have stopped at the second set of samples and 2-3 months, not four or five sets and 12 months, but I didn't know any better and I was desperate enough to ignore the warning signs. I later learned that he did this frequently, just to have wine for free.

Probably the worst experience I have ever had was with an experienced broker in Florida who appeared to offer me a lucrative opportunity for several of my brands. The problem? He was foul-mouthed, rude, sexist and irrational. He seemed to like me and wanted to place the brands, so I persevered with gritted teeth, constantly justifying his behavior with the thought that he was in his late sixties and had honed his skills in the old school liquor distributor days, i.e. he was a dinosaur. It really didn't mean anything, I told myself, although I needed a stress relieving power walk every time I got off the phone with him. Suffice it to say, the brands were never placed, he abusively blamed me for the failure, and I wasted a great deal of time once again ignoring my instincts. Fortunately for everyone else, he is no longer in the business. He recently burned his last bridge.

On the other hand, during my importing career I enjoyed a long and fruitful relationship with a broker in the Midwest. Without him I would not have achieved the same degree of success in several states. He was able to establish distribution I would not have been able to secure on my own.

## My Client's Story

I have a client who is a more naïve version of me in my early days so you can imagine the ways in which he can be taken advantage of. Playing to his strengths of easygoing style and personal wine region knowledge, he has achieved a loyal following and an impressive database for his online sales business. But in two years since he founded his business, he has not achieved sufficient national sales to take it to a more profitable level.

He consults with me rarely these days, mostly for a tune-up when he runs into something unfamiliar. Recently, he told me he signed with a company that he called a "network" of distribution, and he now needed my advice. I haven't seen the contract, but based on the conversation, red flags were readily apparent. A number of hybrid compliance/distribution companies have cropped up in the years since I became a consultant and some of them are reputable and professional and doing a good job for their suppliers. But that doesn't mean you waive your due diligence at any time. It remains your business, not theirs. Based on what he told me, this is a type of broker agreement where they are acting as a middle-man for other states in the hope that these distributors will take on the wines they represent. For that they take a percentage of his sales, plus a base fee.

In the six months he has been affiliated with them, and wisely restricted himself to one state as a trial, they have not made a single sale although they continue to collect the base fee. He hasn't required accountability, nor have they provided him with anything beyond telling him that a prestigious golf course looks ready to place an order.

As an importer, you are a *partner* with your distributor and, until you decide to sever the relationship, this partnership requires transparency and responsibility on *both* sides. His lack of participation may not be important to them because they are playing with numbers and each new client is paying this retainer. Or they may not have as much going on as they imply and don't want to be held accountable. He deserves facts and figures from them and at the same time he must let them know that he is willing to assist them in their efforts using specific examples. At the very least he, and anyone in this situation, should ask for and expect answers to the following:

★ How many salespeople are in this wholesale company?
★ How many are actually showing his wines?
★ What do they know about his brands in general, and particular?
★ What area do they cover, (in my client's case it's a very big state?
★ Which accounts have they seen and will see to show his wines?
★ What are the names of the distributors in other states, in place or in discussion?

He cannot abdicate responsibility because he has a contract with them, particularly since he is paying for the privilege. For example, it is just as important to research each individual, out-of-state wholesaler they might assign his brands to as it is if he assigned them himself. These are independent distributors where no guarantee of performance can be made by the consulting company.

Six months is a long time without results of any kind and without a meeting with the principals to discuss timelines and deadlines, outlook and expectations. It is six months lost, in my view, and continuing this way, because he's reluctant to have the difficult conversation, is likely to produce more of the same unless he takes action.

# CHAPTER 10

# DISTRIBUTION – THE NEXT STAGE

I am sure it has become readily apparent to you that your wine sales participation does not end with the appointment of a distributor. It now requires a vigilant, ongoing, organized strategy to support your customer and manage your assets. Much as you would water and fertilize your plants to support their viability and encourage their growth, your portfolio requires continued attention and nurturing to thrive and grow. There are many wonderful distributors in the country staffed by people who work hard for their suppliers, but in this age of consolidation there is also a burgeoning crop of wholesalers with massive books filled with thousands of wines. There is no way - however magnificent and desirable your wines may be - they will receive the full attention they deserve without your help.

## Incentives – Wine Launch

The first question often asked of you by a prospective customer is: what incentives can you offer to launch the product? This is the question asked in states **where it is legal** to offer incentives. All the points I include for you are important, but this is one of those critical ones. Certain states may prohibit the use of incentive and you do not want to run afoul of the statutory regulations. In some states, offering incentives or providing discounted product can be construed as giving one customer unfair advantage over another. Be aware, through your own preparatory calls to the state board or simply by asking the distributor, whether this state allows incentives of any kind. With legality established, the next question you must ask yourself is whether you can afford incentive.

- Have you built a bit of fat in your margin?
- Have you received an incentive allowance from your winery?
- Has the winery given you sufficient free goods to make *those* cases the incentive, or to be able to support your own incentive program?
- Can you "afford" it, because you've budgeted for marketing in the first year, knowing your initial profit loss will be recouped in the second year?
- Is the prospect of volume worth making a big incentive push now?
- Will the distributor share the launch incentive cost with you?
- What is the distributor prepared to do to partner with you in introducing the brand and starting off on the best foot?

Notice the bold print on that last question. This is because, among critical points, this one is über-critical. For the greatest likelihood of success of your brand, the wholesaler must become invested in its success. In fairness, they may not always have the budget to contribute to an incentive at the time they take on your brand, however enthusiastic and committed they may be. But, as in all business relationships, the most committed parties have a vested interest in the outcome. There are a number of examples to illustrate this in the general business arena: commission structures, profit sharing or simply employees who know that they participate democratically in decisions. These are all incentives for people to work harder towards a common goal. In the case of the distributor, if they share equally in your incentive program, they are more likely to encourage and monitor their sales staff.

Distributors will sometimes commit personnel and marketing resources to the effort either in place of or in addition to a monetary contribution, such as making your brand or portfolio a priority for all sales staff for the first month. This gives you an advantage in your launch while the product is fresh to the market and the salespeople; focus on your brands also gives the distributor an early perspective on how well the brand is likely to perform. The risk in the latter is that the brand may not initially perform well, which may be more indicative of the effort invested than it is a forecast of the brand's future performance. You should therefore make sure to promote your portfolio, either behind the scenes or in concert with the distributor.

Initial incentives should be short-term and designed to generate immediate results. There is nothing less likely to incentivize over the life of the brand, or vintage, as a program that is taken for granted as a static component of the price. My suggestion to those who are on a moderate budget, is to offer incentives on the first order of perhaps free goods or a modest contest. The term of the launch incentives could be limited to either:

- the first order
- the first month
- the current quarter
- when a certain dollar sales volume is reached
- when a designated number of accounts are established

The incentive can be modest or lavish, depending on your budget. It can be one case of free goods on a pallet (or equivalent discount) or a contest for a trip to Tuscany. Whatever the incentive, it must be realistic, meaningful and easily quantifiable. By realistic, I mean to you. The launch of a product cannot bankrupt you nor have you praying no one reaches the target because of your potential financial outlay. If you have the necessary capital to fund a trip to Tuscany or have put together a program with the winery, this is an exciting way to get started. But if you cannot afford it, it makes no sense.

In terms of *meaningful* and *quantifiable*, there is also nothing worse than a program that either cannot be understood, and will therefore be ignored, or has no discernible way to monitor its results. Examples of this type of program could be one that is too general, i.e. has no time limit, or sales goals are not spelled out, e.g. talking about "increasing sales" or "increasing territory" without specificity.

Additionally, the incentive program must be tailored to the circumstances: state, region, distributor's resources, desirability of your brand, ease of selling or contemporary expectations. For example, if your program is to offer $5 for every case sold, this may be a thoroughly appropriate incentive for an inexpensive wine that is likely to be case stacked in stores and generate volume. On the other hand, you may offer $5 a case for a wine that is a hand-sell, high priced, unknown or difficult to sell. Or, in this particular wholesale house, they are accustomed to incentives of $10 a case. I am not suggesting you should do the same; I am making it clear that your incentives should count for something and be customized to the situation. If you see that $10 a case is the only way to get the salespeople's attention but you cannot afford it, *do not do it*. Find another way to promote and support your brand.

It is quite possible to establish and grow your brand on its attributes, along with your judicious management and fostering of relationships within the ranks of the distributor's salespeople. When you receive extra samples from the winery, use that opportunity to pass them along in the form of an incentive.

## Incentives – Ongoing

Ongoing incentives are generally somewhat different from launch incentives. The initial stages are to start buzz for an unknown brand, unknown at least to the distributor you have just appointed. This is an optimistic time. Later, you may be just as confident about your portfolio's positioning at this distributor, but it's time to stimulate sales. Or sales have languished, the brand is getting lost amid new offerings or big brand quotas or you are ready for a vintage change and you want to make room.

As indicated previously, there are states in which incentives or programming, as it is known, is illegal. In the ones where it is legal, some inducements work better than others. I would be guided, primarily, by your contact at the distributor – whether it is the hands-on owner, sales manager or the salesperson with whom you have established a close connection and on whose input you can rely. They really do know what works and what doesn't and how easily it can be managed, given their sales team or their territory.

The programming you put in place after the launch should be at least for a quarter (three months), in my opinion. It can even run all year for a very big contest but a quarter should keep interest high and attention focused while also maintaining a sufficient period for you to realize a significant sales bump. For more immediate impact, with high expectations and perhaps tied in with wine dinners and tastings, a month or even a week can be appropriate. This kind of incentive is most often used when a winemaker or company principal is in town.

**Incentives can additionally be divided into two categories:**

- salesperson
- on-premise (restaurant) and off-premise (retailer)

In other words, what you initiate may benefit the salesperson directly in the form of cash, prizes or trips, or indirectly in terms of free goods to the retailer or a by-the-glass program pricing (wines poured by the glass, rather than sold by the bottle) for the restaurant. Both benefit the salesperson, but operate quite differently.

**The salesperson programming can also be sub-divided into two categories:**

- on-premise sales
- off-premise sales

This is another important distinction, because if you decide to set up a program for volume, for example, the on-premise salesperson cannot compete with it, especially if the distributor sets up their staffing or territory with separate on and off-premise sales teams. For sake of argument, the off-premise salesperson may be able to sell just one retail account fifteen cases of a product for which the on-premise salesperson will need fifteen accounts (or more if split cases are allowed) to accomplish the same thing. To explain the same thing another way, one off-premise account (retail store) could buy fifteen cases of the incentive wine for a case stacking. The average on-premise account (restaurant) would never have the room or need for that many cases of one wine and might even buy six bottles per item, if the distributor allows split cases. The ongoing sales benefit and exposure of the glass pour at a restaurant (offering wine by the glass) may actually outweigh the one-time sale to the retail account but it cannot be quantified in the initial programming period.

Suggestions for programming incentives include:

### Launch or Pre-Sell

> 3% sample allowance deducted from invoice or included in free goods across brands

- large format (1.5L or 3L) bottles as percentage of order or "prizes" for performance
- $5 for each new wine placement on-premise
- $5 for each case in a minimum three case stack off-premise
- $20 for by-the-glass placements (with minimum time frame or case purchase)

Be guided by the distributor and the circumstances. Be aware that you may be setting a precedent for future orders that you may not wish, or be able, to fulfill. Do not fall into the trap of being expected to include standard free goods or sample allowance deduction on each shipment or invoice. This will become absorbed into the price and taken for granted instead of being used as liberal tasting samples, as should be the intent.

### Ongoing: Off-premise

- "One case on ten" i.e., one case free for every ten cases sold – one quarter time period
- "One case on 13" i.e., one case free for every 13 cases purchased. The logic to this is that 14 cases is a "layer" on a pallet. If you take the 56 case pallet premise, it is divided into four layers of 14 cases each. A distributor may say, "I'll take a layer of xxx wine" – as part of an order
- $15 per each (min.) three case stack – one calendar
- $200 gift certificate for highest volume sales over the designated sales period, by brand or portfolio, depending upon how many wines – one calendar quarter

➢ Contest for specified elements of a trip to the country or region of origin for the brand in question. This may be airfare (and winery provides accommodation at their winery) with the winner on their own the rest of the trip. It may be an organized, accompanied, all expenses paid trip. Just spell it out so there are no surprises. Recommended contest period for something of this nature could be whatever your budget dictates but 12 months would be a reasonable timeframe. Since this is an extended program, make sure the sales or brand manager is keeping everyone abreast of progress and it stays at the forefront of their minds.

### Ongoing: On-premise

➢ $20 for glass pour placement – 3 case minimum

➢ $10 for wine list placement

➢ Same as above trip contest but with requirements that are tailored to on-premise parameters, such as number of wine or glass pour placements or hotel or chain placements.

Restaurant placements have some inherent pitfalls in understanding what the glass pour or by-the-glass program entails, which is why you should indicate a minimum order or time period. Preferably, the restaurant will put the wine on their printed list and not on a chalk board which is erased when they run out of the six bottles they brought in as a favor to the rep. It is imperative that you understand how your programming will work. It would be an extremely apathetic or unprofessional wholesale principal (brand manager, owner, sales manager or other similar liaison) who would not advise you as to the incentive that is likely to have the best outcome for you in their market or for that period of the year.

# Distribution – The Next Stage

Figure 10.1 Wines by the Glass

You can see the impact a program can have when the wholesaler matches your incentive so that instead of $5 a case, it becomes $10. Instead of a $200 gift certificate, it can become $400. Not only is the distributor more invested but the salesperson is obviously more motivated to sell your wine.

Whether you have a program in place or not, it's always good business to offer discounts on larger volume, such as for pallet orders of the same wine.

## Sample Allowance and Handling

Wines will not get sold without sampling; this is a simple truth. Except in the case of highly allocated, tiny production, expensive wines rated 100 in *Wine Advocate*, which may be pre-sold to special accounts on the basis of their rarefied desirability. For just about anything else, the customer tastes the wines and makes their decision accordingly. Make sure you keep track of sample usage, preventing wasteful expense through the indiscriminate use of samples, with no accountability.

Most distributors will find the convention of sharing equally in the cost of samples to be acceptable and customary. Samples are handled through a statement called a "billback", which should be sent monthly or quarterly to you from the distributor.

Paperwork, especially at small wholesale houses, is not at the top of a distributor's priority list. Wine sales and the supervision of wine sales personnel is their focus. Therefore, some distributors find that the preparation of billback statements gets pushed back until the end of the year. I find this understandable but not acceptable. Whether billbacks are compiled from memory, from little pieces of paper from the salesperson or from a master list, the longer it takes to organize it into a billable format, the greater the likelihood of error. Despite the fact that the distributor is willing to share this cost equally with you, there can be a tendency to allow sample usage to get away from them. The more time that elapses without access to their sample usage, the less opportunity you have to incorporate it into your budge. Delay also prevents you from reviewing their patterns of sample usage, and putting the brakes on over-sampling (too many samples billed back) if that is the case. The evidence of this will be in the low percentage of sales to samples used.

Conversely, if you inhibit salespeople they will be less likely to promote your wines. If they can't sample they can't sell. If there is a restriction on samples, the salespeople may take the wines out for a certain period of time and then stop. After all, the wholesale house will either discourage the use of samples or require the salesperson to be responsible for their own samples if the supplier is not splitting the cost at all.

In the first edition, I did not recommend allowing the distributor to simply deduct a sample allowance percentage from every invoice because the reasons they gave were usually, "we are too busy to do the paperwork." I felt it took the onus off the distributor to share in the cost to any discernible degree, despite their assurances that this would not be the case. Plus, there can be a tendency to incorporate the allowance into their pricing for additional margin points, just as they might do if you were to run an incentive program indefinitely. However, more recently I have seen a trend towards allowing 2% off every invoice. Since this seems to have become one of those traditions incorporated into standard practice, it's hard to argue with it today.

Another industry norm is for the distributor to charge 100% billback on the following:

- spoiled product (generally corked wine)
- when the supplier (you or the winery representative) work the market
- trade shows.

There is an unwritten code around the use of trade show and supplier visit samples, presumably because they are not dispensed at the company's discretion and are out of their control. There is really no way around this.

Paranoia certainly should not be the basis for your relationship but if your distributor operates on a billback system for samples, I suggest that you monitor the sample usage and require accountability if you feel it is too high. Perhaps a salesperson has been working on an account, or series of accounts, for some time and orders are expected in the following sales period, which is perfectly reasonable. Or perhaps the company principal is not aware of their own billbacks, which are generated by an accounts receivable department, and may find, through your follow-up, that there is a preponderance of samples going to one individual, disproportionate to their sales. If so, this will most likely not be the only indication of this salesperson's lack of demonstrable results.

I also suggest making comparisons with your other distributors' sample usage around the country through their billbacks to you. It is not a scientific method but is often a helpful tool in zeroing in on a distributor sample usage that appears to be an aberration, based on what appears to be more usual elsewhere. Disproportionately high sample usage can then be brought, tactfully, to the attention of the distributor.

On the other side of the coin, there are actually some wholesalers who do not bill back at all for sample usage. I'm not sure if this is largesse on their part or a lack of desire to generate more paperwork. Whatever the reason, I don't look a gift horse in the mouth and am grateful.

## Purchase Orders

The P.O. from the distributor should indicate everything they are expecting from you in relation to the following:

- brand
- vintage
- number of cases
- volume of cases, e.g., 12/case or 6/case
- size of bottles, e.g., 750ml, 1.5L, etc.
- any samples included with shipment (with prior agreement)
- sample allowance (if applicable)
- price for each item
- terms (as already determined between the two of you)
- trucking company
- P.O. number
- pick up point

> notes from distributor, such as "will pick-up remainder of xxx next month." Or "60-day terms on first invoice, as agreed. Net 30 days after that"

A P.O. number is really an essential item from a distributor. Without one there is no way for the trucker to know how to request the order for pickup from most public wine warehouses. A dispatcher releases an order solely based on this specific number.

Notes, if they are included at all, are simply ways in which distributors make sure you are both on the same page with housekeeping issues related to orders.

*The very first thing you do when you receive a P.O. is to check to see that all items are correctly identified, for the correct price and in stock.* If the distributor has indicated 2021 vintage and you are still on 2020, or conversely, they indicate 2020 and you have sold out and have 2021, you must let them know immediately. It may not be important; on the other hand, it could be critical. Restaurant wine lists, special orders by customers, distributor expectations or ratings could all affect how your customer will receive this news. Don't assume it is okay. Don't expect them to accept a vintage they did not order.

If you are completely out of stock of a wine, *let them know.* Don't fill the order, with the exception of the depleted wine, and the first they learn of the issue is when they unload the goods at their warehouse. Call and explain that you unexpectedly sold out and will expect another shipment on such-and-such a date. Or tell them that you sold out of the '19 a while ago (maybe it's been some time since this wholesaler has placed an order) but you will be happy to fill it with the next vintage. Get their okay. You will learn what they really want, and they will appreciate the heads up.

If a price is incorrect, *let them know.* It may be that an incentive program that has expired, a volume discount price that is triggered at twenty eight cases, e.g., or it may be a simple transposition of figures on their part, but they cannot be surprised by your invoice.

If they exceed their allocation and you cannot fill the order – such a happy occurrence! – make sure you let them know. In the case of allocations, this is where you usually don't have enough to supply a particularly sought after, short supply wine and must allocate it in whatever manner makes sense to you. With in-demand wines, distributors will often attempt to put in for extra in the hope the order will be filled. Your inclination may be to wonder if they ever read your allocation spreadsheets or emails, or whatever means you use to communicate, but it's a natural tendency on their part. I've done it myself when I've been given an allocation on a wine in high demand and I've used up my allocation from the winery, and occasionally it has worked. Circumstances may have changed since the allocations were made and perhaps someone else has been late on payment too many times or cherry picked too often or just haven't picked up their allocation. Perhaps you *can* fill this specific order but make sure they know that you know they have exceeded their allocation and that you will not (most likely) be able to do more in the future.

Other P.O. items to review would naturally be to make sure terms state what has been agreed upon and any include sample allowance, incentive goods or discounts.

## Pickup and Delivery

Pickup and delivery of all distribution orders are arranged by the distributor through their own trucking options, either a contracted company or, if they are large enough, their in-house trucks. *The cost of shipping is incurred by them, not the importer.* Your invoice is FOB point of origin – i.e., the warehouse. From that moment forward the wine is in possession of the distributor and becomes their responsibility. Distributors are well aware of this, of course, and will make arrangements that best suit their needs, their pocketbook and the timing of the trucker schedules. My emphasis is to ensure you do not suggest that you ship to them in a mistaken belief that this is customary.

Pickup can often take a couple of weeks for a small distributor if a trucker is trying to take a complete load back to the customer or their originating state or only goes to California every two weeks on a Wednesday. If they miss that date, two more weeks is a long time to wait. In terms of budgeting, be aware that when a distributor puts in a P.O. for "net 30" (payment is made 30 days after trucker picks up product) it may take much longer to get paid because of the pickup schedule, not their tardy remittance. The due date is calculated from the date the order is picked up not when it is put in or is waiting to be picked up.

If it is a first-time pickup for this distributor at this warehouse, make sure they are aware of your warehouse's requirements – such as 48 hours minimum notice, contact email or who to ask for.

As soon as you have determined that all aspects of the P.O. are correct, submit the release order to your warehouse. Then make sure you receive a confirmation or confirm it yourself online on the warehouse website. The worst thing you can do in this situation is to assume the warehouse has your order. If this turns out to be wrong, the trucker misses his window of opportunity in scheduling an appointment, which needlessly delays your order. A delayed order starts a chain of events that affects subsequent orders. It can even result in a retailer or restaurant canceling an order for a particular event or customer because the product did not arrive on time. The other part of the confirmation is to be sure the warehouse also has the correct vintages and product count. As you can see, P.O. confirmations are an integral aspect all the way down the line.

## Invoicing

An invoice from you should mirror all the necessary items from the P.O. from your customer and the release order to the warehouse. It should also now include an invoice number of your own designation. There are no rules about invoice numbers. It is whatever makes it easier for you to readily identify and quantify the orders in your office. Examples of system choices could be:

- 000001, 00002, 00003 (numbering from your first order in sequence)
- SC-00001, SC-0002, SC-0003 or TX-0001, TX-0001, TX-0003 (numbering by state – these indicate South Carolina and Texas orders)
- 22-0001, 22-0002, 22-0003 (numbering from the beginning of each calendar year)

These are just suggestions to illustrate the point. You may think of many other permutations that better suit your style or need.

**The invoice should also include:**
- bill to and Ship to (since these may differ)
- FOB point (this is the location of your warehouse)
- ship Date
- due Date

**You may also wish to include one or more of the following statements:**
- Interest will be charged at the rate of xx% for accounts past due
- Returned checks will incur a charge of $xx

## Distribution – The Next Stage

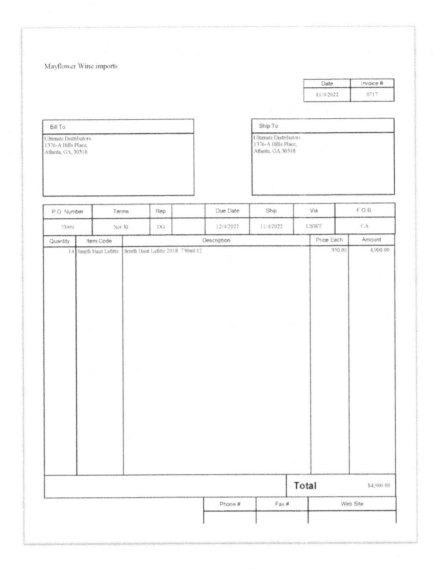

Figure 10.2 Wholesale Invoice

These last two statements are entirely optional but may protect you in the event that the account proceeds to collection. I would not, however, institute any actual interest charges while invoices are past due but the distributor remains in good standing. This will not go over very well with your distributor partner and is not customary.

QuickBooks has a number of examples of product invoices (as opposed to service invoices) and there are others available to download. You can also design or redesign your own using QuickBooks templates options.

Invoicing should be done as soon as the wine has shipped – i.e. the trucker has picked it up. You should receive a shipment advice from the warehouse and once again, through an established system in your office, make sure you have checked the shipment advice against order details. It will become second nature after a while.

If you do notice a discrepancy between these documents, and it happens more often than any of us would like, determine the cause. It can be one of many: boxes left sitting on the dock, miscounted inventory that resulted in depletion of an item or the item simply could not be found. Your first choice would be to have the warehouse call you before the trucker leaves but this is not always possible, so now you are left with explaining the discrepancy to the distributor. Do not avoid telling them or assume that it isn't necessary to do so because they'll find out soon enough anyway. They may have been counting on this item to fill an order, or may end up paying more for what is now an LTL. They will not necessarily be pleased but will be far more understanding because you took the initiative to pick up the phone and inform them. It is also the opportunity to determine how the shortage will be remedied – arranging for another pickup, substituting product, etc.

The invoice should be prepared the day of shipping, as the next stage in your system, and emailed from QuickBooks (or other accounting program). No one uses snail mails these days and emailing saves on postage and mail delays. If terms are 30 to 45 days, you may think you have plenty of time but two things are at odds with that: time goes much faster than you think and the invoice can easily be put aside and forgotten. The sooner you put up your hand for payment, the sooner you enter the wholesaler's queue.

# Collecting

The wholesaler knows very well when the invoice is due but may only have limited funds, an unexpected expenditure or a disappointing sales month. In that case, the supplier whose invoice reaches them first goes into the system first and presumably is paid on an aging basis. Hopefully, there is an accounts payable person or department, which removes both you and the company principal, or executive, from having to deal with financial matters and gives you someone you can contact to pursue a past due invoice.

As soon as the invoice is due, send a statement or resend the invoice with an email request for payment. This is an innocuous announcement that simply reminds the customer that payment is due. If it has already been sent, a reminder doesn't offend and if, by chance, they have forgotten to pay or have not received your original invoice, this alerts them before too much more time elapses.

Presumably, you have done the necessary reference checking prior to the start of the relationship to ensure that the distributor is credit worthy and reliable but circumstances change, as many of us have seen during the recession and the pandemic, and now the invoice becomes quite past due. Stay in touch with the appropriate party via phone. Give them the chance to offer explanations, proffer a new (exact) date and generally bring the account current while retaining your good will. They have agreed to terms, by which you are expecting them to abide, but if their customers are stretching their terms or someone cancelled a large order, they may find themselves in unexpectedly difficult circumstances. You may also find that they are holding invoice payment until *you* pay your billbacks. This is not reasonable, in my opinion, since billbacks are always less than an invoice, but is not unusual.

The more desirable your product and the easier it is to sell (i.e., a "cash cow" for them) the more likely you will be paid. It is also incentive, at some stage defined by your own finances and commonsense, to tell them that no further orders can be filled until all invoices are paid.

There comes a point, of course, when you are acting as their bank with no end in sight, people are avoiding you and the situation has become unacceptable. This is when you realize there is no longer a relationship and cutting your losses with this individual is the only prudent course of action. This is when you issue a final notice and a deadline for collection agency activity. It is an action of last resort, but it does happen and you must be prepared to recover monies due to you. This is when you retroactively apply interest to the entire bill!

I have only found this to be necessary three times in all the years I have been importing and distributing. Each time, if I am being honest, it was because I either abdicated my responsibility in background checking to someone else, or I was reckless in the early days of distributor appointments. The odds that it will happen to you are considerably less because you will presumably be better prepared!

*SUMMARY* — The theme throughout your wine importing career should be preparation, communication and organization. Evaluate potential customers carefully and thoroughly, communicate with them consistently, even when you would rather avoid an uncomfortable situation, and keep all paperwork. You never know when you will need it.

# My Story

I have been very fortunate to have encountered distributors who most often became friends rather than distant business associates. I have stayed in their homes, attended barbeques, gone on shopping trips and mountain hikes with them and been included in family events. I even assisted with the planting of a vineyard – a hobby of the wholesaler – a completely enjoyable day, where a group of us started out diligently planting root stocks in evenly spaced, straight rows and after lunch, where wonderful food and much wine was consumed, continued those same rows in erratically placed, meandering furrows that easily identified what came before and after lunch.

Over the course of my many years as an importer, very few instances resulted in conflict or a breakdown in civil interaction. Most often, wholesalers are just like their suppliers (us) – reasonable, hardworking, honest people who struggle and stress and want to do their best for their customers. Some are incredibly successful and some are experiencing financial difficulties, but all are looking at your wines and you as an opportunity to increase their profits or bring their finances into the black. The fact that they become friends should not deter you from protecting your business but it makes it a lot easier to work together for a common goal.

## My Client's Story

There are many routes to a successful wine import business within a range of budgets. One client has a healthy but not unlimited budget and has wisely chosen to use it to maximum advantage. To that end, she:

★ brings in thoughtfully curated, small volume FCL (i.e. 400-500 cases) across the range of her portfolio, maintaining both warehouse inventory and wine diversity and keeping stock to manageable levels for current and potential distribution

★ travels extensively in the U.S. as required to meet necessary sales goals, to both launch and work with her distributors

★ willingly authorizes depletion allowance (DA) incentive programs (see next chapter) particularly when suggested by the distributor and having examined its potential benefit

★ uses samples prudently but plentifully to establish and stimulate sales.

There are any number of other methods she is employing to ensure the business remains vital and growing into its third year but without this early careful planning her profit margins would be much smaller. It takes discipline to build a strong foundation, and tempering your early passion and enthusiasm with sound financial decisions will serve you far better in the long run.

# CHAPTER 11

# TIPS FOR DISTRIBUTION SUCCESS

Some of these tips are going to appear obvious and others will come as a complete surprise. After all, you sold the wine to the distributor, you have provided them with samples, initiated a launch, given them a competitive price. What else is left to do other than to tell them, "go forth and deplete inventory"? A lot!

These days, distributors are overloaded with product, internal and external demands and maintaining a competitive edge. They *expect* you to help them sell your product. Yes, the wine that took you so long to bring in and find the right distribution for and which you have just happily sent off on its way to its new home. That wine.

## Communication

You've seen considerable mention of this before in the book but I'm saying it again in a different way, for a different reason. I'm talking about the right communication at this particular time in the process. For example, you don't want to communicate so often with the distributor that they are tearing their hair out and regretting the moment they ever said "yes" to your wine. Believe me, this does happen. You don't want to communicate with force, pressure or inappropriate requests. And you don't want to leave them to their own devices and only communicate when you need something. But you do want to communicate.

## Travel Budgeting

This is a reference to time as well as money. Many people feel they must rush all over the country meeting potential customers before any one of them has committed to wine. And if you have the money, well, that fits your budget. However, it really isn't necessary and can bankrupt you in no time. Travel costs will certainly be one of those items that can drastically erode your margin.

Appointing distributors can easily, with the appropriate preparedness, be done via phone and email. If the potential business is enormous – volume, market coverage, etc. – meeting with the company and making a presentation prior to appointment is well worthwhile. They may get the sales team or upper management together and your presence will make all the difference in a life-changing decision for you. It may also be advisable when the distributor feels this step is crucial to the process and it is a company you want to be partnered with. In other instances, you could combine it with a trip to a neighboring state or coincide with meeting two or three potential distributors. But in most initial transactions, it is not critical to meet prior to an order. I used to say that it wasn't critical at a launch either but I say that now with a caveat. There are times when a wholesaler would prefer to get the product launched with their sales people and utilize your assistance at a later date. It could be a soft launch or it suited them to get the wines picked up and into the system but they need to accommodate another supplier at the same time. It could be that they want to test the waters first and not waste time – yours or theirs – with a potentially costly exercise that an orchestrated launch entails.

Aside from that, a launch could be the perfect opportunity to get the wines and your relationship established on solid footing and well worth the time and expense.

Budgeting for travel is essential during the ongoing relationship and for the most part, this should be *at the distributor's convenience.* Suppliers are well aware of the sales bump that takes place during a market visit and are usually clamoring for time and attention. It can become overwhelming to the sales force and burn them out when all they find themselves doing each day is entertaining a steady stream of suppliers. Therefore, most distributors have a carefully orchestrated calendar of visit and if you call far enough in advance (thereby working the visit into your annual travel budget as well) you may have your pick of dates and salespeople. If you leave it till the last minute, prepare to be disappointed. If that is the case, don't be petulant or demanding. There was a system in place long before you came along.

Generally, depending on the wholesaler's size, market coverage, population density, number of wines from your portfolio and several other factors, you may want to visit a market anywhere from once a year to once a quarter. Once a year would be considered essential and this may be determined by the wholesaler's annual trade show or by your own needs. If at all possible, spring and early autumn are optimum times. By spring, I mean from February to end of May, very much depending on the region and time slot availability. It's not necessarily that helpful (or pleasant) to go to Minneapolis in February but Florida or the ski resort mountains of Colorado may be perfect. February to May is the best time to introduce new brands for the year or new varietals for summer, and generally kick off the year. In early autumn, it should be central to your sales budget to have wines positioned for the holidays in both the sales people's minds and in the stores and restaurants.

The basics of market visit protocol once you are on the ground will be covered in a later section.

## Staff Training – In-House

Start with the sales staff if you want them to remember your wines and nurture their growth in your market. This can be accomplished by working with each individual salesperson over the course of the year, but bigger and faster impact commonly requires scheduling a presentation for a Friday morning sales meeting. This is the traditional team meeting held once a week or once a month, depending on the company and, while part of it is devoted to the company's own business and housekeeping matters – quotas, reports, problems, etc. – a portion of the time is typically allocated to suppliers who wish to come in and ply their wares.

➢ First of all, please make your presentation interesting and keep your audience awake. These poor people have frequently been subjected to boring presentations with the same tired product or overly technical discourses delivered in a monotone. This is their time you are taking up. They could be putting it to better use and furthermore will do so as soon as you release them if you haven't made your presentation motivating, intriguing, fun and/or potentially financially attractive.

➢ Stick to the time limit. This could be five minutes or thirty but there *will* be a time limit. There could be presentations before and after yours or they've already spent part of the morning on their own agenda. It is only courteous to adhere to this stipulation and will endear you to the sales team if you do.

➢ Bring wine for them to taste. Not so much that they develop palate fatigue (remember there could be other presentations before yours) but sufficient in number and diversity to reflect your portfolio. These could be wines already in their book or could be new vintages or wines under consideration by management. Tasting through the wines while you describe something of the vineyard, background, style and pricing allows the information to marry with the product. This may be the first opportunity they have had to taste the wines and this may be the occasion on which you find your champion – the one who falls in love with a particular wine and whose mental wheels are turning as to where they can place it and how they can sell it.

➢ Give the sales team key words to use with each wine or the brand in general – phrases that distinguish it from other wines or makes it easier to remember. Keep it simple. Don't overload them with technical information or complicated descriptions. Not to suggest anyone is mentally challenged, but consider you are one of many portfolios in their book and they cannot possibly absorb it all at one meeting. It could be something about the wine or grapes: an unusual, but pleasant simile for the aromatics, age of the vines, yield; about the vineyard: volcanic gravel, source of another brand's success, unique trellising; or about the vignerons themselves: third generation, same winemaker as…, previously made wines at… Whatever it is, try to make it a point of difference and not the usual descriptions they have heard a thousand times before. Avoid obvious hyperbole. Keep the technology and elaborate backgrounds for the handout material or direct them to the website.

➢ Give them more reason to take out your wines. Make the week you are there, or the week following your presentation, a time of monetary incentives for most sold, most placements or $xx a case program. This is not essential by any means, and I have often conducted sales seminars without it, but it is an opportunity for a tangible value-added piece of your presentation if it fits your budget. A non-tangible motivation would be to develop a rapport with all or some of the team so they feel they are aiding the relative success of someone they like and respect. If nothing else, it makes the day spent in their company more enjoyable for both of you. You would be surprised at how often a supplier can be lacking in personality or arrogant or insensitive. Salespeople will tell you these things if they enjoy your company.

➢ Leave them with an invitation to call you if they need more information or have questions. They should each have your business card and email address.

## Staff Training – On-Premise

Initially, it may seem like such a coup to get your wine into the most prestigious restaurant in town…until you look at the list. It is twenty-three pages and that's just the reds. Unless you have a wine on a restaurant wine list by the glass, or the list is very small, you can expect your wine to languish along with possibly hundreds of others. In many states and with many distributors, broken case sales (as in partial case orders) are common and in these instances the restaurant only has to have three to six bottles of a wine they like to put it on the list. Perhaps they wish to qualify for *Wine Spectator's* Award of Excellence, they don't have much room or they simply want a list of a wide range of wines to complement their food.

At any rate, the sommelier may have loved your wine when it was presented but the servers will generally have no clue as to its qualities and will have no reason to recommend it and the lack of name recognition will discourage most people from ordering it. This becomes especially true if it is expensive or an esoteric grape. It is an additional chore for you, one you might rather avoid, instead putting your time to continuing your sales journey, but it can really help move your wine if you can give the servers a reason to recommend it. Preferably, you will have more than one wine on the list to make it worth your while and theirs to conduct the training.

Restaurant staff trainings are usually done just prior to dinner service when the employees have their meeting to review the evening's specials. This means they do not have to be called in on their day off or at a time for which they will receive no remuneration. I believe they actually enjoy this exercise. They benefit from a free drink, or at least a substantial taste, before starting their shift and most servers in fine dining restaurants want to learn more about their wines and feel comfortable making recommendations.

Key words are again important in this setting but not the same words as for distributor sales trainings. In this instance, they want to be able to satisfy a guest's food pairing or predisposition towards a certain style of wine. The server also wants to be able to "up-sell", if possible, since their tip will be reflected in the overall check size. It may be that your wine is more expensive than some, or it could be less expensive, but if the guest's palate is satisfied they will order a second bottle for the table.

Some examples of words that are useful to the guest could be "dry", "complex with blackberry fruit". "full-bodied", "earthy", "rich with fine grained tannins", or ways in which to compare these wines to those the guests are familiar with, if it applies, such as "Rhone style," "Burgundian" or the opposite of Burgundy, such as a pinot that is very cherry, fruit-forward and young. Obviously, the servers will want to present the wines in the most flattering way possible. Steer them away from saying "light" and substitute "soft" if that applies. "Sweet" may in fact refer to the fruit rather than the residual sugar and can be misleading. "Rounded", "mouth-filling" or "ripe" could be a more appealing way to describe the wine.

Once again, your personality and presentation of material will resonate with this group. If they like you they will be more apt to remember you and recommend your wines.

## Consistent Pricing

You may wonder how this element comes under the heading of distribution success tips. Consistent pricing is one of those items that can be overlooked until it is too late and already creating headaches for you and your customers. Developing a well thought out pricing strategy from the outset, one that enables you to absorb exchange rate fluctuations for a time and allows for the vagaries of doing business, is essential.

Once you establish the FOB pricing from which the distributor has chosen, ordered and placed your wines, you cannot come back too soon and say the pricing is wrong, did not take certain costs into consideration, the exchange rate has gone haywire or the winery has increased their price to you and you must pass this along.

You also cannot surprise them with a price increase – no matter how much time has elapsed since the last one – by including it on their invoice or giving them no notice. They are trying to manage their own sales and keep items on wine lists.

My advice is to keep the price constant for at least one vintage. There are many occasions where I did not increase a price over three or four vintages if a winery did not increase to me and the exchange rate did not change. Of course, I have had to institute increases in the usual course of business but on occasion I have even decreased, especially if the exchange rate moved substantially in my favor or the vineyard owners decided to reevaluate their pricing structure. Even if there is a rapid and unanticipated rise in foreign currency, try a manageable increase in your pricing over time. It may not keep pace with your shrinking margin, but it is far better to maintain business at a reduced profit margin than lose the business altogether.

Whatever your decision on price increases, try to mitigate the impact by giving as much notice as you can and offering to preserve the current pricing for orders placed by such-and-such a date, even if they have not been picked up by the price increase date. Or hold pricing on larger orders if you can. Anything to increase orders (which will reduce your carrying costs) and let your distribution partner know you are trying to work with them.

## Relationships Outside the Wholesaler

We have already touched on some of the value-added components to your wine sales. Another one of the value-added items is you! By developing sales and relationships beyond the distributor's workforce and efforts, you will make yourself a more valuable supplier in the distributor's eyes.

Truly, this is not something you should feel compelled to do, nor is it expected. But if you know the sommelier at the upscale resort in town or have connections with a chain, or feel like developing connections with a chain, it can secure a distributor for you during an otherwise fruitless search or endear you to the one you have.

Perhaps you eat frequently at a chain in your hometown that has a varied wine list, such as P.F. Chang's, Ruth's Chris or Roy's. Chains of a specific ethnicity or certain price tier will usually buy on a corporate level for a core list but, regionally, they also often have latitude to supplement for local tastes. Cultivating that buyer could mean a steppingstone for the distributor in another state. Be aware of whether the list is limited to a particular region, or excludes certain countries such as the one whose wines you represent.

Not only is it worth your while for your distributor relationship but who knows what other business your efforts could establish for you nationwide.

## Working Their Market Alone

This can be a delicate area and should be handled with the full cooperation of your distributor. If you start charging around town like a bull in a china shop without regard for pricing or product availability in inventory, you will most likely annoy your distributor and could make it difficult for the sales team if you are going to their accounts without their knowledge.

Working the market alone could come about because there are no more slots left at the time you wish to go into their area, or you have an extra day after your regularly scheduled visit. It could be something you plan on the way to another market or on either side of a trade show when no one is available to work with you. It could be your own home base and you have specific accounts where you have developed relationships.

Set the stage with the distributor beforehand by establishing a balance between what you wish to do and what they would like you do to and, most importantly, let them know you are roaming loose in their territory! Take their price book with you so you quote correctly and learn what products are in their inventory, and don't try to take orders for anything they cannot fill. Instead of just the 'A' accounts that appeal to you the most, go to accounts the distributor may need assistance with or find difficult to get into and you'll be a help instead of a hindrance. If there are incentives available, make sure you don't step on any toes and that it is legal in the particular state.

Done appropriately, with transparency, your distributor will appreciate your efforts and the resulting sales.

## Placement Reports

This one is for you. It refers to the account placements made by the distributor and is specific as to which wine and vintage is placed at what account in their region. It used to be a difficult report to obtain from the wholesaler, especially on a regular basis. It takes time to prepare and provide to you - time they may not wish to devote to something that has no discernible value for them. But I believe that with the increased use of technology to assist information gathering, this is much more doable. Occasionally, wholesalers are reluctant to divulge what they consider proprietary information they fear may be passed along to their replacement in the future. However, many have no problem supplying the information. It can be useful to tie your incentive programs to the quantifiable placements and in the case of restaurant glass pour programs is essential. Knowing where your wines are placed in the market also equips you with knowledge you can use to assist with targeting accounts and stimulating sales. These are the priority objectives to obtaining placement reports, rather than as a means to entice a prospective new distributor.

**Sales by Item Detail**

Accrual Basis — January through September

| Type | Date | Num | Memo | Name | Qty |
|---|---|---|---|---|---|
| Invoice | | 1547 | Wholesale Case - Barossa Valley Estate Grenache Mata... | Blackwell's | 3 |
| Invoice | | 1574 | Wholesale Case - Barossa Valley Estate Grenache Mata... | Blackwell's | 1 |
| Invoice | | 1590 | Wholesale Case - Barossa Valley Estate Grenache Mata... | The Jug Shop | 1 |
| **Total Schild GMS Blend** | | | | | |
| **Schild Reserve Shiraz** | | | | | |
| Invoice | | 1088 | Wholesale Case Price - Schild Estate Barossa Valley Be... | Oakville Grocery Palo Alto | 1 |
| Invoice | | 1433 | Wholesale Case Price - Schild Estate Barossa Valley Be... | Myth | 1 |
| Invoice | | 1475 | Wholesale Case Price - Schild Estate Barossa valley Be... | K&L San Carlos | 1 |
| Invoice | | 1476 | Wholesale Case Price - Schild Estate Barossa valley Be... | K&L San Carlos | 1 |
| Invoice | | 1471 | Wholesale Case Price - Schild Estate Barossa valley Be... | Wine Club Santa Clara | 4 |
| Invoice | | 1480 | Wholesale Case Price - Schild Estate Barossa valley Be... | Wine Club San Francisco | 1 |
| Invoice | | 1519 | Wholesale Case Price - Schild Estate Barossa valley Be... | Carnelian Room | 1 |
| Invoice | | 1548 | Wholesale Case Price - Schild Estate Barossa valley Be... | K&L San Francisco | 1 |
| Invoice | | 1549 | Wholesale Case Price - Schild Estate Barossa valley Be... | K&L San Francisco | 0.5 |
| Invoice | | 1550 | Wholesale Case Price - Schild Estate Barossa valley Be... | K&L San Francisco | 0.5 |
| Invoice | | 1582 | Wholesale Case Price - Schild Estate Barossa valley Be... | Wine Club San Francisco | 1 |
| **Total Schild Reserve Shiraz** | | | | | |
| **Schild Shiraz** | | | | | |
| Invoice | | 1064 | Wholesale Case Price - Schild Estate Barossa Valley Sh... | Eos Restaurant and Wine ... | 1 |
| Invoice | | 1460 | Wholesale Case Price - Schild Estate Barossa Valley Sh... | Mollie Stones Greenbrae | 1 |
| Invoice | | 1546 | Wholesale Case Price - Schild Estate Barossa Valley Sh... | Mollie Stones Greenbrae | 1 |
| **Total Schild Shiraz** | | | | | |
| **Schild Shiraz** | | | | | |
| Invoice | | 1465 | Wholesale Case Price - Schild Estate Barossa Valley Sh... | The Jug Shop | 5 |
| Invoice | | 1466 | Wholesale Case Price - Schild Estate Barossa Valley Sh... | Swirl on Castro | 3 |
| Invoice | | 1467 | Wholesale Case Price - Schild Estate Barossa Valley Sh... | Blackwell's | 6 |
| Invoice | | 1470 | Wholesale Case Price - Schild Estate Barossa Valley Sh... | K&L San Carlos | 4 |
| Invoice | | 1475 | Wholesale Case Price - Schild Estate Barossa Valley Sh... | K&L San Carlos | 1 |
| Invoice | | 1476 | Wholesale Case Price - Schild Estate Barossa Valley Sh... | K&L San Carlos | 1 |
| Invoice | | 1471 | Wholesale Case Price - Schild Estate Barossa Valley Sh... | Wine Club Santa Clara | 4 |
| Invoice | | 1480 | Wholesale Case Price - Schild Estate Barossa Valley Sh... | Wine Club San Francisco | 5 |
| Invoice | | 1485 | Wholesale Case Price - Schild Estate Barossa Valley Sh... | Wine Club Santa Clara | 1 |
| Invoice | | 1481 | Wholesale Case Price - Schild Estate Barossa Valley Sh... | WINE Bar & Shop | 2 |
| Invoice | | 1488 | Wholesale Case Price - Schild Estate Barossa Valley Sh... | Home | 1 |
| Invoice | | 1513 | Wholesale Case Price - Schild Estate Barossa Valley Sh... | Restaurant Gary Danko | 1 |
| Invoice | | 1526 | Wholesale Case Price - Schild Estate Barossa Valley Sh... | Wine Club Santa Clara | 1 |
| Invoice | | 1559 | Wholesale Case Price - Schild Estate Barossa Valley Sh... | Restaurant 1505 | 1 |
| Invoice | | 1560 | Wholesale Case Price - Schild Estate Barossa Valley Sh... | Wine Club Santa Clara | 10 |
| Invoice | | 1582 | Wholesale Case Price - Schild Estate Barossa Valley Sh... | Wine Club San Francisco | 10 |
| Invoice | | 1574 | Wholesale Case Price - Schild Estate Barossa Valley Sh... | Blackwell's | 5 |
| Invoice | | 1590 | Wholesale Case Price - Schild Estate Barossa Valley Sh... | The Jug Shop | 5 |
| Invoice | | 1575 | Wholesale Case Price - Schild Estate Barossa Valley Sh... | Swirl on Castro | 3 |

**Figure 11.1 Placement Report Example**

The reluctance distributors have about handing you the specifics of all their placements can be well founded but this should not be their first concern. If they are performing well to reasonable expectations and honoring their financial commitments, there should be no reason for you to consider taking your brands elsewhere and nor should you. On the other hand, if they are not doing all those things, then you should move on, in which case the placements can come in handy.

**WHOLESALE DISTRIBUTOR**
**Depletion Report - SALES BY MARKET**
**September 1, 2022 - September 30, 2022**

| Vendor | Item Desc. | Item Code | Vintage Year | Liter / Unit | DC Pack Size | DC Qty. Sold | VA Pack Size | VA Qty. Sold |
|---|---|---|---|---|---|---|---|---|
| Braxton | Flaxman's Valley Shiraz | 231926 | 2019 | 0.75 | 6.00 | 1.33 | | |
| Braxton | Roussanne Marsanne | 231927 | 2021 | | | | | |
| Braxton | Eden Valley Riesling | 238792 | 2021 | 0.75 | 12.00 | 0.17 | | |
| Braxton | Barossa Grenache Shiraz Mataro | 231928 | 2020 | 0.75 | 6.00 | 0.00 | 6.00 | 0.17 |
| Braxton | Barossa Valley Shiraz | 231930 | 2020 | 0.75 | 12.00 | 0.75 | 12.00 | 1.25 |
| Braxton | Eden Valley Riesling | 231932 | 2021 | 0.75 | 12.00 | 0.25 | | |
| Braxton | McLaren Vale Grenache Mataro Shiraz | 231935 | 2018 | | | | | |
| Braxton | McLaren Vale Grenache Mataro Shiraz | 231935 | 2019 | 0.75 | 12.00 | 6.33 | 12.00 | 8.50 |
| Braxton | McLaren Vale Grenache Mataro Shiraz | 231935 | 2020 | | | | | |
| Total | | | | | | 8.83 | | 9.92 |

Figure 11.2 Depletion Report Example

# Depletion Reports

Incentive programs should be tied to depletions, translated to mean depletion of the distributor's inventory by means of sales. Otherwise, there is no "incentive" for the distributor to produce records to back up the program. The programming you put in place should hold them accountable, to the extent that programming money is not paid until a depletion report shows the cases sold that month or quarter. This is a basic and good reason for depletion reports but there is more.

It's really in your best interests to see how well the distributor is performing with your brands overall. Depletion reports allow you to see the pace of sales, determine an order point, see where they may require some assistance to move a wine faster and anticipate your own container compositions. Hopefully, this information indicates progress. In some instances, what the depletions show you are that your wines are moving at glacial speed and at this rate you will be three vintages ahead before they are ready for the next order. If this is the case, another order is unlikely anyway. But if you can catch this trend soon enough you can possibly reverse it. Start by calling the wholesaler to see if it is a problem that may be addressed. If the issue lies with how your wines fit in their market or lack of interest from their sales team, better to know when to move on than to languish for additional months in ignorant bliss.

*SUMMARY* — Keys to making your wines a winning combination for you and your distributor can be summed up by one word – communication. If you keep in touch with them, they know it is a true partnership and they will work harder to make it work for you. Listen and learn from them and tailor your programs, presentations and sales efforts to their individual personalities and styles.

# My Story

Or rather, three of them:

➤ In the beginning, I ran around all over my own market in Atlanta selling up a storm for

my new distributor. It was a heady time; the wines sold extraordinarily well; I made inroads into country clubs and restaurants that became new accounts for the distributor and it seemed my portfolio was going from strength to strength. These were the halcyon days of ignorant bliss.

Eventually, I moved my business to Colorado and all those fabulous sales ground to a halt. Apparently, I was virtually the only one out there selling my wines. After all, why should they expend valuable sales force when I was doing so well for them? In those early days of my new career, I did not know the importance of fostering relationships, holding the distributor accountable and all the points I raised for you above, and will elaborate further into the book. It was certainly a hard lesson.

➤ I recall one of the first Friday sales meeting presentations I made to the largest distributor

in New Jersey. I was confronted by a sea of blank faced, bored liquor guys to whom I was just one more in a long line of presentations. Beforehand, one of them had pulled me aside and offered me a free bottle of a new liqueur if I kept my pitch to less than ten minutes. That was the extent of their interest. I'm not saying that anything would have worked with these guys in the old days. Liquor was still king then and wine the also-ran, but knowing my audience, and having more experience, might have allowed me to tailor my presentation to the circumstances, possibly getting in on the ground floor of a burgeoning wine groundswell.

➤ But there's a much more positive story to illustrate this section too. When I first moved to

California, I made a presentation to Costco, where I made a connection with the buyer that resulted in placements at a time when Costco was developing its fine wine program, still somewhat under the radar for most distributors and importers. The prevailing feeling among both groups was that it was not worth the loss of local retailers or potential fallout with a retail account when they discovered that a discount chain was undercutting them. I had no such concerns since my distribution was very limited at the time. I also had a varied portfolio so that I could conceivably offer exclusives of some wines to other retailers to fend off criticism. Running against the grain also made sense to me in this instance. I would rather have dozens, hundreds or possibly thousands of cases to a solid company than make individual case sales and worry about their ability to pay.

That relationship resulted in many years of successful placements and, furthermore, secured distribution in other states through the ability to offer them Costco business within their states. This is one of those chain relationships that brings the "value-added" component to your distribution relationship.

# CHAPTER 12

# MARKETING

There are many things you can do as part of your overall marketing plan that require little or no financial outlay. There are others that are more costly, but an essential part of doing business in the wine world and for which the cost is ultimately recouped. The trick is to find a way to get the most bang for your buck.

## Website Trade Support

Setting up a website is a great vehicle to enable people to find you, to establish the philosophy and mission statement of your company and to provide details of the principals and contact details. But don't expect the wine world to come flocking to your door. For one thing, it takes quite a long time for your website ranking to rise above the chaff of millions of websites out there, even with SEO (Search Engine Optimization) and, unless you have happened upon a prominent brand that inspires people to seek you out, they won't even be looking.

In the beginning, a website is handy to refer prospective distributors to for credibility more than anything else, an imprint that imparts a sense of permanence. I often research importers and distributors on behalf of my clients these days and I am very surprised when I find no internet footprint for them. Unless they are very new and the website is still under construction, this almost raises a red flag for me. It used to be optional; these days it's essential. When you actually have brands in your portfolio with distribution, it is an indispensable resource for your customer. The trade tools the distributor's salespeople are looking for are:

- tasting notes – latest vintage
- tasting notes – previous vintages (if they still have them in stock)
- ratings
- shelf talkers
- labels
- biographical information on the vineyards
- news and reviews

**Tasting notes** can easily be downloaded for sales staff to take out on calls, to familiarize themselves with the wines and to leave with the customer, if required. The information on these notes can bring far more interest to their presentations and increase their knowledge base. Having previous vintages satisfies the needs of those who are still working on a prior release or interested in the difference between vintages.

**Ratings** will benefit the salesperson's efforts if they can mention the consistent pedigree of a particular wine or that the one they are showing a prospect "rated 94 in *Wine Spectator*".

**Shelf talkers** are not essential on your site but very helpful and can quite easily be prepared by you or someone in your office using Publisher or Adobe and uploaded to a "trade section". You don't actually have to print them yourself these days, although I believe they are still a good resource on your trips. If not professionally printed, they can easily be printed on an as needed basis on glossy white card stock, e.g. (which is my preference) and will look as if they were commercially printed. Any distributor sales rep who needs to replenish their supply or replace one of the shelf talkers in a store that mysteriously disappeared after a visit by the competition, can easily download and print them at the office anywhere in the country. Set them up four or six to a page to print and divide without waste. They should not be so large as to obscure, or appear to be referring to, the next "facing" on the shelf (someone else's bottle) and not so small that you cannot fit essential information or they will be overlooked.

Figure 12.1 Shelf Talker Examples

**Labels** are used for the distributor's own marketing efforts and for promotions in restaurants. Distributors will often ask you for a set of labels and it is so much easier for you, less time consuming and costs nothing to direct them to the website, where a PDF or Jpeg is readily available. There are also times when they will need them to register wines on your behalf with their respective states.

Figure 12.2  Front and Back Wine Label Example

**Biographical information** on the vineyards and principals gives the salesperson a story to work with, something – as has been mentioned before – that differentiates your product from every other brand. This point of difference is what the salesperson is always looking for and is an important element, up there with communication and relationships.

**News and reviews** updates the brand with current elements, including personal winemaker awards, magazine articles, changes at the winery, achieving organic status, interviews – anything noteworthy to add to the presentation for the salesperson or to enhance the image for the distributor.

It's easy to make the website fresh by announcing new ratings, recognition or news about brands, winemakers and other noteworthy additions to the front page. It not only educates the salesperson but alerts the distributor, or prospective distributor, to information they might not previously have known.

Some importers add a tab to identify which wholesalers represent the portfolio in each state and this can be helpful, but not vital. It can become outdated or fail to indicate whether they represent a particular brand or wine the consumer or retailer may be looking for. I consider this optional and one that will not measurably affect your sales efforts one way or another. Receiving the odd email or phone call is not burdensome, in my view, and if you are besieged with calls or emails then I'm sure you will be happy to add the information.

# Wine Dinners

In terms of marketing, this takes the subject down to its bare essentials – what does it cost and how does it benefit your wines. As with everything else, it has to make sense. Donating dozens of bottles and flying in for a wine dinner without measurable financial gain is just throwing money away. The restaurant will appreciate the exposure and additional revenue they receive, the distributor will think you inexperienced and you will realize that you just wasted valuable resources.

Wine dinners should only ever be agreed to if you have determined one or more of the following:

- ➢ The cost of wine to you is negligible, nil or reasonable and shared equally with restaurant and/or distributor.
- ➢ There is a tie-in with a local retailer, or with the restaurant's own adjoining wine bar/retail outlet
- ➢ Wine(s) will go on the restaurant wine list or are already there.

There is never any reason to conduct a wine dinner when you are expected to foot the wine bill in its entirety, there is no exposure for either restaurant or wholesaler and there is no plan for follow through. As much as the evening's guests will enjoy the wine and food pairings, the opportunity to learn about the nuances of flavors and your scintillating banter, they will forget the name and what it looks and tastes like as soon as they don their coats and walk out the door. It's just a law of nature. They don't mean to, but once the magic of the evening wears off, they are back to their lives and the wine is relegated to a pleasant experience. Unless they can find it at their local retailer, who has supplied flyers for the dinner with the enticement of 10% off for participants, or who attends the dinner himself. Often, if it is a special event or wines of some note, the retailer will bring their customers to the evening.

At the very least, the wines have to be available in the area. There is absolutely no point in making the effort to do a wine dinner when the wines are not likely to be available for a couple of months because there is no return on your investment in the wine dinner. Unless – the usual caveat – it is an iconic, high demand brand where consumers are waiting with bated breath for the next vintage and this is a privileged insider's preview.  Under that circumstance, they will be very familiar with the brand and feel a connection with the wines, providing a further impetus to purchase them when available.

Determine the quantity and assortment of wines expected, how many people are expected and the number of courses. If you don't have a dessert wine, a cabernet or merlot may take its place with chocolate or cheese, but often the chef or restaurant owner would prefer to have a true dessert wine to expand their choices and finish the meal with flair. In such cases, I have agreed to the inclusion of something such as a botrytis wine, Port, Muscat or Tokay from someone else's portfolio, but this should be simply an addendum to your presentation. A mix of suppliers will normally result in diluting your event and your presentation.

If you know the restaurant, or have access to whomever is organizing the dinner, try to coordinate with them to have input into what will be served and which wines you wish to showcase. At the very least, make sure the distributor gives you as much advance notice of both the menu and the wines chosen so that you can prepare your presentation.

Quite often, the wine dinner is scheduled several months in advance, in which case vintages may have changed. If distributors don't have the wines in stock they usually expect them to be shipped just prior to the dinner. Be aware to follow up at appropriate times to ensure that a.) you will have wine vintages and varietals they wish to feature and b.) the wines the distributor ordered will arrive on time.

Occasionally a wine or a shipment is held up for some reason and not expected to arrive in time for the dinner. Hopefully, this is just one new vintage or one feature item, but in this case you will need to air freight sufficient bottles for the dinner. This is an expensive exercise and makes no economic sense, but it is good judgment in terms of PR, goodwill and smooth sailing for the dinner.

If the distributor does not provide handouts, I always provide a list of the wines, with a brief description of each and room to make notes. Depending upon the venue and access to the room or space beforehand, placing maps of the region or winery brochures on the table helps to personalize the dinner further.

My advice to you about speaking at wine dinners is a little like that for the sales staff Friday tastings: keep it interesting, entertaining and to a time limit. The audience is very different, of course, and the information you impart is packaged for the consumer but the point is to give them a memorable experience that translates into sales.

Formats for wine dinners can be varied but essentially there is a reception wine given to the guests on arrival who might gather in a cocktail pre-dinner setting in a private room or part of the restaurant set aside for the dinner, giving sufficient time for everyone to arrive. This is often the time when the host speaker – importer, winemaker, winery owner, broker, export manager or national sales director – can circulate, be introduced and answer questions about this first wine. It is an informal setting not usually conducive to public speaking.

Once the guests are seated and the first course, and one to three wines accompanying the first course are served, you may want to stand and speak about the reception wine and the first course wines. Usually at this time, I set the scene with background on the region and the winery and perhaps a personal, funny or endearing story about the history and people. Be a little circumspect with these stories. The wine industry is peopled by an eccentric lot and there are lots of stories that may not be appropriate. For example, I imported the wines of a winemaker who threw a tantrum if he wasn't treated like royalty, and a lovely winery owner who accidentally backed over his mother-in-law with his car and killed her. These aren't the sort of stories to tell at dinners, or any other time.

I launch into a brief description of each wine and its compatibility with the course. It is an opportunity to give limited technical information: the difference between French and American oak, what malolactic fermentation means (in its basic sense) are examples of what guests might find informative. Your guests may appreciate a discussion about a particular variety and its role in blends, if blends are part of the tasting selection. Do not delve into technical discussions regarding the entire process of grape to wine. You will see eyes glaze over and it will all be for naught. They are at the wine dinner first and foremost to enjoy good wine and appetizing food and each other's company. In the process, they are hoping to make new discoveries and feel uniquely connected to the winery.

As each course is served, gauge the most opportune moment to get up again and talk about the wines. Keep the talk brief, perhaps even briefer as you proceed. If there are numerous wines, you will notice the noise level increasing commensurate with wine consumed. Eventually, you will be lucky if you have their attention at all, but persevere with your prepared talk because you are a professional and it is incumbent on you to remember that you are performing your job and that is why you are there. However, tailoring the talk to the audience will make it a more enjoyable occasion for them. If you can see they are relaxed and having fun, be relaxed and have fun with them.

Do not become intolerant if they become bellicose; restrain your own drinking so that you do not degenerate to a level that diminishes your effectiveness or image. The wine dinner guests have paid to be there to eat, drink and listen to an expert. Circulate during courses, invite questions, comments and opinions on the wine and thank them all for coming.

# Trade Tastings

This subject should be divided into two very distinct areas: trade tastings and consumer tastings. They are as disparate as night and day, despite the seemingly related format.

## ◆ Trade Show - distributor

In my opinion, the most important trade tasting is the one you do at the behest of your distributor. Not because this necessarily produces the best results and the most lustrous sales at the time – although it can—but because it demonstrates loyalty to your distributor and a willingness to support them in their home market efforts. Which should result in sales down the line. This type of show is an opportunity for direct sales, and to meet or cement relationships with principals and sales staff and learn more about the trade in that area. Pay attention to the distributor's criteria for the tasting. These can include:

- ◆ charging for the booth or table
- ◆ providing a table or section for free

- you providing the wine
- sharing the cost of the wine
- requiring you to supply a certain number of bottles
- optional wine quantities
- requiring that all wine be pulled from stock
- allowing you to bring new vintages or special cuvées
- prohibiting any wines that are not already in their inventory.

Whatever the conditions your particular distributor imposes, respect them. They have most likely gone to a great deal of trouble to put an annual event together, renting space, providing food, printing booklets, dealing with the logistics of wine and people placement, inviting their top accounts and ensuring it is as successful as possible. It does not endear you to them to demand your own table at the entrance to the room, deviate from the wines they have listed in their book and generally behave like a prima donna. Everyone's needs are important, and everyone has the same agenda – to sell wine.

Each venue will be different. I have done trade tastings in the grand ballrooms of fine hotels, a zoo in Phoenix, art galleries in industrial downtowns, an embassy in Washington DC, meeting rooms of moderate chain hotels, tents at the base of a waterfall in Colorado, under canopies in gardens, Soho loft space in Manhattan, an Art Deco theatre in Atlanta and at the distributor's own warehouse. Budget constraints and expected attendance will often dictate the location but the motivation is always to offer a venue and wine selection that will entice the retailer, restaurateur and occasional VIP customer to come to the event or choose this event over another at the same time across town.

Figure 12.3 Distributor Trade Tasting New York

Always arrive early for set-up, to find shipments that may be missing, to open red wines and allow them to breathe and allow white wines time to chill. The basic setup should be in place or will be provided prior to the event. I usually arrive an hour beforehand and, if everything has gone smoothly and I have sufficient time, I can leave and grab lunch, a coffee or a walk.

Wholesalers have differing criteria for the number of wines and number of bottles at their events, depending on space and number of participants. Usually, there are six to twelve wines, although it can be as little as two, with three to four bottles of each one to account for the number of attendees and in case a wine is corked. Wines for these events will have to be approved by the distributor's event coordinator or brand manager beforehand and should be in stock. They will need to print a booklet/price list with the exact wine and vintage, to be able to quote prices to trade attendees and fill an immediate order. In some cases, you may have authorization to show a library wine, new vintage, special cuvée or some other item that is likely to generate interest or excitement. Think about the cost-benefit ratio of this choice. Don't show a wine just to impress if you are unable to import it, it's already sold or the likelihood of anyone being able to afford it is very slim. Housekeeping items I routinely bring with me are:

- posters (if available)
- shelf talkers
- multiple copies of tasting notes/tech sheets and one laminated set
- business cards
- small travel stapler
- packing tape with dispenser
- pens
- depending upon venue, something to decorate the table (e.g. flowers, grapevine, stand)
- depending upon venue, a sign/banner with my company's name
- any really good press that is not on the shelf talkers
- at least two wine keys (because someone will invariably borrow and not return one)
- disposable foil or plastic pourers with collars (depending on your inclination)

- foil cutters
- bottled water, in case it is not provided
- maps of the countries from which your wines originate
- wheeled bag

All events will provide dump buckets, ice tubs (and ice), tablecloths and pitchers of water, for either rinsing or drinking. Obviously, if you are in an art gallery or a tent, you won't have a wall on which to put up posters or banners. You may wish to invest in a collapsible stand for a printed, permanent cloth or laminated banner. They are retractable, fold up to fit easily in a tube and are a relatively inexpensive way to advertise your business or eye-catching vineyard scene.

I place a quantity of inexpensive black and white shelf talkers in front of each wine to both announce any favorable review/rating/accolade and to provide an easy and inexpensive method for event goers to pick up a reminder of a wine they like. People often comment on how handy this is for them, rather than trying to make notes or gathering a larger collection of papers.

If you have background and a group of tasting notes you wish to give out to interested prospective buyers, I suggest stapling them together with your business card.

Clear packing tape, on its handled dispenser, comes in handy either to attach something to your booth/space/table or to close the boxes you have stored under your table after you have filled them with the leftover, unopened wine bottles. The boxes can either be easily transported intact to the next location for a multiple city trade show, returned to the distributor or shipped back to your warehouse.

I sometimes place a laminated map flat on the table, which is a handy reference for people to review the regions. This is especially helpful if you represent wines from an obscure region or wish to demonstrate the proximity of the appellation to other areas or some interesting topographical feature. I also tape one laminated copy of a tech or ratings sheet to the table, just in front of each wine. If they are not laminated, you'll have to keep replacing the sheet as wine and water is spilled on them.

Taking photos of the event in general or having someone take photos of you pouring wine behind your table provides more PR and interest for your website, personalizes you and keeps the website content fresh. Besides, it's nice for you to have a record of the event as well, especially one in an uncommon setting.

A wheeled bag can come in handy to transport any full bottles that either did not come from the distributor's own warehouse, will not be needed for the next event or you are willing to pay for to take with you. Occasionally, you may wish to swap a bottle with another participant and transport that wine out also.

Don't bother with food or crackers. There will be food provided at any tasting, ranging from freshly shucked oysters and carving stations to cheese and bread.

The best salespeople for a wholesaler will have invited retailers and restaurateurs to the show and then steered appropriate potentials to your table and introduced them to you. This focuses their tasting and, if they respect their salesperson, they will pay more attention to the recommendation.

The attendees will most likely come around with their printed booklet and turn to the page you are listed on to start tasting your wines. They may make copious notes or they may make none. If they indicate a particular interest in a wine – asking about availability, telling you they'd like to replace another wine with this, how it will complement a dish, for example – make your own notes and try to get a business card. This information is helpful to the distributor to follow up on with the trade after the event.

On occasion, you will encounter wait staff and kitchen staff of local restaurants in place of the buyer and they will be neither in a position to make a purchase nor make a recommendation. However, the restaurant has chosen to send them and it is incumbent on you to be polite and pour for them as well. It is the right thing to do and you never know when you will encounter them again in a more influential position.

Do not leave your table unattended, unless it is for a brief trip to the restroom, the hors d'oeuvres table or to talk with someone across the room, in which case, ask the adjacent supplier if they wouldn't mind watching it briefly for you. You never know when the premier restaurant or retail store representative will come by and you may not get another chance to show them your wines if you miss them.

Never leave the show early and always make sure you are demonstrating as much interest and effort in promoting your wines as the wholesaler has in putting on the event. It may be tiring or boring. You may have a hangover from the night before or your feet hurt. This is no excuse. For a few hours of remaining engaged, you will reap the benefits – however large or small, concrete or intangible. If you do not demonstrate appropriate courtesy in all areas, they will remember and perhaps consider your wines less of an asset if *you* become a liability.

When you get back to the office, compile notes on the event, send appropriate information to attendees who asked and send a list of interested trade and which wines they were considering to your point person at the wholesaler. Don't wait on this. You are likely to forget or lose cards and the trail will go cold.

### ◆ Trade Show – independent

These are a little trickier. I certainly would not recommend indiscriminately signing up for trade shows around the country. They can be very expensive, unfocused and ultimately a time waster. There are exceptions, of course, and these should be taken on a case-by-case basis.

Government wine organizations promoting trade within the U.S. may be conducting a series of trade tastings around the country or an event at an embassy, for example. Consider the cost-benefit ratio again:

- is this likely to attract the right mix or number of trade potentials?
- are you looking for a distributor in the state or territory in which it is held?
- is the cost for the table/booth within your budget?
- are you able to bring sufficiently diverse wines to make it worthwhile?
- will they charge you per wine?
- does this conflict with anything your distributor is already doing?
- how well-prepared is this organization?
- what is the trade-consumer ratio?
- are there seminars?
- what is your competition?
- is there a theme?
- where is the venue?
- how will it be promoted?

The better organized, more appealing and well publicized the event, the greater the probability it will draw the right numbers and quality of trade. Making sure not to conflict with other, equally appealing events in the same city, or having a series of timely seminars throughout the course of the afternoon, will also increase the attraction.

These events will invariably include a consumer component, either during or after the trade. Including them, at a fee, often helps organizers defray costs or raise funds for a designated cause or allows them to rent a more glamorous venue. Hosting consumers is not financially beneficial to you, but it is often a necessary aspect of the tasting. If the event is primarily consumer and they are expecting fifteen hundred fee paying individuals, the wine requirement is far greater, overall and per head, than for the trade tasting. If you commit to the event you commit to the consumer component, although there is no obligation to supply more wine than you feel comfortable supplying. It is unacceptable to pack up and go home after the trade segment and is considered really bad form. Consumers have an expectation that their event fee includes a certain number of wineries or wines or perhaps they are looking for your wines in particular, having read about them in the press release beforehand.

Press releases for events of this type could be another opportunity for exposure for you, either in conducting a radio interview, or podcast, or having your wines recommended in the food and wine section of a newspaper.

Finding a viable distributor at one of these events could make the whole thing worthwhile so don't discount the possibility if the format and organizational efforts have met with your approval.

If you have a distributor and you really feel this is a meaningful event, try to include them in the trip by scheduling a market tie-in, either working with a salesperson, planning a wine dinner or by connecting with trade at the show that the distributor can follow up on later.

## Consumer Tastings

Anyone who has ever done an exclusively consumer show will attest to the generalization that it is a "drink fest" where an inordinate amount of wine is consumed rather than "tasted", and the likelihood of someone remembering a wine long enough to make a purchase after the event is slim to none. There are always those who ask you to fill the glass to the rim or keep coming back for more and more "tastes", or try to cajole you into giving them the bottle to take away with them. These are usually the people who are barely able to stand and really do not need another "taste," much less a whole bottle.

Nonetheless, I have done my share of consumer tastings and I have occasionally found them to be fun and beneficial and have some residual benefit. Usually, the event space is more aesthetically appealing than the run-of-the-mill trade tasting and in an interesting locale, which certainly makes it more enjoyable. I have also, once again, tied this in with distributor efforts, working the market on days that bookend the event, conducting seminars and doing press interviews.

In this case, dispense with tasting notes and elaborate informational tools but shelf talkers are really helpful and appreciated for those consumers who wish to pick one up as a reminder of a wine.

Those who organize consumer wine festivals and tastings will often recommend the amount of wine to bring with you. I can assure you it will be too much. Irrespective of the number of people they are expecting, you will want to balance limiting your expenditure with providing adequate wine for diverse tastes. I would not bring more than six bottles of each individual wine and less if your range is larger than six wines. If you decide to bring twelve different wines because they represent a cross-section of vineyards you represent, then bring no more than three bottles apiece. Three to four cases of wine is really a generous allowance for this type of event and will still be appreciated.

Figure 12.4 Telluride Wine Festival

Despite the insistence of any inexperienced or aggressive festival goers, limit the pour. The aim is not to get them inebriated and your intent is to stretch the wines throughout the day. If you run out of a popular wine or two, that is to be expected. Just make sure you have an acceptable array of wines for the remainder of the show.

If you can interest the consumer in a prize drawing or sign-up sheet, you may also be able to gather a database of potential wine buyers. Having access to their email and contact details enables you to send an email blast with news and reviews and perhaps even exclusive deals or inside information. Those who respond to your emails and indicate interest in purchasing the wines can be directed to their local retailers. You may even be able to work out a deal with your state distributors to support a discount program (again, where legal) for those consumers who have responded to your emails. It is both an incentive for the consumer and additional sales for your distributor. It is also a way for you to track the effectiveness of such a program.

The same opportunity for publicity may apply to a consumer tasting as well, since it will be in the interests of the organizers to draw as much attention to the event as possible for ticket sales and charity tie-in.

If you decide to participate in this type of event, know what you are getting into and have fun with it. Perhaps it's an opportunity to include a partner to pour with you and go skiing afterwards, attend a gallery opening or try a new restaurant.

## Making the Best Use of Press

Free advertising is one best uses of the press and can take several forms.

As already mentioned, the expanded benefit of a trade show is being able to incorporate a radio or print interview or wine review into the experience. It is free and, in addition to local exposure, can be added to the website or press kit for current and prospective distribution.

Press releases are another way to generate publicity. Not to announce you have a new brand, the latest vintage is out or such-and-such brand released a new wine (yawn). Media get humdrum releases of little importance (to anyone but you) all the time. Think about it from their perspective and the relative widespread value of the information.

- Do you have a renowned winemaker coming to town with something interesting to say or an event to participate in?
- Are you hosting or speaking at a local consumer tasting that is open to the public?
- Have you just opened your business in the area?
- Do you have an innovative slant to the marketing of your brands?

- Have you "discovered" a new wine region, unknown to the general public?
- Did one of your wines achieve something exceptional? (Not just 95 points in a wine publication – something of far greater resonance to the reading public)

The list may spark some of your own ideas. I am not a marketing expert and you may find that hiring or consulting with a firm that specializes in this area will benefit you. But at first blush, the trade show does present an opportunity to market your company and its products for free.

Tailor your approach to the appropriate media outlet. Think about whether your "news" is better suited to a local, citywide, regional or national publication and read sufficiently within that publication to learn more about its tone and the writers. Is there a columnist or a specific journalist who writes about small business, wine or the restaurant scene, e.g.? Submit the press release to them, or call and let them know what you have in mind. A directed approach is often more successful.

High ratings and great reviews may be of limited appeal to journalists in considering a piece on your company, but they will be of considerable interest to your prospective and current distribution partners. Include the ratings/reviews/accolades in nicely organized attachments or on your price list. Keep it brief and attractive and minimize the file size (no multi MB graphics). This applies to all emails in general. It will retain the interest of your busy customers or potential customers if you have a clear and concise message.

If you have new ratings in a recognized (generally U.S.) wine publication, send an announcement to your distributors. It is a tool that makes it easier for them to sell as well, so they will welcome it.

## Point of Sale Material

POS material is an essential tool in the wine industry. Of these, **shelf talkers** are probably the most ubiquitous in the business. Some of the uses have already been mentioned, but as a true "shelf talker" to promote your wines in a store, it begins to work for you to differentiate your wine from the multitude of options on a store shelf. Eye-catching shelf talker wording, color and an emphasis on a high rating (if there is one) can propel the consumer to pick up a bottle of your wine over another, even taking label design into account.

**Case cards** are another way to draw the eye in a store, particularly at a case stacking display. These are stiff, sometimes glossy or laminated color cards approximately the width of a 12-bottle case of wine that is propped up behind the wines in an open case. What you choose to market on these cards can be anything that is of most benefit to you, or fits your brand's style. Again, ratings might be the best and most effective information. Focusing on things like the organically grown origins of the wine, featuring a provocative or evocative logo prominently or highlighting particular features of the wine or the region can all be ways to promote and differentiate the wine and draw the consumer in the display's direction.

**Display sheets** – i.e. a form of shelf talker in a laminated, full size 8 ½ x 11" sheet are very handy for stores, where they allow them, for display in racks or, in the case of Costco, in the fine wine bins. As of writing, Costco prepares its own, standardized printed sheet with an approved rating and which is inserted in a plastic sheath beside the wine. This is certainly helpful to the customer, especially since there is usually no wine steward in their stores, but it does become so uniform as to recede somewhat in view. As of writing, they allow a tasteful display sheet of your own making, tucked in behind the wines in the individual bin. I have found, to my surprise, that despite the efficacy not many people use them. Even if other wines are similarly rated, having this colorful, large sheet tends to draw the eye and the consumer's attention.

**Table tents** are the informational cards you often see on restaurant tables, inserted in Plexiglas sleeves, propped up in their own card base or slipped into menus, usually to announce a special glass pour, upcoming wine dinner or some promotional wine. These are usually provided by the wholesaler, or even the restaurant, using your own logo, the winery label or bottle shot (all of which should be available to download from your website) and put together on a computer program. If you are asked to provide them, and you can do this inexpensively on your own program, they can certainly be worthwhile. It can mean more wines poured or greater attendance at your wine or tasting event. Caveat: in the current era of QR code menus on restaurant tables, and relative scarcity of any material on the table, I'm not sure this is customary any longer, but still worth a mention.

**Brochures** from the winery can be helpful and appealing but were far more common prior to widespread websites and email. They become more of a souvenir at a consumer tasting, a nice addition to a press kit or an educational piece for the salesperson. I would certainly never ask a winery to prepare them for the export market, aware that this will cut into a budget that could be put to much better use.

**Promotional items** are another marketing medium, although they should be used judiciously or you are either wasting the winery's money or blowing your own budget. Polo shirts, hats, aprons and waiter's friends with logo, can all be attractive items to the distributor's salespeople but unless there is an abundance of merchandise, or the winery encourages you to spread them around, I would dispense them only for specific purposes: to supportive sales people, as part of a promotional contest or as a casual wine dinner prize, to the winner of a trivia quiz question or specific ticket number. I don't think there is any value in indiscriminately passing merchandise out at sales meetings or shipping them en masse with wine samples. The original purpose is quickly forgotten and the item becomes simply another article of clothing or a corkscrew rattling around in the bottom of a bag.

**Posters** are lovely but of limited benefit. There are always exceptions to these generalizations, and one case to be made for posters might be a signed, framed image that someone would like to hang in their office. In that case, they are usually of the iconic or sensational variety and valued for that reason rather than simply to promote a particular brand.

# According to Budget

According to *your* budget and a commonsense approach is the way to market your business and the wines you represent. In evaluating wine tastings, trade shows, consumer festivals and charity events, consider also the city or state in which this will take place. Budgetary considerations then apply to:

- **Hotels** – Manhattan is clearly going to be more expensive than Dayton, Ohio or staying four nights more expensive than one.

- **Airfare** – across country will be more expensive than upstate, booking in advance less expensive than last minute.

- **In-town transportation** – will you have to take taxis everywhere or ride the train from another state, or do you need to rent a car?

- **Cost of shipping wine** —air freight, ground freight, taking in your car, checked in as luggage.

- **Quantity and value of wines** – relating to the cost to you for providing it.

- **Service charges, fees for valets, storage** – will you need help with cross-town transport of wine, assistance in and out of hotels, from hotel room to ballroom, charges for storing the wine in the luggage room or having it shipped back to you via the hotel concierge?

- **How and whether you can capitalize with follow up** – the more you follow up the greater opportunity to make sales.

- **Expectations of your distributor in that area** – whether, e.g., they expect you to take the sales team to dinner or lunch, provide bottles for sales calls around the trade show or stay several days to work the market.

- **Tie-in with other markets** – if you can drive or make a quick flight to an adjacent city or state to work that market or attend their trade show it will provide economies of scale.

In evaluating marketing, the considerations are not only whether you can afford it, but does it result in a meaningful return. Broad market, high volume, household name brands do well advertising in *Wine Spectator* to proclaim a new accolade or remind the consumer that they are still the standard bearer of that country's wines but for most small companies this expensive one-off method will produce limited, if any, dividends and eat a substantial hole in the budget.

Expensive, professionally printed four-color, vintage-specific POS is overkill, especially with today's publishing programs. As long as POS material looks professional and is accurate (the right vintage for the right rating!) and omits spelling and grammatical errors, creating them yourself is perfectly acceptable. Print only as many as you need for a vintage or production because you will find that you'll be sold out of the wine and still have a stack of shelf talkers or tasting notes left.

Email blasts can be an effective way to market to both consumers and the trade. Budget will dictate whether you do this by using your own gathered data, pay a nominal charge for limited services or retain a firm that can provide a comprehensive service to a variety of demographics within the industry and outside it to the wine-savvy consumer. This should still be within moderate parameters. You do not want to annoy anyone with constant reminders or appear to be spam.

***SUMMARY*** —Marketing and promotion of your brands and their wines is essential in some sense. They will not sell themselves and marketing assistance is expected. However, the extent of your efforts is at your discretion. If you have a very limited budget, take advantage of all the free, or inexpensive, suggestions I made. Build up a market before you agree to a wine dinner, promote yourself and your business with free exposure, capitalize on all forms of trade and consumer interest and you will find your return is commensurate with your effort, rather than your financial outlay.

# My story

So many wine dinners and tastings, so many mistakes... Early on, in Atlanta, the city of my founding business, I was cheerfully making my lone rounds of the city when I happened upon a restaurant I had not visited before. I was at my most inexperienced at this stage and when they suggested a wine dinner, I readily agreed. From pride more than anything else, I did not query the distributor as to protocol, but plowed ahead on my own with their requests. They asked me to have the table tents and invitations printed, for which I incurred considerable expense at a professional printer, this being prior to the advent of computer publishing. I agreed to provide all the wines. There was no tie-in with any sales, no agreement that they would put the wines on the wine list or any expressed reciprocation for my generous participation.

The night of the dinner, I arrived to find that the wait staff had opened every single bottle – all 72 of them – in advance of the dinner, without any tally of dinner guest numbers. I was horrified, having provided a case of each of the six wines only from which to draw the necessary bottles, and hopeful that they would buy the rest for their wine list. Attendance was moderate, but nowhere near the numbers necessary to consume the volume of wine, none was ever returned to me (I was too mortified at this stage to ask) and no business ever resulted from this disastrously expensive exercise.

> ## My Client's Story
>
> A client new to the wine industry, but savvy about free marketing, has chalked up an impressive array of fairly high-profile interviews in national publications that dovetail with features the publication is already doing. Most of this has centered on a particular wine region that is making a welcome comeback. My client is one of those featured, photographed and interviewed as an example of the new breed of importer of this region and to highlight the quality and diversity of wines being exported to the U.S. In some instances, the wines themselves are tasted and favorably reviewed. It's all positive, free advertising.
>
> This may not be your region's story, but I bet they have one. And so do you.

# PART IV

# CHAPTER 13

# INVENTORY CONTROL

There are various times throughout the process of getting wine from winery to consumer when you will need to be aware of your inventory levels and re-order point. Earlier, I recommended ways in which to evaluate your initial needs. This balancing act and moderate crystal ball gazing goes on throughout your wine career as you make market predictions about the sales potential of your wines.

## Reasonable Stock Levels

This will depend on a range of factors, including:

- **Price points** – if your wines are on the high end of the scale or, conversely, the low end, movement will most likely be commensurate with the cost of your wines.

- **Demand for wines of your region** – if you are on the leading edge of a new trend or riding the wave of heightened demand, you can factor this in as one of your considerations.

- **Demand for your wines in particular** – if you are hitting a great price point for the wines or finding that people are responding enthusiastically to the packaging or style, this may accelerate sales.

- **Distribution** – whether your own wholesalers are hitting their numbers or salespeople are responding well, there is demonstrable growth to the brand.

- **U.S. market coverage** – how many wholesalers you have brought on, which of the concentrated population bases have the wines, etc.

- **Future expectations for the wine** – how you plan on increasing exposure, what markets you may open up, putting on brokers, discount programming, starting your own distribution, e.g.

- **Ratings and reviews** – if you have had or know you will have an outstanding review or comprehensive article in a major publication with the likelihood that this will increase demand. Caveat here is that this was far more likely in years past, such as the time of the first edition of this book. It is far less predictable now, but I leave this factor in because your customer base may rely on ratings and reviews, or the brand has a lineage that historically help sell the wines, or the publicity will be tied with a focused event or limited wine release.

- **Your plans for personnel expansion** – perhaps you plan on hiring a national sales director, regional manager, brand ambassador or sales assistance in the local market.

- **Marketing** – your efforts to promote your brand through advertising, interviews, POS and other tangible means and to what extent they increase sales.

- **Demand from foreign markets** – this is a tricky one, but worth taking into consideration. By this I mean, demand from other countries or the winery's own country. If you anticipate (or the winery has given you advance notice) that the remaining production of the vintage could go to national or foreign distribution, because they have opened up a new market or because, ironically, the stellar ratings *you* have generated have filtered back to them and created demand domestically, then it is up to you to protect your current placements and future sales.

Normally, the idea is to order sufficient quantity of wines to fill the pipeline, with a cushion, so that you neither run out nor get stuck with too much product, racking up storage fees. This amounts to devising your own informal formula, based on the points above (and any that relate to your individual circumstances) to determine what you need to maintain a balance.

## Vintage Management

A distributor will often ask you about what is new or "fresh" in your lineup. They have already presented the 2019 wines to all the prime accounts in their market and want a reason to go back and generate more sales. Or they have been supplying the same vintage for a prolonged period and want the next vintage as a way to stimulate renewed interest. Or because, unless the wine is a venerable, aged reserve treasure, the prevailing thinking in the U.S. is that you should be on such-and-such vintage (especially whites) at a particular point in time.

One minor consideration is when harvest occurs in your sourcing region – roughly February to April in the Southern Hemisphere and August to October in the Northern Hemisphere. Therefore, you could reasonably expect to have a New Zealand sauvignon blanc released in August and in the U.S. market in September, before California vineyards have even picked their grapes. But no one is going to be that fanatical about it. The release of a 2022 white in September 2022 is more of a novelty than a guideline. However, if that same 2022 white is still available in September 2024, there is bound to be a question. It may be drinking beautifully, even better than before and perhaps reviews will attest to its length and depth and enduring quality. You will still have people asking when the next vintage is due, with the same assumptions as expressed above and the further expectation that this next vintage will garner a similarly high rating as the last.

Figure 13.1 Basket Press and Tanks at Creed Winery

There is much more latitude with reds. A cabernet sauvignon may have been aged two years in oak and then left a year in bottle before its release. Therefore, a 2018 wine can be a current release in 2022. It could be such a tannic wine that a later release is anticipated and expected. Conversely, a young, bright grenache and a light, lively Beaujolais will generally be given little leeway because these are wines that will show best in their youth and, if not suffer, at least change with age.

This is to illustrate that there is some play on either side of that vintage expectation, but in general it is perceived as more favorable to have a regular turnover of vintages and a new release each year, a bit like a coming out. This is generally managed by your ordering pattern, based on taking market conditions into consideration for your particular wine.

If your wines are enjoying routinely positive press or pent up demand, there is a further expectation of a regular release of the next vintage. The idea that you still have a considerable supply of the last vintage left at release time will not necessarily inspire confidence in your customers. Market conditions – recession, inflation, terrorism, pandemics, decline in appeal, etc. – often cannot be anticipated but to the extent to which you can plan and ponder the life of each vintage, the more often you will continue to provide wholesalers with positive anticipation. In fact, there are times when you are in a better position if you run out of a vintage, with the promise of the new release in days or weeks, than to still have one vintage when another arrives. Unless the previous vintage is a highly regarded icon that will remain in demand, perhaps exceeding demand for the new vintage, you will find that older vintage languishing in the warehouse until you may be forced to discount it.

The only caveat to this is that you do not want restaurants to run out of wine that is on their list or leave distributors with a lack of supply that they had counted on to fill promised orders. This is going to lose your restaurant placement and annoy your wholesaler.

## Turnover

The concept of turning over the wine quickly enough to create an efficient budgetary model could be incorporated into the previous section on maintaining reasonable levels but really deserves its own breakdown.

It is incumbent on you to monitor the levels of your distributors' stock as well as your own. This reinforces the need for depletion reports and placement reports from your wholesalers. Reports should be used not only to determine if your customer is fulfilling the promises made to you, realizing the potential of the brand and providing you with valuable information about their level of sales, but also to advise you of turnover within the distributor's inventory. This is then incorporated into your own planning for reorder points to the winery – with the usual proviso that this should be weighed with other considerations germane to your individual circumstance.

If you are also distributing your own brands in your home state, then turnover is further micromanaged down to the retail level. When was the last time the restaurant reordered? How long has the same wine been on the local retailer's shelf?

## Reorder Timing From Winery

If that's starting to sound like a repetition of previous sections, let me clarify for you. In addition to the juggling of market factors and conditions, there has to be consideration given to the winery's own logistical capabilities in the event of an order.

- Is the wine bottled?
- Do they have to book into a bottling queue?
- Is the wine labeled?
- Will the printer be able to accommodate your schedule or the winery's needs?
- Is the wine ready to be released? (Releasing too early can be a mistake.)
- Is the winery staffed to handle the order in an efficient timetable?
- Has the label changed to the degree that it will require a new COLA?
- Are containers backed up and therefore require advance booking?

The length of time the wine will spend on the water and overland are of the same importance as they were the first time the wine was introduced. Except that this time there are more people counting on you and, potentially, more to lose if you miscalculate.

# Container Consolidation

This was addressed, to some extent, in the section on containers. However, it merits presenting from a slightly different perspective to emphasize the need to manage inventory and budget by not bowing to pressure to bring in an entire container when all you need is a couple of pallets. In addition to spreading out your invoice payments, if you need 150 cases and not 1000, you avoid the inevitability that the wines will decline before they have found homes.

Developing a relationship with a large, commercially operated, wine warehouse will often bring to light other customers who would benefit from container consolidation. The customer rep or warehouse manager may already know of other importers looking for the same opportunity or, you having mentioned it to them, they will recall your need when someone else expresses the same.

Other opportunities to locate a container partner might be through your distributor, at a trade show or through the trade association (or equivalent) for the country of your wine's origin.

Usually, even if the regions are divergent geographical areas – even different (compatible) countries - it can be less expensive for the party who has the lesser quantity to arrange for transport to the dock of the primary importer's load. It may even be an expense that the winery will absorb, happy to have an order now rather than wait until you need an FCL, which may be months away. There is no customary manner of handling the financial aspects of transport to port, so this is something that becomes negotiable between you and your wine supplier.

My suggestion is that the best way, from both a logistical and financial standpoint, is for each of you have your own MBL (Master Bill of Lading). It only adds slightly to the cost but is still far less than an LCL with a freight forwarder's other customers and gives you far more in transparency. This works even if you only have a pallet and the other shipper has six pallets. The freight forwarder will contact each of you directly regarding your respective shipments and you can follow its progress without either of you relying on the other to provide the information. It also means you are invoiced separately, dispensing with potentially awkward billing issues that can arise from splitting the costs under one MBL.

## Direct Import (DI)

DI implies that the distributor will order a container (sometimes less) of a brand that you represent as importer but control the logistics of the shipment and bear the costs of shipping and taxes. When you achieve considerable traction with a distributor, or you have especially attractive price points, the distributor may reach a point where it makes sense for them to order from you on a DI basis. If you have secured retail chain business, resulting in sufficient turnover in sales for the chain that they want to ensure they have sufficient quantity on hand, they may want to consider a DI order. Under the three tier system, it still requires a distributor to purchase and sell the product to the chain. It is up to you as to whether relinquishing control of the container and allowing the distributor to bring it in under their own license is worth it to you. And for the amount of business it generates, it may well be.

In a DI, the container comes from the wine origin directly to the wholesaler's port and warehouse instead of to your usual port and into your warehouse. It is also cleared with your letter of authorization as the primary source. This clearly has considerable advantages over the usual route in terms of logistics and the size of the sale. Aside from a guaranteed quantity, you also avoid the expenses associated with the container movement and any warehousing costs. The retail chain or distributor in this scenario also expect discounted pricing to account for their additional costs.

The consideration for you is whether you wish to relinquish control over any aspect of the relationship with your supplier, and the implications for the future of your relationship with the supplier (winery). You will need to be confident that this distributor will not circumvent you in any way by trying to secure orders directly from the winery, and that you put something in place to ensure that you are very much a part of the deal. In other words, although they will be the official importer for this particular container, you retain all rights to the brand – arrangements are all made through you and payment for the wine is made directly to you.

You must also ensure you have covered the winery timing aspects (identified in the previous section related to when it will be available) so that sufficient wine is in your allocation and physically at the point of origin for an order of this scale.

The expectation from the wholesaler is that you give them a discount for DI, significant enough to make it worth their while to bring in this quantity and take responsibility for clearance and warehousing. It must certainly cover their costs (which you will not pay) and a further discount, based on what makes sense to you, for the benefit of this order size and minimal handling on your part. They may ask for extended terms or the opportunity to pay in installments. This is certainly something to consider, particularly in a difficult economy, because you have a guaranteed sale of product they have now taken possession of and you won't incur any warehousing fees or inventory maintenance.

As a final note, please be aware that, in keeping with the essential elements of the three-tier system, most states will have a "bump the dock" or "touch the dock" requirement. It can mean different things in each state so always be aware of the individual state's laws. This is especially important to remember in the case of a DI sale to a retail chain and any other sales you might make to a retailer. A wholesaler must be involved in the sale to the extent that the delivery is made to the warehouse. This can mean something as simple as momentarily parking at the distributor's dock and receiving appropriate paperwork to take to the retailer. Or it can mean that the wine must truly be received by the wholesaler. In the case of Arizona, as just one example:

*AZ Rev Stat § 4-243.01 (2020)*

*B. All spirituous liquor shipped into this state shall be invoiced to the wholesaler by the primary source of supply. All spirituous liquor shall be unloaded and remain at the wholesaler's premises for at least twenty-four hours. A copy of each invoice shall be transmitted by the wholesaler and the primary source of supply to the department of revenue.*

***SUMMARY*** — Maintaining inventory levels is much more than just replenishing supply when it is depleted. It is about skillful management of the dynamics of your business as it relates to the winery, balancing your needs and those of your customers, taking the individual characteristics of your wines into consideration and planning for the future. Adopting this considered and thoughtful approach will enable you to maximize your sales potential and minimize costly inventory mistakes.

## My Story

The basic message I have for this section is that I have, like everyone else, been caught with too much inventory of a vintage that became long in the tooth and had to be discounted. Conversely, I have been too conservative with wine orders that became far more popular than I had anticipated, which prevented me from capitalizing on the demand.

I have bought more wine than I should have because "*it's the last of the vintage and the extra 200 cases will finish it up*" or "*the next vintage won't be ready for another month*". Bowing even to subtle pressure or being influenced by the circumstances is almost always, for a small importer, a mistake. Whatever the winery's motivation – and there is no reason to ascribe anything other than they are thinking of their own inventory management, as well they would - if they are trying to talk you into taking more wine than you wanted, or a vintage you did not need, it is time to sit back, think about the practicality and be prepared to say, "no".

No one can predict accurately every time, but a conscientious approach will net far better results than knee jerk reactions in the moment, bowing to pressure or getting carried away with quantities without a sound basis.

## My Client's Story

This is a story for both launch quantities and ongoing reorder timing. One client sources from the Republic of Georgia. This is arguably one of the oldest wine producing countries but wine styles are still not well understood in the U.S. My client understands and appreciates these wines. She has also done her homework, to an extent, by choosing wines to import that appealed to the people she tasted them with in the U.S. However, most of these tasters were not professional wine people but, rather, friends and business associates in her current, unrelated, business. On this basis, she came to me with a proposed container mix that skewed heavily to older, reserve reds with unusual varietal names. I urged her to reconsider her choices. She may be very familiar with these wines and really enjoy them herself but she is viewing them from the perspective of her own palate, rather than what may appeal to the American palate. She will undoubtedly find pockets of Eastern Europeans in the U.S. who will enjoy these wines but finding vast, untapped swathes will be unnecessarily challenging. Rethinking her portfolio will likely lead to greater success.

# CHAPTER 14

# STATE LICENSING

The subject of this chapter is compliance. Each of the fifty states has its own unique licensing system and within each system are entirely different requirements for *in-state* and *out-of-state* importers. For example, if your business is located in Florida, your licensing requirements will be specific to Florida; if you are located in Colorado, you will have a different set of licensing requirements. Each state, a different set of laws. Then factor in the laws for any importer who has their business licensed in their home state and sells to a distributor in another, as importers must do. These licensing laws are also completely different. With fifty states you now have one hundred possible licensing permutations. I postulate that this is the nature of states wanting to wrest control from the federal government and assert their own authority but — whatever the reason, there is no getting around these laws.

This chapter looks at compliance from an importer's perspective. No one person can be intimately familiar with every state's in-state requirements, and they will quite possibly change by the time this edition is published. My goal here is to give you an overview of this tricky topic, some examples of ways to pursue certain actions and the tools to go further with your own specific needs in the states in which you will find wholesalers.

Doing business as an out-of-state importer in any particular state can range from simple one-page forms with no cost, to extensive applications, surety bonds, non-resident seller permits, brand registrations and hundreds of dollars in annual fees. It is essential to comply with a state's requirements and to maintain the licenses in good standing or you may find yourself running afoul of the alcoholic board of that state and unable to ship. We will also look at other considerations that may help you negotiate the state licensing maze.

## In-House or Outsourced

Your decision, at any stage of your business development, is whether to manage your licensing and state reporting from your office or to outsource to a compliance company. Initially, if you have taken on a brand or brands that have no previous history in the U.S., you will be able to start very slowly with one state and its requirements, then the next state and so on. Using the premise that you are carefully and conscientiously sourcing and appointing distributors, this may not be an onerous burden at first. But there are other considerations, even at this stage.

- ➢ Are you starting your business with little or no office assistance?
- ➢ Do you expect to be on the road most, or a significant part, of the month?
- ➢ Are you planning a strong push to put on several states at once?
- ➢ What is your budget?
- ➢ Do you have the patience for this type of paperwork or are you likely to forget deadlines or procrastinate?

Many states have requirements with timelines for monthly reporting. It is essential that these deadlines are met and the money you save from doing it yourself, or with the assistance of employees, is not eaten up with penalties, late filings that delay shipments and issues that take this out of the realm of cost-effectiveness. If you have not registered a brand in a state, a distributor may not order wines of that brand from you. In some instances (Texas, e.g.) an application for brand registration can take up to three weeks for approval. In that time, you've lost momentum if the distributor was ready to purchase and is waiting for your approvals. Distributors have been much more vigilant in recent years about observing state laws and more apt to check your license, brand or label registrations. Verifying state compliance is easily done by going online on the state government's website. As with everything else, online licensing and registrations are more prevalent, although mailed applications are still mandatory in a few states.

If you are on the road a significant amount and unable to find the time or are unavailable to meet deadlines, I would suggest outsourcing, at least until you have sufficient support in the office.

I would stress that there is nothing too complicated or requiring any advanced education that precludes you performing this function yourself, in-house. It is a matter of whether you, or the personnel in your office, will become overwhelmed with the tasks or overburdened, having other functions for which they were hired. Or whether your time is better spent with sales and distribution.

## Compliance Issues

If you choose to take compliance on yourself, a spreadsheet and reminders will be very helpful.

Start a spreadsheet from the very beginning to enable easy tracking of the requirements, whether or not you outsource or complete and submit paperwork in-house. Column headings could include:

| State | License fee | Term | Bond | Label reg. | Label Fee | Price Posting |
|---|---|---|---|---|---|---|
|  |  |  |  |  |  |  |

They could also include the turnaround time for each requirement or whether a state is Franchise or Control, or other relevant information that may be useful to you.

Some licenses are valid for a year, others up to three. Occasionally states require a bond and this can be obtained from a surety bond company that handles bonds of all types for a nominal fee, usually $100 for the minimum requirement. The purpose of a bond is to uphold the contract you have made with the state to comply with their laws. The bond company is effectively guaranteeing your performance with the payment of a fraction of the bond issue.

Label or brand registrations are often in addition to the actual license and may require a fee per label, ranging from $5 to $25 per label. Consider which wines you wish to ship to that state, whether the available volume of wine is worth the expense and, most importantly, which wines the prospective distributor wishes to order. Do not register anything they have not expressed interest in. In some states, registration is annual, so you will potentially have wasted a year's registration while waiting for a distributor to decide.

Some states require price posting each month or whenever a price changes, to set the price itself or the minimum under which the wine will not fall. These states often prohibit variances in prices or any discounts and require uniform pricing for all retail outlets. The next section cover states that require price posting and the ways in which you, the importer, can assign this to a distributor.

## Saving Money – Using Others' Licenses

Licensing in certain states may appear prohibitively expensive until you consider that, in some state, e.g., Colorado, Arkansas, New York, the normal course of action is to allow the distributor's separate import company to "import" and register the brand for you, using what is called a Primary Source letter from you. Instead of a huge licensing fee, you will only incur a nominal cost or, usually, just that of label registrations. You will also avoid price posting difficulties. Assigning rights is a standard operating procedure in several states but something that understandably escapes the notice of neophyte importers. Thinking they're being proactive and following the respective state's regulations, they end up spending far more in license fees than necessary by not investigating better. This is one of many reasons for never beginning the license process until you have lined up a wholesaler. Unless the distributor is also new, they will always know the requirements and, if they're large enough, will have a compliance person who is familiar with the requirements and can advise you. Unlike you, the importer, the distributor has only one state's licensing to stay abreast of and they have numerous brands in their portfolio that keep the regulations fresh in their experience.

There is a caution in this scenario. Where the accepted practice is to utilize the distributor's import license, but it is a franchise state, they become the brand owners of your brand in that state. Investigate fully the implications of using another's license in their home franchise state. It may be the logical and cost-effective way to go but satisfy yourself of this by first doing your homework. Call the state and discuss your obligations with them and ask another winery in your reference checking if they have any concerns about assigning the distributor as state importer.

Contracting with a reputable compliance firm will alleviate these concerns. Professional and experienced consultants will keep up to date on changes in laws and deadlines. There are a number of firms who perform these functions and many of them are very good but, since you will be relinquishing control of the logistics, be sure they have a solid reputation within the industry. Finding out down the road that reporting deadlines were missed can be very costly.

# Monthly State Reporting

At the outset, be aware of your responsibilities relative to reporting because a state will often not advise you and, in my experience, it is not readily apparent on some websites. There is no uniformity of website design and, as with regulations, available resources are not always readily apparent or easily accessed. Some of websites are fabulous and some are so confusing that even with all my years of experience with concepts, terms, licensing and reporting, I still can't make head or tail of them. I never hesitate to call to ask questions or confirm that I have the requisite number and correct types of forms for my clients.

One very important thing that does not vary is that you should not be paying state taxes for the wine you ship into a state as an out-of-state supplier. The burden for state taxes is on the distributor. You are presumably paying your own excise taxes for business within your own state. The shipments that the distributor picks up from you becomes their property in your state. In other words, if they pick up from your warehouse in California, they take possession in California. When you file a report, no matter what the format or requirement, or whether you include invoices or not, if the state asks for taxes, I suggest you call them to find out why. They can misunderstand your position, or you may have filled out the wrong paperwork. It has happened to me, which is why I mention it. Whatever the reason, don't take the request for taxes at face value. You pay enough in federal taxes to get the wine into the country and for state licenses to do business, without also doubling up on taxes that is another entity's responsibility.

As is often the case in this industry, the exception to paying out-of-state taxes is Wisconsin. There may be another, but I haven't come across it. I mention it so that if you sell to a distributor in Wisconsin you won't be surprised by, or push back on the imposition of taxes. It is proportionate to how much you sell there, so generally speaking it will be very little tax, but they do impose it and you must pay it or incur exorbitant fines.

## Change of Importers

Taking on a brand that is already established seems, at first blush, like a beautiful thing. It can definitely have its advantages but there are issues you may face that need to be addressed. There are three distinct areas that should be tackled without delay at the outset and hopefully during the transition from the previous importer to you. Unfortunately, when the brand is not voluntarily given up – whether for legitimate reasons or not – there is bound to be an uncomfortable relationship between winery and old importer, which may spill over to you as the new importer, now old importer's competition and potential adversary. At the very least, it is an uncomfortable time as the previous importer wonders what has been said, if you know the reason they have been terminated is because they owe hundreds of thousands of dollars to the vignerons or if they truly thought they were doing a good job, but you are perceived by the brand owner as being able to do better. None of the reasons are going to be palatable to the prior U.S. representative. At worst, having to now spend valuable time bringing you up to speed only adds insult to injury to many people, or at best is viewed as wasted time when they could be turning their attentions to their remaining brands and finding a replacement for this lost revenue.

> **The first issue** relates to whether you have taken on a brand that has product in the U.S. at the present time. Naturally, to have been admitted to the country, the wine is already labeled with the old importer's details as part of the mandatory label information. There is no reason why you cannot sell and distribute this product (assuming you are comfortable with the wines' provenance and it is a current vintage) but some states require that the previous importer give you permission to register the brand under your license in their state. This requires a letter from the previous importer relinquishing all rights to the brand and authorizing you to distribute wine that is labeled for their use. This is not a Federal (TTB) issue when the wines are already in the U.S. It is a state-by-state issue. Some states will not require anything from you. Some franchise states will require a release from the

distributor. Others will allow you to distribute the wine in their state with a letter from the previous importer. There is no template for this letter but an example that will work is in Figure 14.1.

> **The second issue** relates to wine that may have been labeled in the source country ahead of its required use in the U.S. to save money by bottling and labeling a certain quantity at the same time. Or it may have been done at the request, or insistence, of the previous importer, who wanted to secure a specific number of cases for their future use or who led the winery to believe in inflated expectations for sales. In this situation, hundreds of cases – thousands of bottles – may already be labeled with the incorrect importer details, all boxed up and warehoused somewhere in the home country. Relabeling could well be within the winery's budget and they would prefer to do so, but it is also very likely that budgetary constraints for labor and material costs will incur a hardship for them. In that event, there is a TTB provision for a label "use up" and temporary approval of labels for importation, under the old importer information. Availing yourself of this is accomplished by applying for a COLA online in the usual manner. However, the label jpeg graphic you supply will be the old label and in the section for "other attachments" you will upload a hardship letter. This information is not readily available on TTB's site because it is something that they do not encourage but they will give careful consideration to each request. Taken directly from a November 3, 2003, TTB news release:

*TTB understands that there are circumstances when a company may request to "use-up" labels that do not strictly comply with the labeling requirements of the FAA Act. Reasons may include the sale of a brand to another company or a change of address of the Certificate holder. While TTB does not encourage the use of these labels, we realize that situations arise when temporary approval should be considered. We make our decision about use-up requests of temporary approvals on a case-by-case basis. We restrict approval to situations when consumers are not likely to be misled as* to the identity and quality of the contents of the bottle. In order to facilitate the processing of these requests, please submit a written request containing the following information:

1. Information identifying the affected label(s), including the brand name, serial number or TTB ID number. Please attach the written request to the COLA(s).

2. The reason(s) you are requesting permission to "use-up" existing labels (i.e. explain what is wrong with the labels).

3. The reason you have incorrect/non-compliant labels (i.e. how did this happen).

4. The steps you will take to ensure that this does not happen again in the future.

5. The quantity of labels you have on hand and area of distribution for product you wish to "use-up".

6. The length of time you need to "use-up" these labels (bottle/remove).

7. Suggested alternatives to using incorrect/non-compliant labels, such as the addition of a strip label.

Please provide any additional information that you feel might be pertinent during our review of your request, such as the dollar amount of the economic impact that you would suffer if you had to destroy or could not "use-up" these labels.

Please be advised that if you do not include all the above in your letter, we must then contact you for the additional information. This will increase the time it takes us to process your request. We also suggest that you submit separate written requests when more than one COLA is involved if the circumstances or amount of labels or time needed varies. Written requests should be mailed to:

Alcohol and Tobacco Tax and Trade Bureau

Alcohol, Labeling and Formulation Division,

1310 G Street NW Atten: 4$^{th}$ Floor

Washington, DC, 20220

After we review all the circumstances as you have presented them, we will make a determination as to whether or not we will grant permission to "use-up" existing label stock and for how long, Again, our main concerns are that the consumers are not likely to be misled as to the identity of the product, and that we can determine the company responsible for the product.

---

OLD IMPORTER, LLC

January 24, 2022

New Importer, Inc.

(address)

To Whom It May Concern:

Please be advised that Old Importer, LLC relinquishes all rights and claims to the ABC Brand in the United States. In accordance with your request, we authorize any and all labels currently labeled with Old Importer, LLC importer details to be used up by your company in the United States.

If anyone requires more information on this matter please contact the undersigned.

Sincerely,

John Q. Smith,

   President

---

**Figure 14.1 Letter to New Importer**

Please ignore the instructions to "mail" the letter. Remember this directive was issued in 2003, before the advent of online COLA submissions. Attaching them to the COLA in the manner I indicated above (as "other attachment") is the acceptable and preferable method of submitting this type of application. You should attach both the letter of authorization from the previous importer and the hardship letter. An example of a hardship letter that works is found in Figure 14.2.

---

(your letterhead)

February 4, 2022

Alcohol and Tobacco Tax and Trade Bureau

To Whom It May Concern:

I am currently the authorized importer of ABC wines from Eden Valley, Australia. My Basic Permit number is CA-I-XXXXX

The previous importer, XXX Imports, required that the brand owners, as a condition of their agreement as their importer, bottle and label a number of cases of wine under their import license, for which they neither paid nor arranged for shipping. As a result, the bottles are still in Australia with all the XXX Imports details attached. XXX Imports is no longer their importer.

To require this small, family-owned winery to remove and replace all these labels would be a certain hardship and I request a use-up of these labels. They would be imported under my license, but using the previously printed XXX Imports importer labels. They are the following:

| | |
|---|---|
| 600 cases (12/750ml bottles to a case) | ABC Wines Shiraz 2018 |
| 580 cases (12/750ml bottles to a case) | ABC Wines Shiraz Grenache 2019 |
| 428 cases (6/750ml bottles to a case) | ABC Cabernet Sauvignon 2018 |

I will make every effort to use up these quantities within 6 months. In future, all wine bottled and labeled by ABC Wines will be labeled correctly as imported by (name of your import company).

Sincerely,

Signature

Title

---

**Figure 14.2 Hardship Letter**

These two letter options are the only ones I would consider viable and practical, depending on winery budget, inclination and time constraints. The other alternative offered by TTB, which I mention only to round out the topic, is to cut out the importer's details from each back label and carefully insert the new importer's details in exactly the same place, all the while looking like a seamless and attractive label. I've never heard of anyone doing this and aside from questionable aesthetics, I imagine the sheer time consumption would make other alternatives far more attractive.

**The third issue** relates to franchise states and having to either interest a distributor in continuing with your brand or entice them to release the brand from their portfolio. But first, you have to know where the brand is registered. This is made far easier if the previous importer can provide the paperwork during the transition period to enable you to know exactly where you stand and who you need to contact. It eliminates the need to wonder to whom the brand is registered, if at all. It is conceivable – and I know several instances of it happening – that the importer distributed the brand in a franchise state without ever having registered it. But these days this is far less likely. Or it could be that the importer registered it without ever actually supplying a single case. As one example, I was not made aware of an importer's activity in Tennessee and found, through considerable effort, phone calls and other time-consuming work, that this importer had not registered the brand in Tennessee and had not, in fact, distributed there. However, the *prior* importer before that (now two importers back) *did* register the brand to four different distributors in four different territories. The fact that this was five years previously and not a single case had been distributed since, made no difference to the process of having to obtain a release from all these distributors.

## When to Say No to Distribution

In terms of state licensing, as a separate consideration from your gut reaction to a wholesaler's personality or other red flags, there are instances where the license and brand registration fees outweigh the benefit of distribution. For example, the cost of the license is $1,000, a cost you are incurring yourself, and the distributor wishes to order just two products. Both products have only 15 cases available each at an FOB of $150 per case. The distributor only wants those two items. This sounds like a reasonable order of $4,500, far in excess of your license fee. However, presuming your markup is around 30%, the gross profit on both these wines is $1,350. This is gross profit, not net, and it only just exceeds the licensing fee outlay. It does not take into consideration the samples you have already sent and the shipping costs, the trip you may take to the state and other samples thatwill be billed back to you.

On balance, this may be worth it to you if you believe your prospects with this distributor and the wines' potential may, in the long run, outweigh the slim profits. Base your decision on the strong likelihood of this happening rather than the hope that it will.

*SUMMARY* — There is no right or wrong way to handle state licensing as long as you take the time to acquaint yourself with the details, costs and implications. Don't be intimidated but, as with everything about your business, be aware of what you are delegating and to whom. Licensing and state compliance may be boring, frustrating and without apparent merit, but abdicating familiarity at least with the basics or outsourcing compliance to someone you have not thoroughly vetted, will result – **will** result – in unnecessary expense. This familiarity, and confidence, allow you to outsource, should you choose, and provide you with a professional transition should you decide to bring licensing and compliance back in-house at any point down the road. Some knowledge of the process and confidence in the consultant equips you to know the questions to ask to make an informed decision.

## My story

When I first started, I was somewhat overwhelmed by state requirements, particularly in Georgia. The licensing process for an in-state importer was lengthy and onerous and, on top of that, the state required monthly reporting and the submission of all invoices. I thought the prudent thing to do was to free myself of the state obligations and concentrate on building the sales of my fledgling company. I did not take the time to acquaint myself with the reporting requirements and for a year I paid the compliance company a monthly fee to handle the paperwork. I moved to Colorado with the same arrangement for another year, until one day I received a notice from the State of Georgia that I owed penalties for 12 months of non-reporting. It amounted to $600. The compliance company was either incompetent or unfamiliar with the reporting requirements of an out-of-state company and had filed the wrong paperwork for the entire year I had been in Colorado (if they filed at all). When confronted, they refused to accept full responsibility and I ended up paying half the penalties, in addition to the monthly fees I had already paid the compliance firm to carry out the correct handling of the compliance matters.

In another example, the CEO of a successful importing company called me, after I had taken over my own compliance and found it to be less burdensome than I had envisioned for the few states I was distributing in at that time. He asked me what I paid for my compliance work. I told him that I did it in-house and he was astonished. In all the years he had been in business, it had never occurred to him not to use a compliance company. He had simply reached a point where he felt the cost for maintaining licensing in 40-45 states had become prohibitive. The company he was using charged for every single piece of paper they moved, every call, letter and fax and there seemed to be no economies of scale in piggybacking on their licenses. In my opinion, the revenue he was generating after many years in business was more than sufficient to justify hiring an experienced compliance person in-house. It not only gave him control over the process, it reduced his costs considerably.

Mind you, this is not an indictment of compliance firms – far from it. There are experienced and highly organized companies who competently take care of the complex details for you and relieve the worry. But they are cautionary tales to illustrate the importance of being well informed. Should you choose to hire a compliance company or consultant, compare prices, consider your budget vs. the time it frees up for you to do other things (like sales), get references from other clients, if that is appropriate, and make sure you feel comfortable with your choice before you turn over this important legal responsibility.

# A Client's Story

The new importer in my example is based in South Carolina, and I identify the state because even the people at the South Carolina Department of Revenue were admittedly confused about the status of their laws at the time, based on current and pending legislation. My client, with a raft of legal counsel on tap for his unrelated businesses, had been advised that he could not be both an importer and distributor in South Carolina and wondered why. I hadn't encountered this before and, since importer and distributor are both wholesale licenses that don't contravene the Tied House Rules, this was not something I was willing to accept on face value. I started with the South Carolina website, which was not helpful, and progressed to phone calls with their licensing department and finally to the supervisor. With experience to draw on (and some degree of stubbornness) I persevered at each level until I finally learned that state laws were in the midst of being rewritten. State employees were not allowed to advise potential licensees about the South Carolina licensing requirements while the laws were in a state of flux.

Perseverance paid off. This is a complicated state and the outcome was still nothing I had previously encountered but the conversation with their legal department provided the information I needed to advise the client that they could be both importer and wholesaler/distributor. The moral of this story is that if you familiarize yourself with basic principles surrounding wholesale and retail licenses and how you can legally operate in your home state, you can have a productive conversation to enable you to move forward with your license objectives.

# PART V

# CHAPTER 15

# MARKET VISITS – WORK-WITHS AND RIDE-WITHS

Invariably, no matter what the size or capacity of your distributor, a visit to their market is required. Ideally, this should coincide with an appropriate time of year to work with their salespeople, but it is also an opportunity to meet with the principals and cement the relationship. These market visits are called "work-withs" or "ride-withs", depending upon the inclination of the particular distributor. Perhaps geography has some bearing on this. In Manhattan, the concentration of accounts within walking distance would most likely be characterized as a "work-with" as opposed to a "ride-with." Either way, the concept is the same; you are working with the salesperson, either on foot or more usually by car and typically for the whole day. In some instances, the morning person may hand you over to another employee in the afternoon. Sometimes, this is to give each salesperson a break in the day, a chance to see other accounts and attend to pressing business. More often, it is to give more salespeople an opportunity to work with you within the confines of your visit and learn about the wines.

## Overall Preparation

There are guidelines for these occasions and abiding by them will earn the respect of the distributor; not following the basics of "work-with" etiquette can brand you as someone to avoid or, at least, an unwelcome supplier. It can mean the difference in sales, enthusiasm and the willingness of the salesperson to work with you again. In the world of "work-withs" and "ride-withs", the way you conduct yourself can be a make or break for your wine sales in that market.

The first step is to determine the most appropriate time for the visit and call or email far enough in advance to allow both for your preferences and an opening in their schedule. Less than six weeks would most likely result in an inability to accommodate both. Normally, I try to set up spring visits towards the end of the prior year and autumn visits either in spring or at least by early summer. Often the first visit, presuming it is successful, can precipitate another visit based on the enthusiasm of the salesperson for your product or the desire of the distributor to capitalize on what they now see as a value-added brand or portfolio.

At least one month prior to the date, be sure to communicate with the brand manager, sales manager or whoever is scheduling your trip and find out with whom you will be working and their contact details. An experienced and professional distributor will often have this information sent to you in an email attachment as soon as the dates are scheduled. Others are more seat-of-the-pants operators, not necessarily because they are any less professional and enthusiastic about your visit but most likely they are short staffed and always under the gun.

When you have the information, make your first contact with the salesperson or people and introduce yourself, confirm they have all your details and tell them you are looking forward to working with them. This establishes your professionalism and also reminds them that you are in fact coming to the market, in case they were unaware or had forgotten.

Equally importantly, this is your initial opportunity to make sure all the wines for which they have issued a P.O., or agreed to bring in prior to your visit, will be there in time. There is never a guarantee, but giving this reminder early enables the salesperson to take the appropriate steps if their attention has been elsewhere, and it will be. A gently squeaky wheel is the best approach in dealing with a distributor. If you don't, someone else will take precedence.

This once or twice a year visit is an opportunity to offer discounts for orders placed solely during your visit. It makes the occasion a bit more special and obviously adds a sense of urgency to placing orders while you are there. Offering discounts is not an expectation, nor should you feel any pressure to do so. It will depend, as with every other incentive you offer, on your capacity and budget. If you do offer, e.g., a 10% discount on orders placed for that day or two days, you may find the distributor will step up to add to it. Keep in mind, also, that the offer is for a finite period, that is, during your visit, and therefore the number of cases – the amount of discount – is also finite.

## Wine Dinners and Tasting Preparation

If there are wine dinners and/or tastings during your visit, determine as early as possible what wines are being poured and ensure you have them in stock and they can be picked up in time or that the distributor already have them in inventory. This is such a critical aspect of the arrangements, as noted for the overall visit. The wines may be slightly different from the ones in the portfolio or to be delivered for your visit but overall, since the purpose of any aspect of your visit is to sell wine, they should be available to purchase now or in such demand that a preview will generate more excitement and give dinner and tasting attendees a sense of privileged first look.

If the wines do not arrive in time for the dinner by trucking, avoiding disaster will require making less than desirable changes to the lineup, or an expensive air shipment.

If you do not have the right wines to work with during the day, or sufficient variety, the trip is an expensive exercise that will not produce the desired results. But imagine hosting a dinner in a restaurant, where patrons have paid for an evening of wine and food pairing, along with educated wine discussions. And the wine component isn't there.

When planning a wine dinner, the chef will have certain dishes in mind and would like to select, or have you select, wines that will pair best with them. This requires that you have information on the menu and ingredients in the dishes well in advance. On occasion, they will even develop courses around your wines. I find working on a wine dinner a pleasurable aspect to my trip planning because I enjoy a variety of cuisine and the pairing of flavors. If you are not already comfortable with pairing wine and food, it becomes easier as you identify elements of your wines and consider how this will complement the same elements in foods. In the interim, it is always safe to assume certain standards, such as gewurztraminer with spice, cabernet sauvignon with beef, pinot noir and chardonnay with salmon. But it does require that you take the nuances of your own wines into consideration. Not all chardonnays are substantial enough to stand up to a salmon dish with a heavy sauce. Not all cabernets will go with all beef dishes. Your cabernet might have more elements of sage and eucalyptus and a merlot or syrah may be better with the sauce or infused flavors the chef has in mind. The sauvignon blanc you represent may have powerful tropical fruit and melon; another may have grassy herbaceous characteristics and gooseberry elements.

Don't be overly concerned with the number of wines being poured. As long as you have followed the guidelines I set forth in the section on wine dinners and this is a demonstrable sales opportunity, the more wines poured, the greater the opportunity that guests will find something they like. Generally, five to six is customary but I have had as many as twelve selected by the distributor from several different vineyards.

You will also want to have all the information about the menu and wines so that you can make up a sheet for yourself to capture highlights of the wines and the order in which you will be speaking about them. I sometimes, depending upon the venue and in accordance with the salesperson's wishes, also make up handouts for the guests so that they can record their comments about the wines. I also try to provide maps and brochures for the table, if they are available.

Wine dinners can be a bit tricky in terms of the attendance of one or more representatives from the distributor. It is expected that the restaurant will comp your meal. You are, after all, the draw for the paying attendees and you will be providing your services as the guest speaker. If the distributor has contributed the wine, most likely a representative will also be comped, but they may require payment from the rep for their meal. Only in special circumstances, where I have not provided any wine, it was a very small distributor and I derived a good deal of benefit for the event (not the least of which is good will), have I voluntarily paid for sales reps to attend. I believe it is up to the distributor to remunerate the employee as part of their expense account.

# Time Scheduling

Every market visit is different in terms of what comprises the scope and makeup of the days you spend with each sales rep. A usual time span would be two to three days, perhaps coordinated by you with a trip to a contiguous market so that you may have two days in Colorado and two days in Arizona, e.g. If the wholesaler's region is quite vast, they may ask you to spend a day each in several cities, sometimes even the whole week. I have felt a bit like a relay baton on occasion as I have worked a city or county and been driven an hour or two to the next destination where another salesperson picks me up and so on throughout a week. It has been a very effective way to cover their regions. I have also rented a car and driven myself or taken a flight or train between cities if the distance has been too great, such as in Texas or between New York and New Jersey.

## Account Protocol

The time may consist of a day of restaurant and retail accounts, sometimes one or the other if the sales rep specializes in off-premise or on-premise, where we hope the person has been sufficiently interested and organized to plan a solid day of worthwhile appointments for you. This is not a time for ego massaging, where they take you to accounts that already have your product or where the salesperson can easily get your wines in on his or her own. You should welcome the challenging accounts, the new restaurant or difficult retailer where you have the opportunity to make a placement that the salesperson might not otherwise make. This not only creates additional sales for the salesperson's territory but should engender good will and contribute to their enthusiasm for you and your products.

There are prized accounts they may take you to where they are on very good terms with the buyer and have fostered a relationship that produces large and regular sales, even without your assistance. Undertaken in the right way, this is an opportunity for the sales rep to signal to the retailer that they are important to the distributor and, as a mark of respect, the sales rep has brought the direct representative of the wine (you) to meet them. The retailer, if they are already familiar with the wine and carry it, can now put a face to the brand, even if it is the importer rather than the winemaker, and can ask questions and obtain more information about the wines. It is assumed that you will have been to the vineyard and can provide intimate details about the region, viticulture, winemaking techniques and other items of interest. Perhaps you will be able to tell them why this particular red has a higher percentage of viognier than most Rhone blends, what the vintage was like in 2020 or what measures the vineyard takes to be truly considered biodynamic.

If the retailer does not already carry the wine, this is an occasion for you to make some significant sales. The salesperson, by taking you to this account, has also demonstrated a desire to promote your wines and increase your sales. They could, after all, bring almost any supplier to this account if the relationship they enjoy with the account is a privileged one. They have made an assessment that they believe you and your wines are worth this placement.

The *minimum* day, if conducted appropriately, should comprise approximately six to eight appointments, starting around 10am and finishing at around 6pm, with a short lunch break, unless the restaurant where you eat lunch is also a selling opportunity. In that case, you may spend some time waiting for the restaurant buyer to be free or may be meeting the distributor sales manager for lunch to discuss your portfolio.

There are many other constructs to a day, including a scenario that starts at 8am, when you are picked up at the hotel and driven two hours to the first account, and ending at 11pm when you finish the scheduled wine dinner. It is an exhausting kind of day, but I have done variations on it often and I endure whatever hours and work schedule that has been planned and executed for me, knowing that the time is finite and I will eventually get some sleep. I also respect the willingness of the distributor and the salesperson to put this much effort and time into making my trip successful.

I have met reps at gas stations off the highway or at the first off-premise account of the day and this is perfectly acceptable to me if the sales rep lives closer to the account, it is out of their way to pick me up and if I have rented a car. Most often, the rep will pick you up at your hotel and, depending on the city and the plans for the rest of the trip, you will not need a car at all.

## Expectations

It is customary, and universally expected, that you will pay for the sales rep's lunch. The dedicated professional will either plan the selling opportunity lunch for you or make a brief and relatively inexpensive stop to refuel and be back on the street. Beware the sales rep who brings you to an expensive restaurant for an extended lunch period where they only stock Californian wines and will never consider representing yours. This is the opportunistic sales rep who is looking, literally, for a free lunch and where, once you leave, there is very little post-visit sales activity.

I have been far more impressed by the rep who had me begging for sustenance at 4pm because I was lightheaded from hunger and in their zeal to see more accounts they had forgotten to stop for lunch.

The customary number of wines to take out on these days is six to eight. Too many wines will be off-putting to the buyers who know a large number will take a long time to taste through. However, there are salespeople who may decide to pull upwards of twelve wines from inventory, keep them cool and secure in the car and have available to the accounts the wines they feel may best suit their palates or needs. In my opinion, this is a perfectly acceptable way to conduct the day. Yes, I will generally be billed back for 100% of the samples used during these work-withs but I will also potentially benefit from the greater diversity of opportunity, as long as the samples are used to best advantage. In other words, opening twelve wines of which three to four may be poured for most accounts will result in a lot of leftover wine. Advance planning by the sales rep will result in gathering more people to taste wines at a restaurant at lunch, utilizing the wines at dinner or a tasting that night or making sure they are properly sealed for use the next day on the salesperson's regular route. In some instances, you could also work with the wines yourself during the next day's work-with, but I would normally prefer to start with fresh samples since I'm only visiting once or twice a year and want to show the wines at optimum quality. Of course, some big reds will benefit from aeration and fortified wines will be fine.

# Presentation Primer

I would prefer to assume you have little or no knowledge of the subject area covered in this section and start with some basic principles than leave out areas with which you may not have any familiarity. So, I'll spend a little time with the ABCs of how to "taste" the account, answering questions I had that went unanswered when I started and left me making it up as I went along.

Anticipate spending twenty to thirty minutes with each account to enable you to give the buyer an unhurried experience with the wines and allow you to relate the salient points on background and winemaking. This is a very fluid time frame, however, and there are almost as many variations on this as there are buyers. It will also depend on what the sales rep tells you is the norm for that account or if you are running behind and you want to be guided by the buyers themselves.

There will be the buyer who doesn't look up from his laptop and tells you rudely that he only has ten minutes and he will taste a maximum of three wines. I don't take it personally, but I do take it as a personal challenge; I have started with exactly that greeting and ended up with a tour of their wine cellar's treasures in the basement and having them taste through all 6-8 wines. I met a buyer in Manhattan who pointed to my sales rep and yelled, "*get out*" to him as we walked through the door and ended up with a full, leisurely tasting and a laughing conversation. It's all in the way you handle your "subject".

Remember, you are there to sell wine and have traveled to the location for that purpose. If you let the buyer know politely you are only there for the day and could they spare a few minutes, it can turn their mood around and become a pleasant and worthwhile experience. I'm not saying it will always work but more often than not it will. They are harried and don't want to be taken for granted. Letting them know you respect their time tends to disarm them.

A knowledgeable presentation is one of the key elements of the tasting. Going in unprepared will annoy the buyer and make them feel you are wasting their time, undoing any initial good impression you might have made. Being new will grant you some latitude, but there really is no excuse for lack of preparation.

If you have any time at all before your appointment at a wine store, go directly to the aisle that holds your country's section and check out the competition. Look for regions, price points and sheer quantity of offerings. All of these can be used as part of your presentation to point out differences and deficiencies. You will not want to insult them by suggesting their selection is awful or denigrate the competition. After all, one can assume they made these selections on the basis of their own palate and discernment. But it is appropriate to say you notice that there is nothing from such-and-such region (which you represent) or you happen to have something from a region on their shelves but at a better price point or more representative of the region's style or in limited allocation. Whatever it is that will differentiate your wines from what they already sell.

If you are at a restaurant, look at the menu. It will tell you a lot about how your wines will pair with their dishes. This is made a great deal easier these days by having menus online. Suggest that your Barbera may go beautifully with their mushroom ravioli dish, your lees fermented chardonnay with the roast chicken or a Sauterne with the crème brûlée. They will invariably appreciate that you have done some homework and will be open to the power of suggestion as they taste your wines.

Some sales reps will open the wine beforehand, preferring to establish whether something is corked and to allow reds to breathe. Most buyers will allow you to open them at the first account, so be prepared with a foil cutter and wine key. The sales rep will also have these items, but you should be equipped. I also travel with a hinged closure for any sparkling wines since the cork has expanded when released under pressure and will no longer fit. Remember to put all this in checked luggage if you fly! We've all forgotten that our wine keys were in our carryon, only to have them confiscated by TSA at security.

Market Visits – Work-Withs and Ride-Withs

Figure 15.1 Wine Tasting Czech Embassy New York

Open and pour in the order you feel suits your wines. This is normally lightest whites to heaviest reds and then dessert wines, but there may be a reason why you would open the wines by brand, such as at the suggestion of the buyer or because you feel this is the way to understand the winemaker's intent or the region. The buyer presumably tastes different varietals throughout the day and, with appropriate explanation, will be able to adjust to tasting reds and whites intermixed.

Start opening as soon as you set up the bottles, as long as the buyer indicates that they intend to taste all the wines. At least have each wine open before the buyer tastes so that you can talk without being too distracted. I am a comfortable public speaker but I happen to be easily distracted by the process of opening the wine, even after all these years, so I find that doing this first enables my comments to flow without interruption.

I usually taste, *and spit*, the wines with the buyer when they are first opened, to assure myself they represent the expected wine characteristics and towards the end of the day to see how they are developing. I once poured a verdelho without tasting it and throughout several appointments I was waxing lyrical about it being *redolent with tropical aroma* and having *a luscious passionfruit palate*. Mid-afternoon someone finally asked me to try the wine with them and I discovered that there was virtually no nose and undetectable passionfruit characters. It was not obviously corked but it was definitely closed or possibly so slightly corked that no one was game to mention it. It was embarrassing to me that I had been so explicit about its qualities and must have left a string of puzzled buyers in my wake.

Pour enough to enable them to swirl the glass, to allow the aromas to become evident, and to get a full swallow or two. If they want more, by all means readily pour it. The aim is not to be stingy but not to waste the wine either and perhaps run short at your last accounts. Just as you take cues from the sales rep, likewise gauge the buyer's habits as they assess the wines. No one wants to be told exactly what they taste. They can decide that for themselves. Giving them some background, oak treatment, fermentation, distinctions of the vineyard or perhaps an obscure flavor they may not have encountered is usually welcome. But sometimes they want complete silence until they have finished tasting, preferring to absorb the wines for themselves. In that case, they may have questions at the end, or may be inclined to reject or accept the wines on the basis of price and taste, with a view to their customers' preferences.

Allow the tasting to conclude before mentioning price. This is usually the provenance of the sales rep. It is the distributor who sets the pricing for their business and it is not your place to quote pricing, unless you have memorized the distributor pricing from previous account calls that day and simply repeat what they have established.

While you do have latitude with discounts and special deals for your visit, this is something you will be expected to support through samples or appropriate pricing on the next order, unless you have discussed it with your distributor beforehand. It should not be sprung on the buyer or the hapless sales rep.

On occasion, a discount may make the difference between no sale and a considerable order if you can reach a particular price point. This can be discussed spontaneously, as long as it is understood that you will be supporting this discount. You or the sale rep may need to call the sales manager to verify the feasibility of this one off deal and perhaps to verify you have agreed to provide the necessary billback payment that will result from the discount.

At the conclusion of the tasting, instead of asking for an order, ask the buyer if there was a particular wine that stood out for them. Try to make a comment or two on each wine that designates them as special, for example, because the wine is very small production and there is only a finite amount available, the vineyard is certified organic, the blending varietal is unusual, the region is new, the winemaker previously made wines for such-and-such widely touted vineyard or whatever you can legitimately use to distinguish the wines from others in the store. Don't wait so long at this juncture that you've lost the buyer's attention or they have to move on. Very often, especially if less experienced, the sales rep will leave the entire presentation to you, including asking for the order. At other times, they will know how to step in smoothly and take over, which they should since their commission depends on an order.

There is also the other type of sales rep, usually the completely inexperienced or the unabashedly egotistical (fortunately rare). They cannot help speaking incessantly during the presentation, either derailing your presentation before it has a chance to begin or jumping in where they should just wait. On those occasions, I always wonder what they think I'm doing there. Could they not have just done all this without me? My approach is normally to diplomatically suggest, out of the buyer's hearing, that they use me to the best advantage since this is why I have come all this way. If there is something they feel could add to the moment, based on specialized knowledge of the region or the particular quirk of the buyer, by all means make that contribution. Otherwise, sit back, relax and let me do all the work.

If the buyer happens to be absent, called away unexpectedly prior to the appointment, suggest to whomever is there that you leave a glass or two of particular wines you, or the sales rep, would like the buyer to taste. The glass opening can be covered in plastic wrap, if available, or at least a card of some sort placed on top to keep as much air out as possible. This is often done and can result in sales later. Not as effective as having them standing before you and tasting through the wines but still better than leaving without any opportunity to make an impression.

I take shelf talkers with me on every sales call to leave as a small reminder of the wine they tasted. I suggest you also get used to carrying them with you to tape in front of the wines on the shelf in a retail store if your wines are already in stock. Well worded shelf talkers, hopefully with some impressive press, will likely boost your sales. There are too many confusing options for the consumer and a shelf talker allows them to make a much more informed and comfortable decision.

One word of caution on the shelf talker with the great rating. I am especially averse to using shelf talkers of a previous vintage just because that was the one that garnered the press. I see it often in wine stores but, except when in error, I find it unethical and obviously misleading. If 2021 rated 94 and 2022, the current vintage, rated 89, you cannot leave the 2021 shelf talker. There is no reason to assume that those vintages and wines will be remotely similar, but the consumer will likely think the rating applies to the wine currently on the shelf.

Figure 15.2 Uniform Shelf Talkers

Many wine buyers will eschew wine ratings, and some will simply ask you not to talk about them. But ultimately, as wine professionals, we are all aware of the impact of the rating and while the ostensible reason for leaving the shelf talker is a reminder of the brand and wine tasted, a prominent review or rating will not go unnoticed.

Ultimately, if the sale is not made then it is up to the sales rep to make contact later, assuming the buyer has indicated interest. Take notes about the encounter and follow up with the rep after the visit to see if the presentation resulted in a sale.

# Dos and Don'ts

**Don't drink during work-withs.** Tasting is important, of course, and should be part of ensuring the quality and integrity of the wine. But drinking during the day is another unprofessional way to turn off your accounts and the sales rep. The stories I have been told of importers, brokers and winemakers who drank their way through an embarrassingly unproductive day are legion. These are sometimes individuals whose wines are considered necessary to the wholesaler's portfolio but they are not welcomed happily and these individuals are not relationship building. If the distributor has an opportunity to replace their wines, they will do so.

**Expect to wait at some accounts.** The retail or restaurant buyer may be backed up, they haven't budgeted their time well or perhaps they had a medical emergency. Never become impatient or refuse the opportunity. Take cues from your sales rep as to the benefit of waiting, the likelihood that a sale will result or how to handle the temperament of the buyer. We are there to sell a product, after all. I'm sure we usually derive more enjoyment from our wines than the average office supplies salesperson, but our objective is still to make the sale and satisfy the customer. Occasionally, the buyer may have a cold, just been to the dentist or simply disinclined to taste. This may be a wasted time slot in your limited day but remaining cheerful and open to discussing the wines can also result in a sale.

**Don't load the buyer up with material.** Most of it will undoubtedly end up in the recycling, as the buyers only have so much room or inclination to keep information on wines they may never purchase. If they're really interested, they know that they should be able to go to your website for all the trade information they might need.

**Do ask the buyer if they'd like a tasting note** on a particular wine they are interested in, or will be buying. This often helps them to educate their sales staff or add notes to a wine list.

**Try to engage the sales rep during the day.** Develop a rapport that can be built on during the year and at subsequent visits. I try to find something in common with each individual and ask questions about their interests, experience in the business and how long they've been with the distributor. Irrespective of the personality, there is always a way to encourage conversation and not only make the day more pleasant but help the person you are working with become more interested in you and what you represent. You would be surprised at how many stories I've heard from sales reps about disagreeable suppliers - people who were unfriendly, monosyllabic, uncooperative, demanding, hung-over or unhelpful. These are not individuals who endear themselves to salespeople, who have set aside their day and made an effort to create a successful experience for them. I often wonder why they bothered to make the trip at all.

**Do follow up with the sales rep** after you return to your home base and let the sales manager know, via email, how you felt about the visit if it was positive. They share this with the rep. Call the sales manager if you felt the rep was too inexperienced to make the day productive or if it was a negative experience overall. Better to discuss this over the phone or in person than commit it to writing. You will want to be diplomatic and let them know that you were reluctant to say anything, knowing that you could potentially alienate a salesperson you may work with again, but felt it was in the best interests of the company to do so. They should appreciate it.

**Honor your commitments** to anyone you encounter during your visit. This includes buyers, sales reps and distributor management. If you promised to send them a map, poster or brochure, find out some esoteric information or comply with a special request, they may not remember if you forget, but they will remember if you do send the requested information and it will impress them and encourage support of your brands.

*SUMMARY* — Behave like a professional at all times during your work hours with a distributor and their representatives and remember the key ingredient to this encounter and the success of your work-withs – like everything else in the wine business - is the relationship you establish and foster. This does not mean you can't go out for cocktails afterwards or spend some time socializing with the sales team. It is simply important to remember to keep your eye on the prize during the time you are actually working. These are your sales rep's work hours too and no doubt they would like to make the most of them.

## My Story

Market visits can be tremendously rewarding, fun and productive. They can also be excruciatingly boring, stressful and unsuccessful. I have experienced the gamut of these, but somewhere in between lies the norm – a trip that is usually hard work, but still enjoyable and profitable.

I have been left stranded in my hotel room by a sales rep who was unaware they were working with me that day because the distributor failed to tell them. I've also had sales reps tell me they hadn't booked any appointments because they didn't get any warning about my visit. (I discovered they had.) This is where I learned to always lay the groundwork for the visit, starting with several weeks in advance and following up again the week before I am due. In the latter example, we were still able to salvage the day because they knew the accounts they could go to without an appointment and also called ahead to set up whatever they could while driving. The bleakest of these examples was when I sat with a sales rep in a parking lot in Atlanta, with the car running, while she rustled through papers and her day timer looking frantically for accounts she could call amid an area ripe with good retail shops and restaurants. She called two people, discovered they had no time and gave up. She drove me back to the hotel and I shortly thereafter severed ties with the distributor. This was the last of many, many chances I had given them.

On the other hand, I endured, year after year, a series of wine dinners in one particular city in the Midwest that were extremely stressful, punctuated with periods of stifling boredom, but sufficiently profitable to lure me back every year. The distributor in this case was a man with no imagination and limited conversational skills, partnered with an unpredictable bipolar wife. I suffered through many strange days with them. The main focus of the visit each year comprised three nights of wine dinners that were well attended and resulted in significant sales. Many of the attendees were there to be educated about the wine and to subsequently buy but it was also an entertaining social night for them and the evenings were late. It was often after midnight when I finished. The next day would begin early and sometimes consisted of long drives to accounts. At times I suffered from laryngitis, allergic reactions to the local pollen and lack of sleep, without any consideration from my distributor. But I soldiered on secure in the knowledge that it would end and I would be able to sleep and recover when I returned home. I learned to loathe the expression, "you betcha!", the distributor's response to almost every question, but I also made friends with several of the dinner attendees, who came year after year and bought generously.

These visits took their toll but they did result in upwards of several hundred cases in sales with each series of wine dinners and, for a small importer like me, this was significant. Foregoing the dinners meant foregoing any sales at all with this customer since they considered the dinners an integral part of the relationship. It is for you to decide what your time and effort is worth and to respond accordingly to potential opportunities.

Conversely, my favorite visits were to a small distributor in Asheville, North Carolina and I spent many long days and nights with them driving around the different towns and conducting tastings and dinners. This distributor's fun, cheerful and endearing reps packed my time with worthwhile calls but ensured that I had adequate breaks and downtime and thoroughly appreciated all my efforts, as I did theirs. Unfortunately, they were a victim of the Great Recession and have gone out of business. These were some of the good guys and will be missed.

## My Client's Story #1

This is a recent experience with a client who has now established business in several states. I was privy to some of their paperwork during our consulting relationship and noticed large billbacks from one large distributor that appeared excessive in view of the 2% SA (sample allowance) they had been given on each invoice. I brought this to the attention of the client and we discovered that sample usage records were part of the distributor's standardized billback system and these were being automatically sent, as if there was no SA. In other words, "double-dipping" had been taking place. I'd like to think it was inadvertent but it does demonstrate that you can never abdicate your responsibility for checking your accounts. Start out with recording the individual financial relationships with each distributor, including SA and billback agreements and whether there is a special allowance or circumstance, and you will be more likely to catch costly mistakes.

## My Client's Story #2

I have indicated already that it is customary for the importer to pay for the sales rep's lunch. Further to that, one client asked me a series of trip protocol questions that probably typify all new importer's queries. Here are the verbatim questions:

"In the following situation, who typically covers the event/wines:

- Work-with in market with distributor reps?
- Work-with in market with a winemaker?
- Lunches/dinners for somms/trade with a winemaker in the market?
- Lunches/dinners for somms/trade with a winemaker and distributor in the market?
- Masterclasses with winemaker in the market?
- Distributor sales rep training?"

In all instances, the answer is usually the same. The outside supplier visiting the market, whether it be winemaker, importer, winery/brand owner, is the responsible for lunches and dinners while working the market. Exceptions to this tradition could include hosting an event that benefits the entire distribution company, with expenses far exceeding what should be attributable to one supplier. Anything out of the ordinary should be discussed with you beforehand and agreed on.

Paying for meals in the course of working the market may feel like an imposition or imposing undue financial hardship, depending on your situation but, if you consider the relationship aspect, you are building a rapport with your distributor and sending a message that you understand how the game is played and you are a team player.

# CHAPTER 16

# MAINTAINING DISTRIBUTION

As already stated, it is not sufficient to make the sale and then leave the wholesale company to its own devices. You must nurture and massage and be the (pleasant) squeaky wheel for as long as you have product represented in their house. The importer who does not become a true partner in this process is the importer who will find the early efforts have been for naught and their product relegated to the close-out bin.

## Ongoing Support and Communication

This can be a fairly fluid aspect, depending on the distributor's needs and the dynamics of their company. At one end of the spectrum is someone who expects you to make regular visits, call and email constantly with updates, send samples of new product and vintages on release and be prepared to offer regular discounts and incentives. At the other end, you have a wholesaler who basically wants you to leave them alone to do their job and make one visit a year to work with their salespeople.

The first example may indicate excessive demands based on the volume of business or, conversely, they may be your most valuable customer because comprise 30% of your income. The level of support you provide – i.e., time and money – should be commensurate with what you get back from your distributor. But initially, it is important to make known your desire to be a team player and allow the relationship to develop in an appropriate way. If you find that the orders only come when you work the market, and only to the extent of the sales you make while you are there, then this is not a partnership. Essentially, you are the only one working and the subsequent sales may not be worth the cost of the travel and incentive deals.

At that other end of the spectrum, where the wholesaler basically wants you to leave them alone, it is still in your best interests to be a contributing member of this collaboration. It is vital to provide appropriate sales tools to enable the wholesaler to maximize their efforts. Leaving them entirely on their own can also result in forgetting about your portfolio.

- If you have new press, be sure to send it.
- Include the wholesaler in any quarterly incentives and programming.
- Propose depletion allowances on higher volume.
- Offer to come and work the market at a suitable time with plenty of notice.
- Let them know when a product level is low, or when the next container is expected.
- Direct them to the website where new trade tools, i.e., great press, tasting notes and shelf talkers, are available.

All of this can be conducted via email, of course, with the occasional, judiciously placed phone call. Leaving your distributor entirely alone perpetuates a misconception that you are only marginally interested in their region and eventually they will only become marginally interested in you and your products.

# Expectations

Expectations established at the beginning of the association may morph and modify as time progresses. As the relationship matures, your expectations may change as the distributor demonstrates the extent to which they will support you and order consistently. Their expectations of you may also evolve as the wine becomes easier or more difficult to sell, as they need assistance to move an older product or require help to land a sensitive account. They may expect greater discounts for larger sales or monetary collaboration on a chain proposal, e.g.

Expectations, whether voiced or tacit, are always in play. The trick is to weigh the expectations, provide appropriate responses and maintain equilibrium in the relationship.

# Retail Support and Pull-Through

The first sale is, literally, just the beginning. The wine list placement and the bottle on the retail shelf are nice starts, but small potatoes compared to what you can achieve if you continue to support the account. The goal is the glass pour, the case stack, the end cap (shelving at right angles to the main aisle shelving, facing out with the most exposure) and the consistent orders from the retailer to your distributor. The pull-through. The repetitive sales themselves are significant but it also confirms to your distributor that you and your wines are not a one trick pony. They have staying power. Assuming the wine's QPR is good, much of this will be accomplished by the responses you make to the retailer and the follow up with both the retailer and the distributor rep.

In the previous chapter on working the market with your distributor, I covered the value of responding to the retailer or sales rep's questions and requests, thereby establishing both your reliability and your interest in them. Cultivating a distributor sales rep is also important. This is preferably the go-to person with whom you built a rapport or the one who consistently generates the most sales in the company. This person is likely to respond well to your genuine desire to support their efforts and increase sales – a win-win situation for both of you. Ensure that they always receive personalized emails and the latest news about the vineyard and wines. If they ask for samples for an approved presentation opportunity, send them. This may be the rep some distance from the headquarters and will appreciate that you sent the samples to their home rather than their having to drive a couple of hours away to pick up samples. It could be that the sales opportunity has a deadline, the release is new and not in stock and sending samples directly to the rep will save time and help them meet their goals.

I'm not suggesting you foolishly eat into both your sample allowance and your margin with indiscriminate shipments of wine to an individual sales rep. These are circumstances that stand on their own merit, after you have evaluated the person and the situation. Be cognizant of the sales rep's credentials.

- Are they a standout seller, or have they used up their sample quota from the main office and are looking for a way to circumvent the system?

- Did you get a good feeling about them during your 8+ hours together on a ride-with or did they seem to be driving around aimlessly without a plan for the day?

- Do they have a proven track record or are they new to the company and inexperienced?

Taking a chance once or twice may yield meaningful results. If not, you will have to reevaluate the wisdom of doing it again. I have experienced disappointment several times, but would still be willing to make the determination on a case by case basis and take a chance on a valuable return.

Retailers and restaurants can achieve a favored status to you, and you to them, also by your establishing rapport and continuing to maintain the relationship. Perhaps it's the account you always call on when you are in the area and have taken the buyer to lunch to thank them for the previous sale or to taste them on wines away from the hustle and bustle of the store. It may be the restaurant that held a successful wine dinner and attributes the success to both the wines and your personality. Whatever the reason, they will support you and your wines and, aside from the benefit of spending time with someone whose company you enjoy when you are in their market, you are almost guaranteed that they will be receptive to your next release, new brand or something else from your portfolio. They may even save a spot on the wine list for you or ask their rep if you have something from a certain region because they want to continue the relationship. Don't let them down if they have your wine on the list and order consistently. If you are going to change vintages, give them plenty of notice and try to save an appropriate number of cases of the current vintage for them, since this is what they selected and is in print on their list.

In addition to communication and spending time with them on a market visit, try to think of other ways in which you can let them know you appreciate them. It could be a winery polo shirt, apron or cap, things you have received for free from the winery. Or it could be a tiny allocation of a special wine that you can only supply to five distributors in the whole country and you have asked the rep to show it to this particular restaurant, knowing they will love it and it is perfect for their cuisine. Regardless of what it is, you are demonstrating that you consider them to be an important customer.

## Diversifying Portfolio Placements

Much of the time, you will want to have all the brands you represent in the one wholesaler house in the state. But there are certainly situations that call for diversification among distributors within the same state and this can be the savviest way for you to maintain distribution. The reasons why you might consider diversification are:

- if the distributor is too small to take on several brands at once
- if the distributor is too new for you to gauge their effectiveness
- if you have too many brands for any one distributor to focus on them all
- if the distributor only covers a specified area or territory
- if certain of your brands are allocated premium and others are high volume value priced
- if you want to evaluate the effectiveness of two or more distributors
- if the distributor has expressed interest in only a part of your portfolio.

In most of these examples – and there can be others – the decision is yours. Make it without an emotional attachment. It is so easy to think you can check off that state and move on. You like the wholesaler, you hope for the best and in time they will sell greater volume or venture into other brands. This may happen, but it also may not. The distributor themselves may even tell you they will never be able to sell such an expensive brand in their state or they have too many wines from one region you represent. *All* your wines deserve your best efforts at representation and it is up to you to dispassionately assess your options.

# Winery Visits to the U.S.

This is a far different animal from your market visits to the distributor and most definitely requires its own section.

The winery owner or winemaker will invariably decide at some point in the game that they need to come over and assist you with sales. This is said with the best of intentions, but sometimes with an inflated sense of how valuable this visit will be. For some reason, despite all your experience and familiarity with the U.S. market, the occasional winery owner, who is often the winemaker, will be absolutely convinced that their brand will somehow flounder and fail without their hands-on efforts. In fact, they may even believe it is imperative to the success of the whole U.S. venture that they come over and shepherd its passage through the three-tier system. And it requires two, extended, multi-city visits a year to accomplish this.

I welcome the "face of the winery" at most times, but usually discourage a brand representative from making this visit when the wine has just arrived or has just been launched. They are understandably chomping at the bit. The venture has taken months to get off the ground and the wine is finally on its way. However, this is a critical time for you - registering the brand, perhaps obtaining new licenses, getting samples out, researching more distributors, making sales and capitalizing on what may be a critical season. Once you enter the winery owner in the mix, you become a travel agent and event planner and your own carefully laid plans must go on hold. There also may not be much the winery representative can do given the limited number of markets that have the wine and depending on whether these markets are ready for their own launch.

At the other end of the spectrum, there are winery owners you will have to coax to come over at all. They cannot find the time to leave their vineyard businesses or are so reserved that they do not feel comfortable in an unfamiliar social setting. I once represented a brand for over ten years and not once did the winery owner, who was also the winemaker, make a trip to the U.S. It was a good, solid brand from an organic vineyard but it would undoubtedly have benefited from his appearance. If nothing else, he would have witnessed the changing U.S. palate styles and updated his wines accordingly. The wines were excellent quality, but somewhat old fashioned and sales eventually suffered.

So, while I encourage most winemakers or brand owners to visit (with exceptions, discussed later) because they do create a bigger buzz and are the actual people who have their hands in the soil and their feet in the juice – so to speak – the timing has to be right. If the visit is scheduled properly, with notice, the supplier will usually be very welcome and distributors will make space for them and invest effort in seeing that their time is well spent.

# Initial Planning

Notice to you of the proposed trip by the winery representative is imperative. You will need time to select the most advantageous locations, give the targeted distributor as much notice as they'll need to put on an impressive and worthwhile visit, schedule the trip and, as already said, put on your travel agent's hat. There really isn't any other alternative. Even if you tell the winery representative exactly which states and cities you wish them to visit, it is understood that they will not know where to stay, what connections to make, how long they need in each place and many other details. The Marriott downtown, e.g., may not be the best choice. It could be the little inn closest to the rep they'll be working with or the chain motel near the wholesaler's headquarters on the other side of town.

Establish at the outset how long they plan to be in the country. If it is one week, then you will be better off keeping them to one general geographical area to minimize travel and maximize working time. If they indicate they'd like to be here for three weeks, but only want to work in your home state with you and in Manhattan, for example, this has to be discouraged. Working within your own state will presumably necessitate monopolizing all your time, unless you have a full complement of salespeople, and now you have someone doubling up on a market you have already covered, potentially making their presence less effective. Perhaps Manhattan is a new market for you and there is limited potential for this brand, or it is too soon to send a winery owner or the distributor is already overbooked. It may require a brief day in Manhattan and the rest of the time in New Jersey or upstate New York. Even though you must work within their time constraints and availability, you cannot allow the winery representative to dictate the areas they will visit, although most don't try to do so. Dayton, Ohio or Denver, Colorado may be far more attractive alternatives for this brand or distribution. You are the expert in this situation and ultimately both of you will benefit from your choices through increased wine sales.

Determine which airports they will enter and depart from. The points of arrival and departure may be at opposite ends of the country. Possibly they are arriving in New York and may be going on to British Columbia to spend time with their Canadian agent. Or arriving in LA and departing from New York to attend the London Wine Fair. Such scenarios are quite common and all has to be taken into consideration when planning the supplier's visits. You won't want to have them ending up in California when they need to get back to New York the next day to take a flight to London.

I have also found it surprisingly common for less experienced winery owners to schedule a seven day visit and expect to be busy for all seven days. I do understand the desire to maximize every moment they spend on an international business trip, especially one of such short duration. But there is very little that can be done on a weekend and usually nothing at all on a Sunday, with the possible exception of a trade show that has been scheduled and registered for months in advance. Wine dinners, advertised afternoon tastings at stores or wine bars and casual store tastings *can* be organized, but again require a good deal of pre-trip planning and the willing cooperation of the distributor. There are some wholesalers that simply do not have the time, nor the appropriate state licensing authority, to conduct tastings on the weekend. In addition, Saturday night is usually a restaurant's best attended night and the restauranteur may be reluctant to give it up for a less well attended wine dinner.

The winery representative on a longer trip will often appreciate a Saturday to travel from one location to the next and Sunday to rest or see something of a city.

## Trip Logistics

First of all, it may appear to be appropriately courteous to accompany this winery representative to each location to pave the way, introduce them to the distributor principals and make their trip in a foreign country a smooth one. In fact, as I write this, it sounds as if it is absolutely the right thing to do! But unfortunately, unless you have an unlimited budget and plenty of time, the reality is that it is far more practical for you to send this person off on their own to *enhance* your efforts, not monopolize your time and incur additional expenses in duplicating effort. This is not to say you cannot meet them somewhere or have them start or end their trip in your home state to discuss business or see some accounts, but to accompany them on every leg is impractical. I have found that, once I explained this to my suppliers, they are understanding and ready to meet the challenges of negotiating the country alone. After all, I have arranged for every contingency, including which airports they arrive and depart from, what mode of transport they will be using, whether someone can pick them up, the hotels, contact details for all persons with whom they will be working and arrangements for functions. Regional managers, when you are in a position to appoint them, are the individuals who will be best suited to escort winery representatives during their trip and will most likely learn a great deal more about the wine and its origins in the process.

# Maintaining Distribution

Below is an example of the actual itinerary of a couple who travelled together, both being owners: one was the winemaker and the other managed the vineyard operation and marketing. They had made previous wine trips to the U.S. to other locales and this was a two week visit to supportive, secondary markets, with the aim of using their time to best advantage with additional tastings and wine dinners. Although they had down time over each weekend, it was still quite a packed trip.

---

**Mr. and Mrs. Winery Owners' itinerary**

**Arrive September 7th** – Wednesday - LAX
**Depart same day for Phoenix, Arizona** (Sky airport) from LAX
    Accommodation at Marriott in Old Town – short shuttle ride from airport
    3311 North Scottsdale Rd, Scottsdale, AZ, 85251 (8 miles from airport)

ARIZONA
**September 8th** – Thursday – work Phoenix with XXX Distributing salesperson (you will be picked up at hotel)
**September 9th** – Friday – work Phoenix with XXX Distributing salesperson (you will be picked up at hotel)

COLORADO
**September 10th** – Saturday – depart for Denver, Colorado (shuttle from airport)
    Accommodation at Four Points Sheraton Cherry Creek – close to distributor and shopping mall/restaurant area—600 South Colorado Blvd., Denver, CO, 80246
**September 11th** – Sunday – free day in Denver
**September 12th** – Monday – work with XXX Cellars salesperson (pick up)
**September 13th** – Tuesday – work with XXX Cellars salesperson (pick up)

NORTH CAROLINA
**Depart the evening of September 13th for Asheville, North Carolina** from Denver airport.
Accommodation at XXX Distributing guesthouse, Asheville (no cost to you – taken to location by sales rep who will pick you up at airport)
**September 14th** – Wednesday – working Hendersonville and Black Mountain
Event at Merry Wine Market that evening (sales rep pick up)
**September 15th** – Thursday – working Asheville (as above)
Event or dinner that evening (TBD)
**September 16th** – Friday – depart for San Diego, CA
Accommodation at Inns of America Suites, 5010 Avenida Encinas, Carlsbad, CA, 92008
Shuttle from airport.

CALIFORNIA
Tasting event at Wine Street, Carlsbad, (wine store) begins at 5:30pm. (I will pick you up and take you to event.)
**September 17th** – Saturday – free day on your own or outing can be organized
**September 18th** – Sunday – barbeque at my home for key accounts
**September 19th** – Monday – XXX Portfolio Tasting, San Diego
Event is 3:30pm to 7pm. Dinner following for suppliers at Oceanaire restaurant
**September 20th** – Tuesday – working with sales rep in San Diego (pick up at hotel)
**September 21st** – Wednesday – depart San Diego for LA

---

Figure 16.1 Sample Supplier Itinerary

## During the Trip

Much of the same protocol applies to the winery owner/winemaker/principal as it does to you, the importer, regarding transport, the sales calls and other facets of conducting a successful sales trip. I have enormous respect for the winery/vineyard/brand owner whose wines I have chosen to be part of a select group in my portfolio and have taken pains to ensure that we are a good fit. However, it does not mean they are fully conversant with U.S. market visit protocol and it is incumbent on you to both advise the winery representative and, if necessary, prepare the wholesaler. I perhaps go into excessive detail on this aspect. You may benefit from reading it all or glean what is useful to you depending on your situation.

- **Advice to the winery owner**, especially if this is their first trip, should concern expectations regarding the sales call and their particular presentation, who pays for lunch (they do), rundown of tipping in the U.S. and a general overview of the markets they will be visiting. I also try to prepare them by offering suggestions for a diplomatic presentation at an account. For instance, how not to bore or inadvertently insult the buyer!

- **On boredom** - having the direct winery supplier at the store is normally a unique and welcome opportunity for buyers to pick the supplier's brains on a region, ask esoteric questions and generally add to their knowledge of the brand. However, buyers do not want to be lectured or talked down to. They do not always want to be given tons of technical information and have the winery owner talk in explicit detail about their vineyard and techniques. They do not want to hear a supplier drone on about their fabulous chateau in Tuscany and be shown 8x10 glossies of this magnificent palace. As this particular story was told to me, the off-premise buyer declined to buy the products of the chateau owner "because *he* obviously doesn't need the money and I know other suppliers who do". A winery owner must, within reason, be just as sensitive to the situation and the personalities as you, the importer, have to be.

- **On diplomacy** – the last thing a potential buyer for a wine wants to hear is how much better this particular wine is than anything else they have in the store. They don't want to have their current selection ridiculed or denigrated nor be the recipient of negative gossip about a certain vineyard's practices whose wines they happen to have prominently displayed in a case stack or end cap. On one occasion, to my great discomfort, I was in the presence of a winery owner who proceeded to tell the store buyer that the reason they had selected this particular Chardonnay to export to the U.S., out of the five or six they produced, was because "*the U.S. palate is not as sophisticated as the average Australian palate*". Needless to say, no sale was made at this account.

➢ **Preparing the wholesaler** might involve giving them a synopsis of the winery's own expectations for their market and any quirks, foibles and idiosyncrasies of the individual. By now I have made a point of establishing the importance of working with people you enjoy and with whom you can form a good working relationship. This still holds true but that doesn't mean suppliers don't have distinctive traits that, once conveyed to the distributor, might make for a more enjoyable and productive trip. These might be very positive attributes, such as this winemaker likes to work long hours and would really appreciate having evening events scheduled as much as possible. It may be that they have never been to the U.S. before, so it may take them a little time to adapt, but they are excited about the prospect of helping with sales, or that English is not their first language, but they speak it fluently.

Ultimately, you will have no control over the conduct of your supplier and the success of their visit but planning ahead can save some headaches and misunderstandings.

# Winery Expectations of the Trip

As discussed earlier, you may have to – nicely - disabuse the winery owner of the belief that their mere presence in the market will herald spectacular sales. I don't mean to sound cynical, but you may also need to help them understand that everyone will (usually) be especially polite to them as they make their way through on-premise and off-premise accounts out of respect for their role and the distance they have come to see the account. The buyer may also, in their misguided attempt to compliment the winery owner, tell them how much they love the wines and suggest that they will be purchased just as soon as they can find room in their inventory, on the floor or on their wine list. This may or may not be true. However, to the uninitiated winery owner, this is a sign that everywhere they go people love and buy their wines. So why haven't you sold more?! (Yes, that has been said to me.) I believe it is far more useful to the winery owner to hear how their wines are perceived as a result of either market forces or the wine's own characteristics and I encourage them to ask for honest feedback. Empty promises don't sell wine and don't help the brand owner understand the market or help them make adjustments in areas such as planting, production or allocation.

In time, as a result of your diligent efforts and if you have chosen well, the wines will speak for themselves and the winery owner will appreciate what you have done to broaden their reach in this part of the world. Their trips are a welcome adjunct, much appreciated and somewhat essential, but management of this market and the bulk of the U.S. sales will still rest with you.

***SUMMARY*** — Staying on top of your distribution in each market is most likely the difference between success and failure. It is certainly the difference between small and large sales numbers, between infrequent and frequent orders. Distribution, without proper cultivation, can easily fade away. Foster the relationships and maintain a balance between too little contact and too much.

# My Story

Once again, I probably have as many stories as there are personalities, good and bad, amusing and disastrous.

I once had two winery owners from the same region come over at the same time, despite my best efforts to get them to stagger their trips. Due to their intense dislike of one another, my job was to make sure they were never in the same city at the same time while in the States! It was very early in my importing days and I only had limited markets so this was an almost impossible task. After ten days of considerable angst, things had gone about as well as I could expect. Unfortunately, they were scheduled to leave for home at the same time and I had to chauffeur them both to the airport. They sat in stony, uncomfortable silence for forty-five minutes. Following the trip, they were always in competition to see who had sold more in each of the markets they had visited. The end result of the trip was that their diligent follow up actually stimulated sales; the end to the story is that they were both much too high maintenance and I discontinued their brands.

I have also had:

- a winery owner's son who set fire to his hair while exploding illegal firecrackers on top of a downtown Atlanta high-rise roof
- an export director who drank all the samples during the day so that the salesperson had to make an unscheduled stop at his house in the middle of the day to pick up more samples
- winemakers who got lost and showed up so late to appointments or events they missed them entirely or who slept in and missed their connections to other cities, where carefully orchestrated events had to be cancelled or rescheduled, thereby disrupting the subsequent events and segments of the trip
- one winery owner (just one, fortunately!) who was so offensive I was asked by the

distributor never to let him back to the markets he visited. He had actually *cost* them sales

- a winery owner who refused to leave the airport until someone came to pick him up, despite the fact that no one was available and he had been asked to take a taxi or shuttle to the nearby hotel.

These are the (mostly) funny stories. But, quite honestly, I have most often dealt with industrious, entertaining, warm, dedicated individuals whose aim is the same as yours – to sell more wine and give their brand greater exposure. They may have partied late into the night, but worked equally hard during the day and never allowed their lack of sleep to diminish their cheerfully passionate presentations. Most were such assets that sales reps asked me how soon they could return.

## My Client's Story #1

Taking advantage of the opportunity to enhance the relationship with the distributor is something one client has taken to heart. Whenever a winemaker who has effective stage presence and speaking ability comes over, he organizes a "Master Class" in one or more cities, inviting sommeliers and influential decision makers to an informational tasting. Any importer could do it, if the winemaker was so inclined. Sommeliers always want to learn more. The class could be theme-based: for example, Riesling verticals of the vineyard for the past ten years or a blind tasting of new varieties planted in a region. It could be the range of styles from the vineyard, with an in-depth look at vineyard management and winemaking.

An invitation to such a class can be popular for those in pursuit of their Master of Wine or Master Sommelier, or at any stage of their education, as long as it lives up to its billing. For the importer, it is an opportunity to introduce your wines to sommeliers, perhaps surprise them with the quality and diversity of your portfolio and of course fulfil the hope that providing an event like this will be sufficiently appealing to make a sale. At the very least, it introduces the importer to the influential people of the area or cements a developing relationship.

## My Client's Story #2

In the vein of the previous comments on winemakers who are perhaps a little too impressed with their wines, one winemaker has my client pulling out his hair. The winemaker insists on calling each distributor constantly from his home country (and can't understand why they don't always call him back) and wants final veto power on distributors under consideration. He makes calls to sommeliers he has "heard of" and takes their advice over that of his importer. This is an ongoing situation at this stage that may work itself out if the brand owner wants to continue as part of the portfolio, but it may also result in a parting of the ways. If this happens, the negative consequences for the winery are far greater than for the importer, who is building an impressive portfolio. The winemaker has been lulled into taking his early success for granted, not realizing that finding any importer is a challenging exercise, much less one who shares your vision, works tirelessly to make sales and pays for the wine.

# CHAPTER 17

# WHEN IT'S NOT WORKING

## How to Recognize the Signs and Move On

There may come a time when you realize that your distributor is no longer a true partner. This may become apparent because they:

- indicate apparent disinterest in your brands by ordering less and extending the time between orders,
- do not extend their commitment to your portfolio by ordering any new products as they become available,
- stretch their invoice payments beyond the normal boundaries, until it becomes intolerable
- dispute invoices on flimsy grounds,
- abuse sample allowances,
- rarely return your calls,

- create obstacles to your coming to the market,
- take on other brands that seem to compete directly with yours, resulting in a loss of focus.

In defense of the average, well-meaning distributor, the lack of attention to your brand may be simply a business decision created from necessity. Your brands are losing focus for the salespeople because there is something changing in the market or the price point is no longer attractive. It makes it a tough sell for them, despite their efforts. Early communication is the first order of business to nip any obstacles in the bud, but if you find your concerns are being deflected or repeatedly not being addressed, it may be time to consider a change.

It is important not to react from anger or with a knee jerk reaction to their lack of interest or even if they are ignoring your statements and owe you money. Your objective is to do what is best for your brands, get paid in the process and gracefully exit. This also means lining up another wholesaler if at all possible. Just as in the job market, where it becomes easier to find a job when you have a job, the time to find another distributor is before you leave the last one when presumably market momentum and brand familiarity will be an asset to the new partner.

Many distributors, once you speak to them, will be agreeable to the change. It may be something they were anticipating, either at your initiative or their own. They will most often make this a smooth transition for you, especially when your products no longer work for them and they can move on without further obligation.

Whether or not you have a replacement company, or whether it was their decision or yours, avoiding burning bridges during this process is to your advantage. The wine world is ultimately a small place and a sales manager at one place could end up setting up their own distribution company where they may be receptive to representing your brands when they recall how they enjoyed working with you.

## During the Transition

In most states, the withdrawal of a brand from one distributor and the appointment of another is a relatively simple procedure. There are many variations on this theme, of course, as they relate to the different state's requirements. But essentially it is a painless process, with the possible exception of franchise states if you encounter opposition. In that case, you may be dealing with a distributor that knows they have the upper hand because of franchise laws, and try to take advantage of you. Opposition is not common, but I remind you of the franchise states again so that you appoint distributors in those states with special attention to the laws. Be sure to factor in the time it will take for the state to re-register the brands or handle a new license application, if necessary. Presumably, this will be shorter than the initial license application, but not always and something to prepare for.

In certain situations, the exiting distributor will expect the remaining inventory to be picked up and transferred to the new distributor. This may be a problem because there is no guarantee that the wine has been stored properly or that vintages are current. We can normally anticipate that if the situation has devolved into one that requires a severing of the relationship, there is very little remaining inventory because they haven't ordered in some time. Whatever the case, you don't want old (potentially unsalable) inventory to be a deal breaker with your new wholesaler. You will certainly want to start off on the right foot with them, as you would with anyone. In this case, work out an attractive price for the new distributor or offer incentives. They will not be surprised by this turn of events and it may have happened several times before but they will still wish to make a prudent purchase of new product they anticipate being able to sell.

> (Letterhead of Importer)
>
> Date
>
> Georgia Department of Revenue,
>
> Alcohol & Tobacco Division,
>
> 1800 Century Center Blvd., NE,
>
> Room 4235,
>
> Atlanta, GA, 30345-3205
>
> To Whom It May Concern:
>
> XXX Distributing voluntarily releases the brands Pikes Peak, Merlin's Magic and The Legacy registered to XXX Distributing by TNT Wine Imports, Inc. This release is contingent upon pick up and payment for any remaining inventory of TNT Wine Imports products as well as the payment of any outstanding invoices due to XXX Distributing by TNT Wine Imports, Inc. Sincerely,
>
>
> Thomas Beckett, III
>
> President
>
> cc: TNT Wine Imports, Inc.

Figure 17.1 Distributor Release Letter for Franchise State

If all else fails, you may have to arrange for your own trucker to pick up the product and bring it back to your own warehouse. This will depend on whether:

★ the product is worth salvaging,

* the cost of freight is outweighed by the value of the goods, or
* the old wholesaler requires you to pick up inventory as a condition of its release.

The last factor is most likely in the case of franchise states where a distributor will often expect compensation or sometimes another brand in trade from the new distributor – as long as it is a brand they want. This can really be a financial hardship for you, but something you cannot get around unless you forego the new distribution or are willing to wait a period of time with no distribution – therefore no sales – in that particular state for anywhere from one to four years.

If you really encounter a distributor in a franchise state who refuses to release your product under any circumstance, e.g. in Georgia, there is an appeals process. Usually, this requires that the distributor has failed to meet the standards set by the state and that you can prove this to be the case.

Figure 17.1 is an example of a typical release letter from a distributor to the State of Georgia, with a copy to the importer:

Release letters do not necessarily include the last sentence, but be prepared for its appearance.

*SUMMARY* — Understanding each state's position on distribution laws and moving brands, *at the outset,* will help considerably with the management of your brands in that state as you go forward and how you approach the need to change distributors, if that time comes. This goes back to ensuring that you take the time to familiarize yourself with all aspects of your business, regardless of whether you outsource compliance or keep it in-house. And the importance of keeping track of all your paperwork is illustrated in the story below.

# My story

Over the course of many years as an importer I feel fortunate to have encountered very little difficulty transitioning away from a distributor. I believe that maintaining a cordial rapport with them throughout the entire relationship will go far to mitigate any problems, but they do occur. I encountered one situation where I had to send a particularly intractable wholesaler to collection after he refused to pay me for invoices totaling several thousand dollars. I consider a collection agency to be a pretty drastic measure and have only resorted to this option twice since 1992 because to do so is to recognize that this is an irretrievable situation and burning bridges is the only option. It is also expensive. In this case, the wholesaler simply refused to pay without reason, and it was my last resort. Repeated efforts by the collection agency yielded no results and I was told the only option left was to sue which was included in the collection agency's fee.

I came to court armed with a thick file of documentation that refuted his claims. In short order, the judge awarded in favor of my complaint and ordered the defendant to pay my invoices, plus interest, plus damages.

Before I had an opportunity to collect on this judgment, the distributor sued me for spoiled wine – the same wine for which I sued him for non-payment, a year after receipt of goods. Back I went into court, again armed with a comprehensive record file.

He maintained that he had been unable to sell any of this allegedly bad wine. Luckily for me, I am a conscientious record keeper and, although this had now progressed about three years beyond my initial sale to him, I was able to produce a depletion report from the distributor that showed a sale of this exact wine to a large Chicago retailer. The distributor argued that one sale was all he was able to generate and only as a favor to him. I produced more depletion reports showing more sales. He tried to contest their veracity. They were originals he had mailed to me with his signature. The judge naturally ruled against him and I eventually received a partial settlement of my original claim. Lessons can be expensive, but this one taught me the value of good recordkeeping.

# PART VI

# CHAPTER 18

# HOME STATE DISTRIBUTION

At some point, you may want to start distributing all or some of your products in the state in which you have based your business. This has some distinct advantages:

- You benefit from the additional margin as wholesaler.
- It increases the scope of your sales.
- You are able to exercise more control over the distribution of your products.

My initial inclination is to suggest that you take this step– at least in any meaningful way – after you have established a chunk of your out-of-state distribution, or you may find yourself bogged down with in-state distribution at the expense of larger volume sales. Consider the Pareto Principle – also known as the 80/20 rule. In the case of national vs. state distribution 80% of your sales will come from 20% of your customers and this is still where you should apply the majority of your focus, at least at first. However, when to establish in-state distribution, if you choose to at all, will depend on your own situation again in terms of your approach t budget, resources and connections and whether, in fact, you find you prefer selling to retail more than wholesale, establishing closer relationships and deriving satisfaction from faster sales.

The economic benefits of home state distribution are compelling when you combine it with importing your own products, breaking down something like this in terms of **gross margin**:

FOB (your cost + 30-35% markup) + wholesale (FOB + 45-50% markup) = price to retail

Using the lower markup, an example of $150.00 FOB to a wholesaler means you can now charge $217.50 to the retail account. Your overall gross margin has just become much more attractive. The retail price will also stay on parity with retail in other states when you sell to distributors and you take one margin and your distributor takes for the other.

However, the additional markup isn't all profit margin; there are a number of expenses that are fundamental to a distribution business and these will be covered in the following section.

## Distribution Basics

### Licensing

The licensing requirements for your home state (i.e. the one in which you are licensed to do business with the address of your Federal Basic Permit), will be very different from those in place for you as an out-of-state importer. As a general rule, the latter usually comprises simple paperwork, a fee of a few hundred dollars, registering brands and assigning distribution to each state's wholesaler. The objective of the state is to track your sales to the distributor within their state and ultimately, to make sure excise tax is paid to them. You can have out-of-state licenses in fifty states, but only one home or in-state license.

In most cases, the requirements for in-state wholesale distributor are comprehensive. It may include fingerprinting, background checks, site inspection, interviews and considerable paperwork. You are now setting up distribution of alcohol in the state in which you will also be selling, delivering and responsible for sales and excise taxes. Fees vary by state — no more than a few hundred dollars in California, e.g., to several thousand dollars in New York. The home state could also differentiate between a wine and beer license and a spirits license, so be aware of what you want to do before you apply. In New York, e.g., the wine distributor license is $3,750 for a three year term; the wholesale license to distribute liquor, for the same term, is $27,280.

# Facility

Decide how large you wish to become in your undertaking, which basically comes down to three choices:

1. Full-service, state-wide distribution. This will require additional licensing (beyond the one referred to above), large storage space, a good inventory software package, additional personnel, equipment and overhead.

2. Limited, but wholly controlled, distribution in your area. This will require additional licensing but a scaled down storage space and less personnel.

3. Expansion of your sales into a local area distribution network, but outsourcing the services. Additional licensing of your own storage facility won't then be necessary, but success will depend upon the quality of the outside services you contract.

The first choice will require a fairly hefty budget for warehouse and office personnel salaries, sales reps, insurance for both personnel and facility, transportation costs, trucks (or rentals), facility rental or purchase, forklifts, racking, utilities and so on. The starting overhead will be substantial but, if you have the right sales team, it means you can ramp up pretty quickly. Assuming you have available product, it enables you to realize some large volume sales, which may eventually outstrip your national sales. This is the most ambitious example and should not be undertaken without in-depth research and the understanding that a budget of several hundred thousand dollars will be necessary as an underpinning to your first few months of personnel salaries, expenses and plant overhead.

In the second example, distribution and storage is still under your control but in a more economical and scaled down version. You may, for instance, have sufficient space in your own rented office that can be dedicated to storage of a few hundred cases and be able to replenish your stock as needed from your main warehouse by regular delivery from a trucking company. Consideration must be given to:

- your location and whether it is zoned for such an enterprise
- whether state licensing permits it
- whether trucking companies are able to access your street and storage area
- whether you have a loading dock or will need delivery trucks with lift gates.

In this scenario, you can hire your own sales personnel or use local brokers as independent contractors. Distribution must necessarily be circumscribed to a manageable geographical area from which you can easily deliver to your accounts using your own resources, rented trucks or local delivery services.

In the third example, you will need to find a good, local, appropriately licensed storage facility, which will be quite different from the large, bonded warehouse at which you store the bulk of your product. It will need to be well-organized, efficiently run, responsive to fast turnaround needs and be able to deliver regularly to all the counties or towns you have designated as your distribution area. Costs will be much higher for storage than for your general, public warehouse because their main service is deliveries, but you have that second margin (the state distributor markup) to absorb these costs. Cost-conscious case volume should be considered in this option to allow for ample availability without eating up margins through storage.

Since there will be far more stock movement and smaller, finicky deliveries than the national distribution example, it is imperative that this storage and delivery facility employ people who conscientiously pack and load each wine. They must cross check for correct vintages and quantities, including filling partial case orders. It requires far more attention to detail and reliable truckers, also employed by the warehouse. Delivery drivers will be handling money in COD cases, so they must be trustworthy and bonded by the warehouse. These entities are available and this is actually a viable and manageable alternative when you are starting out. It can be a value-added piece to your national distribution, without deviating too much from the Pareto principle.

## Taxes

In any scenario, you will have excise taxes, applied to alcohol and tobacco, on the goods you have sold within your home state. There is a huge variance on rates between the different states so be sure to check with your own state to factor this cost into your budgetary considerations. Usually, these taxes are paid when you bring the container into the country and then refunded when you complete excise tax forms to report which sales have been made outside your state. In the case of state distribution, of course this means you will not be refunded the tax you have paid. Depending on the state, you may also have local taxes and fees.

## Account Selection

The natural inclination is to focus on the "A" accounts, followed by the "B" accounts and, if you have sufficient salespeople to cover them, the also-rans, the mom and pop operations or the local, out of the way places that are usually under the radar. Everyone would like to promote the fact that their wines are on the hottest restaurant lists in town. The point is that *everyone* wants to do that but not everyone will be able to find a place in these top tier restaurants. There may simply be too many distributors for the buyer to see, lack of space or a list that is dominated by one of the big wholesalers, who also supplies the well-brand liquors (the house pour) or the "must have" specialty liquor. Even if you do get in, this may not be your bread and butter and will require far more attention and massaging than the quantity or value of the orders deserve (again, the 80/20 rule). It is still important to have some significant accounts, since they can elevate your profile and add to the winery's cachet, but they should not be the entire focus of your portfolio. That can come later when you have established yourself as a specialized distributor of "must have" fine wines.

You would be surprised at how much you can sell to the little neighborhood restaurant, especially if it is *your* neighborhood and they know you. These can be opportunities for glass pours that result in a couple of cases every week or their wine list is so small that if someone orders a cabernet, chances are 50:50 that it will be yours. Even if it isn't your neighborhood bistro, it may become a place that you or your salesperson will get to know and where you or they can befriend the owner, manager or beverage buyer. Some local grocery or specialty stores have a nice little selection of wines and this may be your niche, since they are often neglected by bigger wholesalers.

## Account Presentations

This has a lot of the elements of presentations you make on out of town work-withs, but you are now responsible for the entire presentation and assumption of risk and follow up. You, your sales rep or a broker will all have the same considerations for the presentation. Therefore, reference to "you" is taken as including anyone filling these roles.

- Are you showing appropriate level wines for the account – i.e., the right price point, region or style?
- Have you researched the account to determine if they fit your profile focus – i.e., within your geographical scope for attention, deliveries and time?

- Do you have sufficient availability, or any in stock at all, of the wines you are showing? This is not always a necessity, especially if you are generating pre-sell buzz for a hot wine or you know the restaurant or retailer will not have room for a few weeks, but is certainly something to determine and convey from the outset.

- Is your book (the representation of your portfolio) up-to-date? You will need to bring a price list and leave it with the account. Are the vintages you are showing the same ones in the book? Does it show all the available brands? Is the pricing current? Your book does not have to be professionally bound in 4-color (in fact it is too expensive to have this done as often as your products and vintages change) but it should be professional, accurate and updated regularly.

- Do you have a credit application (if applicable) or any other paperwork to leave with them?

- Is this an account that requires you to bring your own glassware? (I have encountered this occasionally, believe it or not). If you don't bring your own, they are likely to rummage up a dirty waxed paper Dixie cup that makes the wine taste terrible! I traveled once with a distributor rep in New Jersey who brought his own Riedel stemware to accounts; this is by no means necessary or the norm, but it conveyed to the account that the rep felt the quality of his wines deserved specially made glasses.

- Have you determined whether they conduct tastings by appointment, only on the third Thursday of the month or as a drop in any time as long as you are prepared to wait?

- Knowing the name of the buyer on the first visit is courteous and will make an impression, but it is more important to ensure that you know it on subsequent visits.

- Get a feel for the temperament of the buyer. Adapt your style accordingly. You can be genuine and still accommodate their personality to make the time more memorable and enjoyable for the buyer.

- If they are in a rush you should be well prepared and give an abbreviated presentation. Presumably, there will be other opportunities to develop a rapport or take more time. As a general rule, talking less at first is better than talking more. They can always ask you to expand on the information, but it's a lot harder to ask someone to stop talking (although most buyers don't have trouble letting your know their time constraints). They may have five other suppliers to see after you, or are expecting a delivery any moment.

- *Establish credibility from the beginning.* It is much harder to regain it later. If you do not have a wine in stock, say so. If you are not clear on a price, say so. If you do not have the exact percentages on the blend, the type of oak or what the vintage was like, tell them you will find out. *Do not wing it.* It's not worth it in the end. They will not really care if you know now whether it is 15% or 20% cabernet franc, but they *will* care if you told them 2019 was a great vintage in a remote region and they found out later it was one of the poorest in a decade.

# Home State Distribution

Figure 18.1 Featured Wine in a Local Wine Store

## Other Issues

Determine whether you wish to impose a minimum order quantity or will "break" cases – i.e., deliver less than a case of a particular product. When you are new and your wines are relatively unknown, it might be more appealing to have a low minimum quantity, such as two cases or a minimum order value of $250, which still allows you some economies of scale on the delivery. Some small distributors have minimum order quantities of 5 cases or $500, so you will still appear reasonable by comparison.

Broken cases are usually at your discretion (except in COD states where it is the norm), but if you outsource your logistics this will require more handling and higher expense at the warehouse. You might offer broken cases on high value or dessert wines, such as Port, either of which might take the restaurant a while to deplete. Restaurants often have very limited room to store wine. In the event you are warehousing your own product, by all means accept broken case orders, as long as there is some reasonable minimum on the total order. It may even work to your advantage if the retailer or restaurant orders six *half* cases of six different wines, instead of three *whole* cases of three different wines. The number of bottles is the same, but you have just achieved twice the wine list exposure or shelf facings.

At the time of an order, do not leave the account without the necessary license details as they pertain to your state (in the case of California, for example, their ABC number and reseller certificate). Not to have these on file may run you afoul of your own state licensing body. At the very least, it tells you that they are licensed to sell alcohol. To sell to an unlicensed account would most definitely incur heavy penalties for you, if not the loss of your license.

Each state has different requirements regarding payment from the account, but generally they fall into two categories – COD or 30 days. If COD is the requirement, then a check must be picked up at the time of the delivery by the truck driver. Not to do so violates state law. In the case of 30-day terms, you will need to determine that the account is credit worthy. This should be done by obtaining a credit application. You may find that certain high-profile accounts will refuse to complete one, maintaining that there is no need to do so. Personally, I allow them this vanity. Accounts such as these are usually unlikely to be in any financial difficulty. Whether references are obtained or not, I suggest that you establish a maximum dollar exposure for yourself until there is a history of timely payment.

Go above and beyond to make a good account happy. If they run out of a wine for the weekend and delivery is not scheduled until Tuesday, get that case to them yourself, even if it means disrupting your own plans outside normal working hours. A salesperson expects to conduct evening tastings and wine dinners and catch the restaurant buyer, who may be the chef or head bartender, after the dinner hour rush.

Delivery errors are a reality, so it is important to be responsive to the customer and correct the error at the earliest opportunity with a cheerful attitude. Even if it is the customer's mistake, e.g., miscommunication between sommelier and restaurant manager, take back the goods or make the exchange. Far better to retain an account for future orders than lose them over one correctible incident.

In states where terms are extended, be prepared to go and collect the check for an account that is late or where they tell you they will pay when you bring them the replacement for the corked bottle.

Drop in on the restaurant account whenever possible, even if it is just for an appetizer, a drink or a light lunch. There is a symbiotic culture in the wine industry, especially at this level, and when they see you supporting their establishment, they are more likely to support your wines.

On the other hand, try not to get sucked into too many local tastings in the early stages of your import company and your distributor model, especially before you have a sales team. It is very tempting to accept a request from an up- and-coming wine bar or a friend's restaurant to do a wine dinner or tasting. As the distributor, supplier, co-organizer and speaker, you are now far more involved with the event than if you were coming in from out of town to work with your distributor on an event they have organized. Without sufficient sales support and local infrastructure, this may well be to the detriment of your national business, which still requires the bulk of your focus. Again, the 80/20 rule applies as you consider the amount of work and return for the local event vs. the work and return on a national level. Tastings and wine dinners become an essential component of your core distribution business, but must be evaluated in context. It is flattering to be asked but you will not lose the account or the opportunity if you tell them that you would love to do this dinner, but unfortunately you have a conflict until a date down the road (when you will be better prepared). Dinner or tasting guests also need to have somewhere accessible to buy the wine after the event. Establish retail store accounts nearby.

# Sales Personnel

Establishing your business as the sole employee is normal, but there quickly comes a time when you will have to bring on help, either because the business is growing too fast or it can't grow at all with just you as its only employee. At this point, based on preference and circumstances, you decide whether to hire your own sales team or retain the services of independent brokers. Both of which have pros and cons that can be broken down this way:

### Salesperson - Pros

- Works exclusively for you and therefore all hours and commitment is to your company
- Focuses exclusively on your product, instead of being spread around several portfolios
- Will show all products, and those you determine require increased focus
- Can be trained in your systems as they relate to order entry, office requirements and pitching in where necessary to make a sale happen
- Is assigned accounts and territory according to your needs
- Will adhere to a company philosophy and ethics as part of their employment and while being the face of the company in the field
- Can grow within the position as your company grows and, as products are added, or if a sales team needs a leader, there is someone within the company qualified to take on the responsibility

◆ Loyalty and job satisfaction are engendered with appropriate salary and benefits package and fair treatment.

## Salesperson – Cons

◆ Initially and for some time, there may not be adequate sales potential to justify the salary and benefits

◆ If there is insufficient product – either in diversity of items or volume - to sustain a full-time employee, there is either wasted salary or a disgruntled employee who cannot live on the bonus structure

◆ May not be experienced in retail sales and require extensive training

◆ May not know the local accounts

◆ Difficult and expensive to discharge an employee who is not performing well

◆ Requires adequate supervision.

## Broker – Pros

◆ Independent contractor not subject to salary, benefits or bonuses

◆ There is an established 10-15% commission based on sales and no hidden expenses

◆ Since commission is directly linked to sales, will work hard to ensure sales to desirable accounts

◆ Understands retail sales

◆ Already familiar with, and has access to, local accounts

- Whatever the limitation on the size of your import portfolio, it can be integrated into their existing representation, because it is part of a larger income stream for them

- Has built up a sales territory and relationships that could provide immediate sales.

- Can work independently with little supervision.

## Broker – Cons

- Portfolio diversity means less attention to your wines

- Can pick and choose which wines they wish to show, based not on your needs but on their own inclinations

- The accounts they service may not be your preference

- May choose not to involve themselves at all with accounts receivable collections, maintaining this is your responsibility and it interferes with their ability to preserve a positive relationship with the account

- Has own philosophy regarding presentations and image, which may conflict with yours

- Can give up your brands at any time, leaving you without a replacement and with the resulting loss of business.

On the surface, it may appear to be far more advantageous to hire your own sales team, but this would be looking at the weight and number of the pros, without considering two important deal breakers of the cons – your portfolio may not sustain a full-time person or team, or you may not have the budget. Your choice has to make sense for you and your situation. Local brokers are a very viable option for any small company and I can recommend them, when the situation is right. However, there may not be any available or reputable brokers in your area. One option is to advertise in an online publication, like the job section of Wine Business Monthly: www.winejobs.com, or www.indeed.com for someone who is willing to work commission only. It could be someone with a second job or who is willing to forego salary for the chance to gain more experience.

Ideally, you want someone with established accounts who has experience, but this is not always possible. When hiring an employee, I always say think about the *qualities* more than the *qualifications*. Although a well-qualified and well-rounded individual is the ideal, you may find that someone with a certain wine sales background is not necessarily the right fit. For example, and only as an example and not meant to be a rigid principle, sales people who have worked in wine stores *buying* product do not always make the best person out there *selling* it. A sales mentality has to be the first consideration. Wine store employees are accustomed to:

- being in one place
- working within an established range and number of hours
- having people come to them
- buying product
- selling a huge range of products from around the world.

A distributor salesperson has the exact opposite working environment. They are accustomed to:

- traveling around all day
- working fluid and extensive hours

- going to the buyers to make the sales
- selling product
- representing a limited range of wines.

This is not meant at all to denigrate the experience, qualifications and motivation of the wine store employee. While the opportunity to be fairly independent and closely aligned with a select group of wines could appear attractive to some, they may discover they are not natural self-starters, the portfolio is too limiting or they are uncomfortable asking for the sale. On the other hand, it could be the perfect breakout chance for an individual who started with a wine store to gain experience and is grateful for the opening at an up and coming distributor to prove themselves.

A sales rep making a lateral move from another distributor may not be a better choice. Yes, they have the experience, the orientation to the type of job they will be doing and perhaps even familiarity with local accounts. But why are they making the move? Were there problems with the last employer? Did they underperform or have issues with management? Or it may simply be a move from a big distributor where their sole responsibility is to wake up at 5am and stock grocery shelves to a small company where they have a ground floor opportunity to make a difference.

Are they experienced, but brash, opinionated and overly self-confident? This personality may have worked well at a behemoth distributor whose products are necessary to an account's survival. But if you are like me, you want this individual to be mirroring your own values of excellence and relationship-building in a small, growing company, not someone who is likely to rub people the wrong way and get them barred from the account.

The point is that you will save yourself a lot of wasted time, expense and headaches if you make a little extra effort to really take a look at a candidate, ask for references and conduct a pretty comprehensive interview. Give them a trial period and see what develops.

## Office Personnel

Aside from obvious salary and benefit considerations, the more sales people you have out there the presumption is the more you sell and the more you make. Not so with office personnel! They are an essential, vital part of the business and without their expertise and contribution it would be impossible to function. But employ too many and you will collapse under the weight of your non-revenue producing overhead.

Again, the model you have chosen will dictate the number of office staff and their roles. Assuming you have intended to take a serious run at being a distributor, and have the budget, two people in the office could divide up roles within logistics and compliance, e.g.. If you import all the wine you distribute, you can expect the container shipments to increase as you require more wine to divert to your own distribution. This will also increase the paperwork at both the winery and retail account end. The following are now the responsibilities of your integrated import/distribution office:

- purchase orders to winery and tracking of fulfillment.
- container logistics
- inventory control at, potentially, two warehouses and your office
- warehouse and delivery logistics
- order processing of calls from accounts and calls/emails from salespeople/brokers
- coordination of the salespeople or brokers roles

- reference and credit checking of wholesale and retail accounts
- invoice preparation and disbursement
- accounts payable
- accounts receivable, including phone and email collection
- filing
- purchasing
- coordination of compliance, even if it is outsourced
- excise tax information gathering, preparation and timely submission
- marketing and promotion, including POS materials and website
- bookkeeping
- shipment of samples to prospective wholesalers
- payroll (which can also be outsourced to a payroll service like ADP).

While day to day bookkeeping should be done in the office, periodic accounting, financial statements and tax preparation are best left to your own outside professional. QuickBooks will be able to provide you with excellent tools, including financial statements, if information is input correctly on an ongoing basis. Accounting and tax professionals are accustomed to working with QuickBooks documents that can be backed up and emailed to them in compressed files when necessary. Prompts are easy to follow.

# Hiring Basics

The following are my own personal philosophy and recommendations based on years of hiring people in the wine industry and, prior to that, when I managed around 130 employees in another industry.

For any new hire, make sure they understand exactly what the job will entail. Do not spring something on them after they have accepted the position or they will feel they have been misled. Understanding that the distribution division is in start-up mode and there will be a couple of days of inventory management each week until the company expands is different from being told the job is a full-time sales position, only to discover that three days a week they will be operating the forklift. Company mission and guiding principles should be clear in your own mind and conveyed in conjunction with expectations.

I once saw a job description that did not mince words, but really gave a clear understanding of the position. This is just an excerpt:

> *"We are looking for 3-4 visionary leaders to be the future senior executives of The Company as we grow and expand our unique cutting edge business model around CA and beyond. Please do not apply if you are looking for a comfortable big company wine sales job. Right fit will be driven professional with a long term view, willing to trade some short term benefits for huge long term opportunity. The Company has all the tools you'll need for great success, so your hard work is all that's missing."*

I believe in stressing a policy of cross training, to a degree, and this should be explained to each new employee, especially office and warehouse personnel. It engenders heightened team spirit and transparent understanding of mutual expectations from the beginning. Although it is within reasonable limits to expect sales reps to also prepare their own POS material and submit detailed reports to management, the purpose of their position is to generate sales. If they are stuck on the phones in the office because someone is on vacation, it is inhibiting your growth.

The cross training should take into consideration the aptitude and experience of the employee, so that the creative marketing person is not expected to take on bookkeeping and a sales manager is not filling in for the receptionist.

Overall, specific job assignments are recommended in the office so there is continuity and accountability. However, with the need to pitch in where necessary as the work ebbs and flows, crossover and cross training can and often should be part of the equation.

As the sales and paperwork increases the time will come to consider other hires, but unless a rapid increase in sales from a specific source is anticipated, I suggest that you wait until there are unmistakable indications that workload cannot be handled by current support personnel and perhaps initially consider a part-time hire or temp to take up the slack. Workload has a habit of expanding to fit the hours and people available, so evaluate whether this is truly adding to your bottom line in a meaningful way.

Depending on your choice in storage, delivery and sales model, you may need warehouse personnel, drivers, sales manager, etc. Increased orders may necessitate a second order entry/customer service person, or someone for marketing and handling social media.

## Account Protocol

Whether it is you or your sales rep, visit the retail store regularly to make sure your brand is prominently displayed, hasn't been obscured by store marketing and has the appropriate shelf talker prominently displayed. Determine how you can achieve better placement, such as at eye level on the shelf or on an end cap.

If you are developing a marketing plan, be very aware of the constraints the Tied-House laws place on you to promote your brands. These are the basics:

- The phrase "nothing of value can be given to a retailer from a wholesaler" is the bedrock of Tied-House rules.
- This means there can be no mention of a retailer by a wholesaler in a tweet a retail event promoted by the event itself or another party. This, for example, is not allowed: "come and try our wines at XXX wine bar on May 16th".
- No photo of an event can be published on Facebook, or on a blog or a website, either before or after the event, if the name of the place is mentioned or any signage is visible. Even if nothing is said, if the retail establishment can be identified in your photo it is a violation.
- You cannot mention any retail account in a tweet (e.g.) to indicate that you've sold to the account, plan on selling to them, or that the wines can be found at this account now or in the future. For example, you cannot say, "We're proud to have our wines in XXX store" or "If you've been having trouble finding our wines, they will soon be available at XXX store".
- You cannot mention that XXX store loves the wine. For example, "Joe, at XXX store, said this is the best NZ sauvignon blanc he's tasted all year" or "Cheryl, at XXX wine bar, loves the new vintage of our syrah".
- There can be no mention of a tasting you've done, or publishing a photo of a tasting, if it's at a retail location. The retailer may not even be carrying your wine, but if the event is a retail location, which is now tweeted or posted to potential followers, it is considered that you have provided something of value to the retailer, thereby establishing a de facto favorable relationship between wholesaler and retailer.
- A tweet by another party cannot be retweeted by the wholesaler to promote an event at which the wholesaler's wines will be poured or sold.

To round this out, many states do allow something "of value" to be given to the retailer in the form of product displays, samples and signage, but TTB (Alcohol and Tobacco Tax and Trade Bureau) defines these as items that are specifically for the promotion of alcohol that is bought by the store. It cannot be intended as an inducement to favor placement for the wholesaler and cannot be greater than $300 in value.

Today, promotion of wine is ubiquitous on the internet and every wholesaler must be familiar with Tied-House regulations to understand how they can promote their wines legally. If you are engaged in social media for wholesale distribution or importing business, before you post that photo, tweet that tweet or comment on your website, consider whether you are in fact promoting a retailer in the process, even seemingly innocuously and tangentially.

## Outside the Single Account Model

The pursuit of an edge over the competition, especially as a startup business, can sometimes be very difficult. The behemoths have their account dominance on occasion for reasons stated earlier; the well established companies with good product and great customer relationships already have that edge over you in the single on-premise and off-premise account. What's a newbie to do? Thinking outside the box may be the way you can increase your volume and begin to allow you to make some inroads.

## Chains, Resorts and Country Clubs

In addition to national chains, there are statewide chains where the buyer is accessible and a relationship can be developed, much in the way you would nurture a relationship with a single retailer or restaurant. Because they are within a reasonable drive from your office, you can make appointments to see them on a regular basis to make presentations. California seems to have a preponderance of chains, but there are head offices in other states and some states that have a significant number of restaurants, even if the head office is elsewhere. For example:

- Cheesecake Factory's head office is in Calabasas, California, but there are 308 restaurants in the US (2021), with fourteen restaurants in Florida and ten in Texas, e.g.

- McCormick & Schmicks Seafood is based in Portland, Oregon, where there are six restaurants, but there are also six restaurants in Illinois. There were eighty throughout the country, pre-COVID, but some have closed. This may be the case for others, so research online when considering chain options.

- P.F. Chang's is based in Scottsdale, Arizona, but also has 192 locations (2021) throughout the country, with a majority in California, Texas and Florida, but still sufficient in most states – eight in Colorado, five in each of Tennessee and Illinois, e.g., to make securing their regional business very worthwhile.

- Costco's head office is in Issaquah, Washington, but they have regional offices across the country. These area offices make all or most of the fine wine decisions (those wines that go in the wooden bins) and many of the floor stack decisions. The regional buyers accept appointments for presentations and can be powerful allies in your distribution business. Often, if the wines selected in one region do well, they become strong contenders for sales in other states.

- Whole Foods' head office is in Glendale, CA, but the core product wine buyer is currently in GA. One of the best ways to get attention for a product is to establish it at the store level, then regional and then state, especially for unknown brands that may not meet a below $10 price point. Like many other national chains, Whole Foods often wants to see traction before they make a bigger commitment.

Most states have resorts and private country clubs that present wonderful opportunities for wine placements and volume business. There are world renowned spa resorts in Arizona and Disney's Epcot in Florida as prime examples. One of my first accounts in Atlanta was a country club that not only put several of my wines on their list, but held tastings for their members who then bought cases of wines they particularly liked. The incentive for the club was to have good, interesting wines on their list that kept their members coming to events. The members, in turn, were able to buy wines at a low markup. These people often love the opportunity to be in a semi-exclusive position with wines at insider prices, a perk of their membership.

Subscribe to free newsletters such as Shanken News Daily and Wine Business Monthly that give you the latest news on various aspects of the market, whether it is interviews with winemakers or label innovations. In the Shanken News Daily I read an interview with the head of ABC Fine Wines & Spirits, which operates approximately 150 stores in Florida. He said competition is his biggest hurdle these days. The stores are losing some ground to supermarkets at the lower end, but doing a great business in higher end wines and spirits. To remain competitive, they've also increased their lines of private label products. These types of opportunities could dovetail with your own import portfolio. Or you may have access to other wines that would be perfect for private label.

## Wine Clubs

Although California is a haven for wine clubs, they exist all over the country and are easily researched online. Some wine clubs are connected to stores and others only send wine and wine related gift baskets through a virtual store. Many of these clubs have regular customers who receive monthly or quarterly offerings. The clubs are looking for constant turnover with new and intriguing wines to offer their members. Wine clubs often order in increments of sixty cases each of red and white or have tiers of wine pricing where they might purchase fifteen to twenty cases of a top tier and up to one hundred cases of a lower tier.

# Military Bases, Cruise Lines and Hotel Chains

These are all additional prospects that are often missed, but do require a good deal of research, understanding and possibly outside resources, such as brokers who specialize in these entities. I mention it now simply as a resource you may want to investigate a bit further down the road, once you have your core business stabilized.

*SUMMARY* — In your basic distribution model, your main concern should be to offer excellent customer service, a reliable alternative to the many distributors the accounts already see and QPR on your wines. Home state distribution can be a worthwhile adjunct to your import business and really take your business up a level. Try not to waste money on extraneous purchases in the beginning, be creative in expanding your home base and make your money work for you as much as possible with the largest return for your investment of time and wine.

# My story

My very first retail account was a local "mom and pop" specialty grocery store with a small wine aisle, tucked down a secondary road in a neighborhood. They offered readymade gourmet foods and high-end essentials for local high-end clientele. This was not a conventional A, B or even a C account. But they were close by and I got to know them from quick trips in to pick up takeout food on my way home. From the first appointment they were willing to make a big commitment to my portfolio and, ultimately, my unknown wines from my small, new portfolio comprised 80% of their stocked wine. For me it became an "A" and valuable account.

A popular, busy restaurant with excellent food and, especially for 1992, an eclectic, daring wine list was one of the first restaurants I ventured into to sell my wares in Atlanta. I was treated politely, but the buyer did not buy anything. I loved the casual atmosphere of this local treasure and because I'm just determined to turn "no" into "yes", I was on a personal mission to make it onto that wine list. I persevered through three or four tastings without a purchase. Eventually, I started dropping in to do paperwork at the bar and order a glass of wine or a bite to eat as I worked. After about eight trips to the account, the buyer (who happened to be the chef and the owner) openly acknowledged that I had paid my dues and he was ready to make some purchases. He was testing me, just as accounts will test you or your salespeople. Not always to this extent, of course. But this buyer knew that he was a desirable account and I was so new I might not last long enough to warrant the change to his wine list. They want to make sure you will be around for the long run and that they will not have wasted their time getting to know you and your wines. Again, this developed into one of my better accounts and the owner became a good friend. You will not necessarily have time for this much massaging and cultivation of a potential buyer, but the point is that you cannot afford to dismiss an account because it does not seem to fit a profile. It is also important to recognize that symbiotic relationship between the distributor and the retail accounts.

## My Client's Story

This is a story of two clients, one in Northern California and one in Illinois, in similar situations. They both have connections to local restaurants, sommeliers and retail opportunities. In Northern California, the client has a close friend who owns three busy restaurants. This is a perfect opening for wines on the list and BTG, with built-in sales to launch their state distribution. In Illinois, my client has access to a high volume chain where the buyer tasted the wines before they were imported and expressed a preference for certain wines and styles. Both clients were understandably anxious to take advantage of these guaranteed sales and it made sense to get that going even before any national distribution sales. In addition, I pointed out that, to them, this is a great proving ground for the wines, both to see which ones work particularly well in the market, and to attract distributors in other states who will now see the local success of their wines.

# CHAPTER 19

# DIRECT TO CONSUMER

In the first edition I included a couple of paragraphs on internet sales under the next chapter "Other Thoughts". In the second edition, I expanded that section, but it now deserves its own section. In recent years, almost all new clients ask me how to make online sales to consumers. Occasionally, it is their sole goal in becoming an importer.

The latest report from major alcohol industry lender Rabobank stated that online sales doubled from pre-pandemic levels, reaching $6.1 billion nationwide last year. Online sales now represent 23% of the $7.2 billion in revenue from U.S. direct-to-consumer wine sales. Rabobank forecast that the online channel is set to be the biggest driver of industry growth for years to come.

## Where You Can and Where You Can't

First and foremost, before we get into what you *can* do, I would like to dispel the misconception that wineries and importers have the same license to sell online. They don't. So many people see websites, blogs and commentary devoted to the huge potential of online sales and the vast swathe of country they can sell to and think it applies to them as an importer. *It doesn't.* "Why does this winery distribute all over the country and also sell their wines at a tasting room?" Because winery regulations are very different and the latitude that wineries may enjoy in California, Washington, Oregon and elsewhere do not, in the same way, extend to importers and distributors.

Until *Granholm v. Heald* (2005), a Supreme Court decision that allowed wineries to sell directly to consumers out-of-state, wineries were historically allowed to ship to consumers only within their own state. The legislative power that individual state wholesalers had amassed since the end of Prohibition and signed into law, required wineries to sell to a wholesaler in each state, preserving the three-tier system and, more importantly, giving wholesalers the power to allow a winery into their state or not. After an eight-year battle by small wineries contesting the states' ban on interstate sales, the Supreme Court decision declared the state laws unconstitutional, allowing wineries to bypass wholesalers to sell to consumers in other states, and giving consumers domestic wine choice. No such rights extend to importers (just in case I wasn't clear before!).

If you intend to be a wholesaler within your own state and also want to sell online to consumers, there is an exception in California where it can be combined as a hybrid with your distributor license through the California ABC. In this instance, there is no "bricks and mortar" store. Unlike a licensed store, it is not based on an area's liquor license density nor your licensed premise's proximity to schools and churches. You cannot have customers come to your location and you cannot hold tastings, either in your office or at another venue, under your license. This license is issued strictly to sell online from a website. It can be administered from your own import/distributor offices and fulfilled from elsewhere.

One issue with selling online to consumers, as an importer and distributor, is managing the online business so that you don't appear be competing against the distributors and retailers to whom you already sell or wish to sell. Wineries have been doing it successfully, of course, by selling to consumers at their cellar door or through a wine club with exclusives for members. In selling to distributors, the key for them, and you, is to maintain price integrity so that the consumer is essentially paying the same price online as they would at a retail store, with the exception of specials and exclusives. Undercutting your other customers, i.e., wholesalers and retailers, will end up adversely affecting what is normally the importers' core business.

In the event you pursue this option, my suggestion would be to set up a separate site for online sales that does not conflict with your primary trade website. A website for direct-to-consumer (DtC) sales would also look different from your wholesale website and could be under a DBA or another trade name. It will need a shopping cart system and shipping policies, and be a dynamic site to include new products, vintages, updated availability, and specials. Your importer website should not list prices, unless you have a trade-only, password-protected section where you house your "trade tools": FOB pricing, POS material, etc.

Even with an approved online license, there are a limited number of states to which you may ship, often limited volume, out-of-state licenses to obtain in each state to which you ship, and excise tax to pay to the states in which you are licensed and sell. This is something to consider in the budgeting for your DtC business model.

Since the advent of COVID and its attendant lockdowns, DtC sales have increased dramatically. Along with that, the number of companies offering third party compliance and logistics has exploded. The key, again, is to determine if their services are geared to wineries or include importers. Most don't, but because this is an area outside my comfort zone, I went on a search to find anyone who could provide that platform for importers to sell directly to consumers.

## Working Within the Three-Tier System

Recently, I spoke with Ben Bradley of Thirstie, who was kind enough to give me some of his valuable time to explain Thirstie's concept and how it works. Thirstie is now one of the leading alcohol e-commerce sites and, clearly, they offer a valuable service. They have an extensive network of independent, licensed retailers around the country where orders are fulfilled for consumers in their respective states but shipping is from California. They assume liability for shipping and handle logistics and compliance. Thirstie's technology ensures that these all-important aspects are handled correctly and expeditiously. As I've already stressed throughout the book, regulations are embedded in every transaction within the alcohol industry. Thirstie can take the burden off the customer by ensuring compliance with the countless laws in each state and county in which their retail network is operating. They collect metadata on sales which they provide to their clients, allowing brands to strategize and focus their efforts on building sales. But. Big But. Their customers are wineries, distilleries, and breweries, who want a broader reach for their brands. An importer will still need to have distributors in each of the states from which their product is fulfilled by a retailer, and Ben Bradley stressed that a marketing budget is essential for success. It is through a marketing effort that includes ad creation, paying for clicks and impressions, photos, etc., that data capture maximizes future sales targeting.

Other e-commerce platforms operate in a similar fashion to Thirstie's, although no other company I contacted responded to my request for information, so I can't be sure.

I investigated different websites that were recommended by Sevenfifty. There are fulfillment companies, such as Drizly, VinDelivery and eProvenance who have identified a personalized, consumer delivery niche between retailers and consumers, and their relationship is strictly between these two. Their marketing, variously, is to provide fast, temperature-controlled and touch-of-a-button easy wine ordering.

From their website, Speakeasy appears to operate in much the same way as Thirstie, e.g., acting as a facilitator for wineries, distilleries, breweries and brands, and offering technological and marketing advantages in their delivery model. Data and analytics figure prominently in their website, as do the ease of use and simple integration with their client's current sales vehicles, i.e., website, trade shows and cellar door.

Speakeasy's website makes clear their relationship with their customer (bold is mine):

> ***Our role in the transactions** contemplated by these Terms and Conditions **is that of a marketing** and **service provider** that enables you, the Customer, to purchase alcohol and related products from Licensed Retailers via the Sites ("Services), and to participate in the Services and/or any other product offers offered on the Sites. The sale and delivery of orders are executed and fulfilled by licensed third-party retailers that hold valid licenses issued by state alcohol beverage agencies allowing for the legal sale of alcohol ("Licensed Retailers"). **You acknowledge that you are purchasing alcoholic beverages from a Retailer licensed in the state in which it is licensed, and not from Speakeasy.** Thus, all orders of alcohol and related products you place through the use of the Sites are processed and fulfilled by such Licensed Retailers, as the actual sellers of the Products.*

Vinoshipper, based in California, state on their website:

> *Vinoshipper is dedicated to making your job easier by simplifying compliance and increasing direct sales across the country. We work with all types of producers & sellers including wineries, cideries, meadiers, sake brewers, importers, distillers, and retailers."*

They are spelling out their role in integrating the full range of alcohol licensees, including importers, into their business model. They offer seamless website shopping cart integration, licensing compliance in each state in which they have licensed partners, and sophisticated wine club, shipping and data collection technology. This still limits the type of importer client they can take on, but is a valuable service if you meet their criteria and want to farm out DtC to a third party.

This is just the tip of the iceberg of companies that provide a bridge between wholesale and the consumer. You can Google them for more ideas, but now that you know a little of the criteria, look for the wording. If wineries, distilleries and other alcohol manufacturers are their customers, then this is likely not going to work for you. However, it can't hurt to talk to some of them and make your own assessments, adding to your knowledge base.

Regardless, all of these DtC fulfillment companies promise to do the "heavy lifting" of consumer sales, while the client concentrates on growing their business. There is peace of mind in having all licenses, taxes, order fulfillment and customer service in the hands of a knowledgeable and experienced company. Budget is a big factor, as is your ability to reach these consumers because this is your responsibility.

Knowing of a Washington State importer who appears to have a robust online sales business, I spoke to an agent at the Washington State Liquor and Cannabis Board about the licenses available there. He was adamant that an importer license in WA does not allow sales to consumers. For DtC sales the licensed entity must be either a winery or a separate retailer owned by different principals from the import business. There are no allowances, as in the CA license, for online sales. Still, if you look at WA online retailers such as Fat Cork, which holds licenses as an importer and distributor and a separate retail license, it seems to be a very viable option. Fat Cork, e.g., has been in business since 2010 as a champagne specialist with a healthy wine club sales component. They entice their customer by inviting them to "take a trip" and "transport yourself to Champagne", with lyrical descriptions of region, geography, vineyard soils and vigneron families. They are constantly updating their site with more user-friendly information and skillfully-taken photos to captivate the reader, allowing them to feel connected to Champagne, and foster a desire to try new offerings from small growers. After reading these articles, I felt quite ready to purchase a few bottles myself!

*SUMMARY* — Always contact the licensing entity of your particular state. If your business is in a state that allows importer and retail licenses and you want to utilize them to sell DtC, you still have your work cut out for you to market your website, brands, and individual wines. If you don't have a readymade base, you must first attract the customer, and that takes a barrage of social media, well-placed ads, and professional, captivating content. Once that is accomplished, the company that engages with their customer on a personal level, *and on a consistent basis*, is going to keep the customer coming back and grow their business. Find that marketing balance; a well-known online wine sales company became wildly successful through his hyperbolic descriptions of wine in his newsletters and sales pitches; on the other hand, there is always the risk of turning people off with too much hype. Can you deliver the substance to back up the hype? You must. There is too much competition out there. Integrity, quality and follow through are as necessary to your consumer business as it is in every other segment.

# My Story

I have some experience with third party online sales through the representation of a client as their importer. They own a vineyard and an established trout fishing resort, hotel and restaurant in their country of origin. They serve their wine to their guests, most of whom come from the U.S. This perfect combination of having enjoyed good quality wine and retaining fond memories from their experiences at the resort, propelled the guests to ask where they could buy the wines in their respective states when they returned to the U.S. As a result of a long wait and no idea how to get the wine exported legally, my clients had built up a substantial backlist of waiting customers. It posed a unique situation for me, but one that dove-tailed well into my business model. For the past few years, with the exception of one imported brand, I have focused on consulting, writing and teaching. With this new client, I could provide the appropriate licenses, logistics and compliance, and they had all the sales they needed in the consumer customer base.

Still, it was something of a steep learning curve for me. I had to find the California company that could provide the bridge between wholesale and retail and the all-important fulfillment piece and understand how that worked, legally, within my own license framework. The setup was quite intensive, but once that was up and running, the fulfillment company had everything in place to support customer orders, and deliver wine club options and logistics.

While I wanted to make sure my client's needs were met, I was determined not to become involved in the operation in a more hands-on way. I can sometimes get pulled into situations that require more time and effort than anticipated, with the result that I feel overworked, or am not meeting my obligations to other clients. I caution you not to do the same in any area of your business. Going back to the 80/20 rule, if you feel that you are spending a disproportionate amount of time on something or someone that represents a small fraction of your income or business potential, take a look at whether you should continue down that path. It may be something that you want to pursue because of connections you're making or greater sales potential, but if it continues to be a drain on your resources (time, money, or personnel), without producing the desired results it may be time to pull the plug (no pun intended).

As for this new client, it was important that I have the necessary licenses: a Federal Basic Permit and the CA licenses to import into the state and distribute. It was also important to warehouse at a CA ABC Type 14 warehouse, where inventory could be stored until trucked to the fulfillment warehouse.

# My Client's Story

When a certain couple first approached me with their idea, I was skeptical. Initially, it sounded like any another client who wanted to sell online without having a firm grasp of what that might entail. Especially since they both came from completely unrelated professions and wanted to concentrate on just one local area of a European country with which they had fallen in love. Of course. But the more they talked about their plans and the way in which they intended to target potential customers – through their own professional associations, wide range of friends and acquaintances and their adult children's fraternities and sororities – the more it sounded to me like the idea had legs. This was the catalyst, but every business idea must be followed up with solid, consistent effort and they did. They also used creative content in email newsletters, on their blog and on their website and sourced a diverse collection of wines from that small region. With honed, specialized knowledge of the region's wines and access to those unknown gems, they built a portfolio that was able to change and grow with their customers' tastes. Their website and marketing outreach incorporate folksy tales of their countryside searches and include wine pairing recipes. They have also set up three levels of wine club with attractive value-added features

I was only involved with their business's early foundation, but have followed their journey. Four years later, they have an inviting tasting room (with a different Washington license under someone else) where they can showcase their wines, and events to draw in locals and longtime customers, to add to their customers from around the country. Despite the very challenging past three years living with the pandemic where many businesses have understandably failed, these clients' business has continued to grow and develop new ways to attract customers.

# CHAPTER 20

# OTHER THOUGHTS

We have now gone from the very first glimmer of thinking about importing wine, through the process of establishing and developing your business. Now that we have reached the end, I thought I would round out the picture by briefly discussing other aspects that may come up in the course of your journey. Some of these ideas were controversial ideas at the time I was writing the second edition, but are now mainstream, some are more recent, and others are simply expansion thoughts from both post-Recession and mid-COVID developments that are new to this third edition. Most of these changes, or innovations, have significantly affected how the market behaves in recent years.

## Millennials

The reality is that millennials – according to the US Census, those born between 1985 and 2000 –significantly impact today's market demographics. They represent a block that is now larger than baby boomers and their tastes and mindset are very different from the previous generations. Millennials become the single-most important marketing focus of the current industry and are considered the future of the business (until the next generation rises).

How are they different? There has been an enormous amount of research conducted in the past few years, driven by the knowledge that millennials were becoming influential wine consumers. Baby boomers grew up in a time before the internet, when wine drinking was fairly unsophisticated and information much less readily available. By contrast, millennials have information at their fingertips and their choices are far greater. The prevailing thinking is that they:

- are much more likely to rely on peer recommendations for wine
- are less loyal to brands and more willing to make adventurous wine buying decisions
- are unwilling to compromise on quality
- have a casual approach to drinking wine that transcends traditional social norms of previous generations
- don't like to be actively marketed to; they'd rather feel they've made their own discoveries
- like to explore to become more informed
- want wines that align with their personal values
- demand transparency
- find wines that support sustainability generally more appealing
- are attracted to less conservative brands.

In short, they present an opportunity for anyone who takes the time to relate to this consumer and embrace their culture.

They generally ignore the 100-point ratings system they associate with boomers and will be more connected to the stories and history of unique discoveries. This does not mean you throw out your 92-point shelf talker. Baby boomer and Gen X wine drinkers still collectively make up the majority of wine buyers. But if you want that millennial customer base, you need to engage them on their playing field. Social media is fundamental. Blogs, Instagram, word-of-mouth, and key influencers such as retail wine store consultants and restaurant sommeliers, are more likely to impress them. Interestingly, they are captivated by the historical significance of regions and the mystique of people behind the wines. Tradition can still capture their imagination. Wines by the glass on restaurant wine lists are a terrific way to allow millennials to discover new wines with minimal expenditure. Restaurants are responding by offering higher quality BTG wines, which broadens the base for a new importer's wines as well.

Perhaps the best way to promote your wines to millennials is to seek out original, interesting wines with a compelling story at a good price point, to appeal to both their sense of romance and their budget-conscious tastes. Don't underestimate them. They'll engage all that social media content and their contemporaries recommendations to make savvy decisions.

## Current and Future Trends

There are so many trends right now, and the trick will be to focus on those that make sense to your model and be somewhat cautious in your embrace of something that could turn out to be a passing fad. Ideally, the current trend will be tomorrow's mainstay of your portfolio and remaining open to future trends could allow you to catch a leading edge. Here are some current and future trends for you to consider. These are only examples, but indicative of how wide-ranging they can be and food for thought for your new venture. In no particular order:

- ❖ *Natural wines*. In response to consumer trends towards healthier foods and minimalist intervention, a number of brands have adopted variations on vegan, gluten-free, non-GMO. These don't have to be organic wines, although organic is farming is part of the whole movement. Biodynamic and sustainable vineyard practices are all at the fore.

- ❖ ***Sparkling wines from all regions.*** This is not a new trend, obviously, but the category has continued to grow. Look for cool climate areas that might be starting to produce their own sparkling for the first time. But also take into consideration the higher import taxes you will incur.
- ❖ ***Uncluttered labeling*** – and no frills for premium products, suggesting quality that exceeds the price.
- ❖ ***Bordeaux Redux.*** Bordeaux had fallen out of favor in recent years. Prices have been too high for questionable quality and the wines have been faced with competition from, well, everywhere. En primeur (futures) is not something many people want to invest in these days. But classics rarely go out of style permanently and Bordeaux is no exception. Sometimes a classic becomes complacent, until the market forces it to reevaluate. Pricing has stabilized to some degree and recovery is in process. In addition, Petit Chateaux and Crus Bourgeois are more affordable options that have been driven by younger palate demand for wines that the consumer doesn't have to wait years to taste.
- ❖ ***Israeli wines.*** I said this was a category to watch in the 2$^{nd}$ editions. Significant strides have since been made in winemaking quality that have elevated Israeli wines into a mainstream choice. Winemakers have traveled to other regions and, as a result of expanding their knowledge, have adopted wines that are more suited to their climate, such as native grapes and strains that can withstand dry heat. They have also introduced higher acidity whites, emphasized sustainability, and promoted small, family vineyards. Kosher wines have managed to cast off their previous reputation for poor quality and there are now an array of excellent options from Israel and other countries. An exciting time for this country's wines and a potential niche for you.
- ❖ ***Lower alcohol wines*** – specifically, better balanced, more nuanced wines. These adapt well to cooler climate regions, which have increased exports to the U.S., but warmer climates can and do offer wines with more restraint

too. A trend that has been ongoing, but shows no sign of slowing.
- *Rosé* remains popular. Dry, Provence-style rosé has elevated this category to appeal to more sophisticated drinkers and pairs well with food and occasions. Rosés from many different regions are now offering good value at every price point.
- *New Zealand* – has long been the bastion of sauvignon blanc, but demand for more options has created a market for chardonnay, pinot noir and pinot gris in particular. With varied climates and terroir in a small country, there are pockets that offer exciting cabernet sauvignons and Bordeaux-style blends. Right from the start, New Zealand promoted quality wines, even at lower price points for the ever popular sauvignon blanc, and this image has carried them through the introduction of other varieties.
- *Red blends*. A custom that is hundreds of years old, if you consider the time-honored tradition of Bordeaux. But they are becoming very popular from old and new world with distinct fruit character and soft tannins.
- *Cider*. There have been gains and losses in this sector, but capitalizing on artisanal and organic alcoholic cider could be your story.
- *Beer*. We have seen the proliferation of artisanal beers from all over the U.S. and although it is a saturated domestic market, there is still room for imports. Locally sourced herbs and spices and unusual infused ingredients have expanded this exciting category and created momentum for imports from all over the world. Note: importing beer (malt beverage) can easily be accomplished with your Importer Basic Permit, although there are some differences in approach, both logistically and in terms of compliance.
- *Private labels*. Finding, or having access to, a customer who could benefit from the advantage of an exclusive brand on their shelves or wine list could be your own niche. Private labels can also give your portfolio a distinct edge in maintaining control over your own brand. There are private label winery specialists with enough volume to offer a number of different clients with

exclusive labels for their own brands. Or you may establish a relationship with a winery that is willing to offer the same wine as their own brand, under a different label. This is an area that can be too challenging for the new importer, but is one trend that is always worth exploring now or in the future. A private label can secure a brand identity for you and your customer, and ensure it won't be taken away from you on the whim of a supplier, or through the efforts of another importer.

❖ *Climate change.* This deserves a chapter of its own, but I don't think anyone in the wine industry, or about to embark on a wine business career, is unaware that global warming is impacting the world's wine regions. As a direct result of the variance, there are dramatic shifts in the types of wines being made in appellations that, for generations, were strictly regulated to make only certain types of wines. As a matter of economic necessity, regions such as Bordeaux have introduced new varieties for the first time in their history to try to combat rising temperatures. In Champagne, where warmer seasons are resulting in naturally ripening grapes, they are now producing excellent champagnes without the need for added sugar, but they worry about the future. Growers in Champagne are also experimenting with hybrid grapes.

There is no denying climate change is here and its impact is increasing. I bring it to your attention as a consideration for your portfolio, not to suggest you avoid warmer climates but to become aware of what proactive growers are doing to combat climate change in their vineyards and to broaden your portfolio to include new regions, particularly cooler climate and higher elevation. Any of these options might be an innovative advantage in winemaking and marketing.

❖ *Content-driven social media* – emphasis on *content-driven*. Everyone wants value in their reading, but millennials are accustomed to getting their wine recommendations, stories and reviews through social media and it is important not to simply sell to them. Providing interesting background, wine information or winemaker tips through QR codes, as an example of social media on bottle labels and case cards, can be a way to extend your reach. Instagram stories that capture the essence of the wine, history and background with winemaker interviews is another effective way to reach your audience. You Tube videos with a winemaker or viticulturist to discuss specific qualities of wines, vintage or conditions could be inserted into your website for viewing by trade or consumer. Consistency and interesting updates, rather than repetitive bombardment, is key.

- *Canned wines.* In the last edition, I didn't even mention this as an alternative under the heading about packaging, and now I'm giving it its own heading. The concept of packaging wine in a safe, lined container was invented in 1996 in Australia at Barokes Wines winery, but only caught on with the rest of the world about four years ago. Wine spritzers were made popular by younger consumers, but the trend for canned wine has burgeoned since COVID lockdowns restricted restaurant-going. It became apparent to wine brands, including those of premium wines, that this was an exciting new opportunity. There are many advantages to canned wine, including reducing the carbon footprint and keeping white or rosé wines colder longer. The cans are easily recyclable, lighter, and a portable alternative to bottles. Al fresco dining, which was born of necessity during COVID, has become so prevalent that temporary solutions to a pandemic problem are now becoming permanent fixtures, bringing additional seating for restaurants and cafés and creating more demand for patio-friendly beverage containers. Sports venues and resorts have now become hot prospects for wine of all quality. If 97% of all wine is consumed within three days of purchase, canned wine seem like a perfect way to appeal to today's consumers.

- *Packaging.* Inventive labeling, unusual bottle shapes, bottle etching, printing labels directly onto the bottle and biodynamic materials are no longer "emerging" as alternatives to conventional packaging, they are firmly entrenched. More specifics on that in "going green".

Figure 20.1 Bizzarro Spritz Canned Aperitif

# Think Green

**Going green** and preserving our resources is beyond trendy these days; it is about survival and reducing our carbon footprint. There is an abundance of organic foods in stores now, recyclable products everywhere, energy efficient appliances and entire homes powered by alternate power sources and built from recycled construction materials. Businesses are recouping taxes and claiming credits through energy efficient practices and utilizing renewable resources. The idea of sustainable living is becoming more and more a part of our way of life as population and pollution explodes. In the wine industry, being on the leading edge in sustainability is one way to stand out and be environmentally friendly at the same time. This includes seeking out biodynamic vineyards and organically grown grapes.

**Tetra Paks** (generally individual cartons) and boxed wines (3L as the norm) is another packaging alternative that deserves more than a mention with wineries embracing this technology in sustainable packaging.

In comparison with traditional glass bottles, Tetra Pak containers requires 92% less packaging material, uses 54% less energy over the life cycle of the container, 80% fewer greenhouse gases and 60% less solid waste volume, and take 40-50% fewer trucks to deliver the same quantity of wine than that delivered in traditional glass bottles. Although glass is also recyclable, it is often less expensive for a winery to use "virgin" glass rather than recycling.

Initially, Tetra Pak was criticized for being less recyclable than glass and because some communities do not have facilities to handle their waste. Tetra Pak created a *Corporate Social Responsibility* program committed to responsible forest stewardship and overseeing the entire supply chain to decrease waste. This might be an area of interest to explore with your supplier, but do your own research on sustainable practices.

**Boxed** wines have increased dramatically in use as well. They are no longer confined to inexpensive wines of marginal quality. Premium wines are now much more prevalent in this type of container and packaging them in this way is finding acceptance at all level of consumer.

Figure 20.2 Garçon Flat Wine Bottles in Case

**Flat pack** wines are one of the most exciting new innovations, another of those born of necessity, the brainchild of Santiago Navarro, the owner of British company Garçon Wines, who was trying to build an online retail business but finding that delivery costs were too expensive. A flat pack wine bottle is made of 100% recycled and easily recyclable PET material. Because they are flat, it allows twice as many bottles to fit in a standard case and many more cases can fit on a pallet, reducing freight costs and emissions. They are virtually unbreakable and preserve wine well. Although wines that need to age to reach their drinking peak will still benefit from being in a glass bottle, the high proportion of wine consumed within three days makes this another attractive packaging alternative.

# Clearing Wine

*There is no provision to clear wine under your import license that is not label approved or intended for trade show or as bona fide samples.* Those are my italics, for emphasis, but TTB makes the parameters very clear when a licensed importer submits a trade COLA waiver request to clear wine that has arrived by air or outside normal customs clearance channels. TTB ask the importer to attest to making the request only for the reasons stated above. In other words, you may bring in wine on your own behalf (as a licensed importer), or a licensed importer may do so on your behalf if you do not yet have a license and want to start the ball rolling to assess samples, send to potential distributors to assess or for a specific trade show, which must be documented to IAD's satisfaction. Period. There is no allowance made to clear non-compliant samples to give away at an event, to give your friends, to sell or for any other purpose. I've covered COLA waivers in its own section earlier in the book, but I am often asked about "clearing" wine for other purposes and I thought it was worth addressing here.

Quite often, travelers will either buy wine in another country to ship to the States or go online to order from the winery's website and expect it to be shipped to them. This is not allowable under U.S Customs regulations. The only way to buy wine for personal consumption, is for it to be imported legally, or as below.

There are certain provisions made by U.S. Customs for consumers to bring accompanying wine with them into the country after a trip **for personal use only**. However, some of the wine can be subject to duty. This is what U.S. Customs says on their website, (https://www.cbp.gov/travel/international-visitors/kbyg/customs-duty-info):

"***Alcoholic Beverages*** *One liter (33.8 fl. oz.) of alcoholic beverages may be included in your exemption if:*

- *You are 21 years old.*

- *It is for your own use or as a gift.*
- *It does not violate the laws of the state in which you arrive.*

Federal and state regulations allow you to bring back more than one liter of alcoholic beverage for personal use duty-free. However, states may allow you to bring back more than one liter, but you will have to pay any applicable Customs duty and IRT.

**While Federal regulations do not specify a limit on the amount of alcohol you may bring back beyond the personal use exemption, unusual quantities may raise suspicions that you are importing the alcohol for other purposes, such as for resale.** CBP officers are authorized by the Bureau of Alcohol, Tobacco, Firearms and Explosives (ATF)laws, rules and regulations, and are authorized to make on-the-spot determinations that an importation is for commercial purposes. If such a determination is made, it may require you to obtain a permit and file a formal entry to import the alcohol before the alcohol is released to you. If you intend to bring back a substantial quantity of alcohol for your personal use, you should contact the U.S. Port of Entry (POE) through which you will be re-entering, and make prior arrangements for importation.

Also, state laws might limit the amount of alcohol you can bring in without a license. If you arrive in a state that has limitations on the amount of alcohol you may bring in without a license, that state law will be enforced by CBP, even though it may be more restrictive than federal regulations. We recommend that you check with the state government about their limitations on quantities allowed for personal importation and additional state taxes that might apply. Ideally, this information should be obtained before traveling."

Wine can also be included in your household goods container for an international move, in which case you must include it on your Unaccompanied Personal Effects form and complete an Alcohol Inventory Declaration with quantities and retail value. I only mention this to round out the subject of "clearing" wine into the U.S. It really doesn't pertain to importing for resale.

# Export

This is allowed under your Federal Basic Permit obtained through TTB. There is no additional cost (at least at this writing). However, there is a considerable amount of paperwork, all of which is explained in detail at: http://www.ttb.gov/itd/exporting_documents.shtml.

You begin by submitting the Export Certificate Template through the International Affairs Division. There are certificates and customs documents that apply to each individual state or the European Union as a collective. Drawback forms to complete and submit to the National Revenue Center to claim a refund on taxes paid in-state are also available, when applicable. There are also compliance and label laws to learn in the destination country, all of which should be investigated through that home country's wine governing body. (But I would venture to say, none of which will be as complicated or rigid as the U.S. laws)

The obvious choices for wine export would be American wines, since presumably other countries will have their own export program at the winery, just as they have exported to you in the U.S. My personal opinion is that it only really makes sense for you, as the purchaser and not the producer of the wine, to investigate exporting when the U.S. dollar is weak enough to make the exchange rate and the resulting price attractive in the export country of choice. It is something else to consider and you may find a wine that is so inexpensive it makes it worthwhile, irrespective of exchange rate.

# Grey Market

Everyone who deals in, or has contact with, the so-called "grey" area of wine importing (not to be confused with the "over 55" consumers!) seems to have a strong opinion on it. There is no "grey" area when it comes to opinions. I will attempt to dissect the meaning of this term and make sense of it.

Wikipedia defines grey marketing as *"the trade of a commodity through distribution channels which, while legal, are unofficial, unauthorized, or unintended by the original manufacturer."*

This defines it perfectly for the wine industry. Grey marketers are licensed importers who obtain label approval for the wine through TTB, so that it is cleared lawfully through customs, but who have not been assigned as an importer by the particular winery. The Federal government has no way of determining which COLA is being submitted with authorization from the winery, nor do they police grey marketing importation. States that require a letter to prove that the importer is the appointed agent for the brand in the U.S. will not allow a grey marketer to register the brand nor obtain a license, but this is a state by state issue.

Wikipedia goes on to say that grey marketing is commonly engaged *"when the price of an item is significantly higher in one country than another"*.

Price disparity is a common misconception when it comes to grey marketing. Consumers who buy grey market goods assume they are paying less than they would if bought through "white" channels, i.e., directly authorized from supplier (winery) to importer, to distributor, to retailer. The fallacy in this thinking is that either the three-tier system is being circumvented or the authorized importer's pricing is so high that buying grey market goods means a savings. As if the grey market somehow comprises altruistic individuals who just want to make more wine available to the masses.

You may surmise from this I have a problem with grey marketing. Not in theory. I do have a problem with the aforementioned thinking. Some of this thinking seems to derive from the custom of many champagne houses to create artificially high pricing in the U.S., whereas the same item may be purchased less expensively in Europe. This has encouraged unauthorized importers to purchase from Europe and sell in the U.S. at a lower price, while still maintaining a profit margin.

In the case of wine, grey marketing occurs most often when a wine has achieved a high U.S. rating and is (generally) in extremely short supply. Unauthorized importers may have access to distributors in the country of origin or find the wine in Europe, e.g., where there happens to be excess supply and the wine can be bought for a discount. When the legitimate importer has carefully allocated a limited supply of stock to customers and suddenly more wine makes its way into the market, it can make the importer look disingenuous, as if they have created a false or misleading claim for the sake of generating demand. It also circumvents the relationship between the authorized importer and their authorized distributor, which can result in further disruption in the market between distributors and retailers.

I believe the common objection to grey marketing from importers is that they have taken great pains to source and establish wines through the origin – the winery or vineyard. They have often made several trips to the destination and spent countless valuable hours working with the winery on wine selection, pricing, labeling and so forth. The relationship has been established with the express understanding that the importer is the exclusive representative of the winery's wine over here (unless it has been disclosed that the country will be divided in agreed-upon territories). In other words, all the things we reviewed in some detail in the early chapters are in place.

The appointed importer has warehoused product, submitted to publications (from whence the great rating derived), put in the hard yards through previous vintages and a range of wines to establish the brand and finally, one wine gets the exposure they have been waiting for in the form of a high rating or significant review. The grey marketer sees an opportunity to capitalize on all this groundwork and finds a way to source just this one wine, knowing that it will sell quickly.

Normally, the only time the price may be less from the grey marketer is when they sell directly to retail in their home market, foregoing all or part of the second margin, since there is very little overhead connected with their enterprise. Otherwise, unless the importer is gouging, the price should not vary significantly and can sometimes be greater from the grey marketer.

A potentially legitimate complaint from consumers regarding grey marketing relates to provenance: that there is no way to validate the origin of the unauthorized wine or whether it has been properly stored. When the wine passes through so many hands – authorized or unauthorized – there is often no way for a legitimate importer to determine that the wine's integrity has been maintained either. Was the wine too close to the sunbaked window in a retail store? Did it sit out on the dock too long at the distributor? Were the trucks that transported the wine always temperature controlled? Reputable, conscientious importers always try to make sure wine is properly transported and stored and make decisions regarding transport and distributor appointments accordingly, but control passes on and absolute certainty is not always possible.

My last point on grey marketing is to suggest you consider what your philosophy and mission statement is going to be in your import company. Will you disrupt the marketplace in which you sell your product? Are you sure of provenance and integrity of the wine? Does it fit your business model? I am not discouraging you from availing yourself of grey market goods. I simply pose these questions for you to ask yourself.

*SUMMARY* — Negotiating the maze of legal requirements in a highly regulated industry is cumbersome and frustrating but worth the effort to determine that you are in compliance with the laws and regulations that affect your license, your livelihood and your good name.

# My Story

On the subject of grey marketing, there were two instances in which I was aware of a product, for which I was the authorized importer, being brought into the country other than through my own channels. In both situations, it was the same item, a fairly priced wine with a sudden high rating and national exposure. Unfortunately, there was a finite amount of this vintage and I had to carefully monitor its access and distribution.

In one instance, the grey marketer was an importer I had known, and liked, for several years. To my knowledge, he brought in one pallet of this wine (56 cases), bought presumably from a local distributor in the country of origin, and it was quickly sold without any backlash to me or disruption to my business.

In the other instance, an importer went directly to one of my best customers, a retail chain to whom I had just sold what I told them was the last of their allocation, and attempted to sell them somewhere between fifty and one hundred cases. To add insult to injury, he tried to undercut my price, which was understood by the chain to be the best price I could offer. To this day, I can't imagine where he found the wine at all, much less at a lower cost, and I suspect forgery.

Fortunately for me, the relationship with the retailer was strong enough that the buyer called me. She was not happy. I looked very foolish at best and duplicitous at worst. With considerable anxiety on my part at the potential jeopardy this created for my business, I was able to explain what had occurred and to their great credit they refused to purchase the wine from this grey marketer. When I confronted this particular importer with the problem he had created for me at this account – not the issue of grey marketing overall – he dismissed me with these words *"Grow up; it's just business."* Well, it may be to him, but because of the relationship I enjoyed and had fostered with this important retailer it was not "just business" to either one of us.

# CONCLUSION

Once again, no coverage of a subject as vast and multi-layered as this can be all encompassing, despite another comprehensive revision, and more pages added! This is also *my* story and a subjective look at my triumphs, travails and tribulations in the wine industry. In the course of this personal journey on which I have taken you, I have tried to adhere to sound, concrete guidelines of starting and running a wine import company. If you follow these principles, you may not know everything, you may not be wildly successful, but I guarantee you will be way ahead of any learning curve you would encounter had you not read this book.

This is a business that, despite everything – economy, recession, inflation, pandemic, trends, regulations and competition – remains exciting, fun and rewarding and is populated by fascinating characters. It holds the promise of a treasure trove of fabulous, yet to be discovered wines. I began importing wine in 1992 and continued importing a portfolio of Australian and New Zealand brands until around 2011, when the recession made it all but impossible in terms of exchange rate and boutique Australian wine pricing. I am still a fully licensed importer and keep my hand in with two imports, one from Australia and one from Patagonia. I feel fortunate that I can apply my experience to helping others on their new import journeys. Yes, competition is stronger than ever, and we face other hurdles outlined in this book, but alcoholic beverage choice, distribution options and technological advances keep this industry dynamic and energized. With a whole new generation to appeal to.

In conclusion, in this third edition, I continue to wish you success, unforgettable experiences, great adventures and above all, remember: it is *still* about relationships!

# INDEX

*Figures*

Figure 1.1 Early morning overlooking a vineyard, 6

Figure 1.2 Example of Australia's Unique Vineyard Wildlife, 8

Figure 1.3 A Story in Labels (Courtesy of Journey Wines), 14

Figure 2.1 Groskopf Warehouse, Sonoma, California, 29

Figure 3.1 The three-tier System, 36

Figure 3.2 Letter of Intent with Foreign Suppliers, 40

Figure 4.1 Biodynamic Wine from France, 51

Figure 4.2 Waitiri Creek Vineyard, Central Otago, New Zealand, 58

Figure 4.3 Mark Creed of Creed Wines, 64

Figure 5.1 Purchase Order example, 79

Figure 5.2 Example of limited American Source (Appointment) letter, 84

Figure 5.3 Example of exclusive American Source (Appointment) Letter, 85

Figure 5.4 US Compliant Labels where the "brand label" is the back, 91

Figure 5.5 COLA Waiver Request Example, 94

Figure 6.1 20-foot container, 100

Figure 6.2 Shrink-wrapped Pallets in Partially Loaded Container, 103

Figure 6.3 Data Logger (Courtesy of MadgeTech), 104

Figure 6.4 Authorization Letter, 112

Figure 7.1 Pricing Tables for Australia and Europe, 128

Figure 8.1 Tasting note/tech sheet Example, 146

Figure 8.2 Wine Spectator Website, 155

Figure 9.1 Brand Lineup Ready for Tasting, 174

Figure 9.2 Credit Application, 178

Figure 10.1 Wines by the Glass, 199

Figure 10.2 Wholesale Invoice, 207

Figure 11.1 Placement Report Example, 223

Figure 11.2 Depletion Report Example, 224

Figure 12.1 Shelf Talker Examples, 231
Figure 12.2 Front and Back Wine Label Example, 232
Figure 12.3 Distributor Trade Tasting New York, 239
Figure 12.4 Telluride Wine Festival, 247
Figure 13.1 Basket Press and Tanks at Creed Winery, 262
Figure 14.1 Letter to New Importer, 280
Figure 14.2 Hardship Letter, 281
Figure 15.1 Wine Tasting Czech Embassy New York, 299
Figure 15.2 Uniform Shelf Talkers, 303
Figure 16.1 Sample Supplier Itinerary, 321
Figure 17.1 Distributor Release Letter for Franchise State, 332
Figure 18.1 Featured Wine in a Local Wine Store, 345
Figure 20.1 Bizzarro Spritz Canned Aperitif, 382
Figure 20.1 Bizzarro Spritz Canned Aperitif, 384

## A

ABC Fine Wines & Spirits, 360
Account Protocol, 294, 356
Adobe, 23, 230
Alcohol and Tobacco Tax and Trade
    Bureau (TTB), 40–43, 45, 86–90,
    92–94, 97, 156, 277–78, 280–82,
    358, 385, 387–88
Alcoholic Beverage Control (ABC), 38,
    46
Alcohol Inventory Declaration, 387
Alcohol Tobacco Tax Bureau, 112
Appellation Contrôlée (AC), 5
Appellation d'Origine Contrôlée
    (AOC), 5
Argentina, 7, 22, 173
Argentine malbec, 4
Argentine Peso, 129
Arizona, 84, 268, 293, 359
Arkansas, 275
artisanal beers, 379
Asheville, 307
Atlanta, 32, 226, 238, 255, 306, 332,
    360, 362
Australia, 7–8, 17, 30, 32, 128, 281,
    381, 393
Australia's Unique Vineyard Wildlife, 8
Austria, 16

## B

baby boomer, 375–76
Barbera, 298
Beaujolais, 262

billbacks, 200–201, 209
Bioterrorism Act of 2002, 81
Bordeaux blends, 16, 63
Bordeaux fanatic, 157
Bordeaux Redux, 378
Bordeaux-style blends, 379
brand manager, 198, 240, 290
brokers, 10, 182, 184–87, 236, 260,
    303, 342, 349–50, 361
customs, 45, 82, 113, 115, 130,
    152–53
export, 52
foreign, 42
independent, 348
local, 184, 340, 351
budget, 114, 119–20, 192, 194, 198,
    212, 214–15, 217, 251–53, 338,
    340, 350, 353
Bureau of Alcohol, Tobacco, Firearms
    and Explosives (ATF), 386
business model, 22–23, 25, 27, 29–31,
    33, 37, 39, 119, 370, 372, 390
broad market, 45
business relationships, 192
*Buyer's Guide*, 140

## C

cabernet sauvignon, 16, 142, 151, 262,
    292, 379
Moldovan, 9
Calabasas, 359
California, 7, 29, 32, 38, 46, 276, 339,
    346, 359–60, 366, 368–69
California importer/distributor, 169

397

California State License, 46
California vineyards, 261
carignan, Mexican, 9
Certificate of Compliance, 179
Certificate of Good Standing, 179
Certificate of Label Approval (COLA), 42, 44, 86, 89, 92–94, 98, 279, 281, 388
Certified Organic Farmers, 143
chardonnay, 98, 292, 379
   Cowra Estate Reserve, 116
Cheesecake Factory, 359
Chile, 7, 10, 155, 173
China, 109, 114
Cider, 379
Colorado, 38–39, 84, 215, 226, 238, 271, 275, 284, 293, 319, 359
compliance, 24, 86–87, 94, 271, 273, 283–84, 353–54, 368, 372, 379, 387, 390
   outsourcing, 47, 283
Compliance Issues, 273
consignee, 78, 112, 115
consultants, 62, 90, 125, 188, 275, 285, 377
consumer wine festivals, 246
control states, 37, 127, 182–84, 186
Cooper, Michael, 140
Coppola, Francis Ford, 15
Cost, Insurance and Freight (CIF), 105
Costco, 133, 227, 250
Côtes du Rhône, 4
country clubs, 226, 358, 360
currency, 68–69, 129

Customs and Border Protection (CBP), 101
cuvées, 238, 240

# D
Dayton, 252, 319
*Decanter*, 140, 144
Denver, 319
*Denver Post*, 39
department of revenue, 268
depletion allowances (DA), 212, 312
de Rothschild, Baron Philippe, 15
Direct Import (DI), 266
display sheets, 250
distributors, 28–33, 35–38, 119–26, 131–33, 167–69, 175–78, 183–86, 191–209, 212–15, 218–22, 224–27, 232–33, 263–67, 273–76, 282–83, 289–95, 304–9, 311–20, 326–31, 333–34
distributors and retailers, 115, 125, 159, 367, 389

# E
Eiswein, 16
Employer Identification Number, 39
Epcot, 360
Euro, 11, 127, 129
European labels, 14
European Union (EU), 387
exchange rate, 8, 11, 68–69, 131, 133, 219–20, 387, 393
Export Certificate Template, 387
export manager, 236

Ex Works (EXW), 106, 129

**F**
FAA Act, 278
Facebook, 357
FCL, 107, 109–11, 130, 153, 265
FDA approval, 93, 117
FDA registration renewal, 83
FDA website, 82
Federal Importer Basic Permit, 39
FedEx, 30, 43–44, 96, 122
fees, 3, 30, 42, 115, 153, 245, 252, 274, 338–39, 341
  advertising, 160
  brand registration, 282
  license, 3, 275, 283
  warehousing, 18, 27, 267
Florida, 187, 215, 271, 359–60
Food and Drug Administration (FDA), 81–83
France, 5, 9, 13, 51, 63
franchise states, 180–83, 186, 275, 277, 282, 331–33
Freight on Board (FOB), 62, 105–6, 129, 133, 150, 172, 204, 206, 283, 338

**G**
Galloni, Antonia, 155
Georgia, 32, 180, 183–84, 270, 284, 333
Gewurztraminer, 292
Gisborne, 16
Glendale, 359

globalization, 7
goods, clearing, 45
Google, 51, 145, 169, 370
Great Recession, 307
Grenache, 262

**H**
Halliday, James, 144
Health Warning Statement, 88, 90
Hickenlooper, John, 39
Homeland Security, 101
Home State Licenses, 45
House Bill of Lading (HBL), 112
Hunter Valley, 17

**I**
Illinois, 25, 168, 359, 363
importer markups, 107
incentives, 68, 124, 127, 131, 133, 191–95, 198–99, 209, 222, 224, 311–12
Indiana, 25, 168
insurance, 27, 105–6, 116, 339
International Affairs Division, 95, 387
International Trade Fair for Wine, 55
*International Wine Cellar*, 156
Intuit, 148
inventory, 122, 149, 151, 221, 259, 265, 269, 291, 296, 324, 331–33
  control, 261, 263, 265, 267, 269, 353
  levels, 31, 259
  maintenance, 267
  management, 147–48, 269, 355

399

miscounted, 208
mistakes, 151
tracking, 149
warehouse, 212
investors, 2, 21–22
invoices, 63, 67–68, 148–51, 153, 196–97, 200–201, 203–9, 268, 276, 332, 334
  dispute, 329
  service, 208
  shipped, 31
Israel, 378
Issaquah, 359
Italy, 55, 138

**K**
Kentucky, 25

**L**
Letter of Credit (LC), 63
Letter of Intent with Foreign Suppliers, 40
licenses, 23, 25–26, 28, 38–40, 42, 46–47, 272–75, 277, 281–84, 286, 365–66, 370, 385–86, 388, 390
  beer, 339
  broker, 179
  spirits, 339
Licensing and state compliance, 283
Loire Valley, 3, 5
Long Beach, 100

**M**

Manhattan, 238, 252, 289, 297, 318–19
maps, 235, 241, 293, 305
market demand, 120
marketing, 50, 54, 129, 131, 229, 231, 233, 248, 254, 260, 354, 356, 368–69
  grey, 388–91
marketing assistance, 254
marketing budget, 368
marketing efforts, 232, 368
marketing expert, 249
marketing materials, 147
marketing medium, 251
marketing outreach, 374
marketing plans, 160, 229, 357
marketing resources, 193
marketing tool, 140
market research, 63
markups, 52, 119, 125–26, 129, 131–33, 283, 338
Marlborough, 16
Marriott, 318
Martinborough, 16
Maryland, 157, 182
Master, 73, 140, 327
Master Bill of Lading (MBL), 111, 113, 266
Master of Wine, 327
Master of Wine or Master Sommelier, 327
McCormick & Schmicks Seafood, 359
McDonalds, 180
Merlot, 63, 142, 234, 292

Mexico, 9
Microsoft, 23, 171
millennials, 161, 375–77, 380
Minneapolis, 215
Mississippi, 182
Moldova, 9
Muscat, 234

**N**
Napa, 29, 56, 156
National Organic Program (NOP), 91
National Revenue Center, 387
Network Solutions, 145
New Jersey, 25, 28, 32, 226, 293, 319, 343
New York, 25, 28, 54–55, 72, 275, 293, 319, 339
New Zealand, 11, 16, 30, 52, 58, 63, 261, 379, 393
Non-Resident Seller's Permit, 179
Non Vessel Operating Company (NVOCC), 112
North Carolina, 307

**O**
Oakland, 29
Ohio, 25, 127, 132, 183, 252, 319
Oregon, 84, 359, 366

**P**
packaging, 10, 12, 140, 173, 260, 381–84
Pareto Principle, 337, 341
Parker, Robert, 157

Penfolds Grange, 8
Pennsylvania, 28, 127, 182
Perotti-Brown, Lisa, 157
personalities, 19, 50, 56–57, 217, 219, 225, 315, 322, 325, 344, 352
P.F. Chang's, 221, 359
pinotage, 9
pinot gris, 379
pinot noirs, 16, 292, 379
Point of Sale (POS), 23, 253, 260
port, 62, 65, 94, 99, 102–3, 105–6, 109–10, 114, 117, 122, 129, 152–53, 265–66
Portland, 359
port of origin, 6, 62–63, 102, 123, 129, 139
Power of Attorney (POA), 44
press, 66, 68, 240, 245, 248, 302
pricing, 5, 7, 59, 69, 120, 125–26, 132–33, 136, 216, 219–21, 300
  by-the-glass program, 196
  discounted, 266
  impressive, 4
  level, 133
  model, 119, 184
  scenario, 133
  spectrum, 125
  strategy, 219
  structure, 220
  suggested retail, 155
  uniform, 274
Prohibition, 36, 39, 180, 182, 366
purchase orders, 77–80, 113, 148, 151, 161, 202, 353

## Q

Quality Price Ratio, 11, 122
QuickBooks, 78, 148–49, 151, 208, 354

## R

Rand, 129
ratings, 14–15, 120–21, 135–36, 139–40, 147, 157–60, 172, 175, 178, 230, 260, 302–3
regulations, 35, 47, 53, 82, 86, 93, 275–76, 368, 386, 390, 393
  enacted, 101
  federal, 386
  statutory, 192
Release letters, 333
Republic of Georgia, 270
resources, renewable, 382
restauranteur, 320
restaurant manager, 347
restaurants, 36, 134, 137, 195–96, 198, 215, 218, 232–35, 263–64, 292–96, 298, 315, 346, 358–59, 362–63
retailer markups, 131
retailers, 35–37, 47, 123–26, 131–33, 167, 169, 185, 195–96, 233–34, 267, 294, 313–15, 357–58, 367–69, 388–89
Rex Goliath, 13
Rhode Island, 180
riesling verticals, 327
Robinson, Jancis, 140
rosé, 379
roussanne, 4
Royal Melbourne Wine Show, 144
Roy's, 221
Ruth's Chris, 221

## S

sales manager, 172, 184, 195, 198, 290, 301, 305, 330, 356
sales managers, 184
salesperson, 195–96, 199–201, 232–33, 242, 245, 251, 289–91, 293–96, 305, 342, 347–49
sales personnel, 184, 340, 348
sangiovese, 57
Sardinia, 16
Sauterne, 298
sauvignon blanc, 16, 292, 379
SCORE association, 148, 157
Scottsdale, 359
Search Engine Optimization, 229
semillon, 7, 17–18
Shanghai, 55
*Shanken News Daily*, 360
shareholders, 22, 26
shelf talkers, 156–57, 159, 230–31, 240, 246, 250, 253, 302–3, 312
shiraz, 7, 136
sirah, 15
ski resort, 215
Small Business Administration (SBA), 148
social media, 161, 356, 358, 371, 377, 380–81

sommeliers, 73, 218, 220, 327–28, 347, 363
Sonoma valley, 29
South Africa, 9, 30, 52
South Carolina, 206, 286
Starbucks, 180
state brand registration, 86
state compliance, 283
state websites, 183
Stories
    My Client's Story, 19, 33, 73, 98, 117, 138, 188, 212, 256, 270, 308, 309, 327, 328, 363, 374
    My Story 17, 32, 72, 97, 116, 135, 187,
        211, 226, 255, 269, 284, 306, 325, 334,
        362, 372, 391
Supreme Court, 181, 366
Switzerland, 13
Sydney International Wine Competition, 144

## T

table tents, 251, 255
Tanzer, Stephen, 156
Tasmania, 16
tastings, 141, 157–58, 237, 242, 245–46, 296–97, 300–304, 307, 319, 357, 360, 362, 366
taxes, 3, 26–27, 106–7, 126, 130, 133, 252, 266, 276, 326, 341
    excise, 276, 339, 341, 367
    federal, 276

higher import, 378
state, 131
tax preparation, 354
Tennessee, 183, 282, 359
territory, 195–96, 221, 244, 282, 316, 348, 389
Tetra Pak, 382
Texas, 206, 273, 293, 359
Thirstie, 368
three-tier system, 36–39, 267, 317, 366, 368, 388
tied-house laws, 38
Tokay, 234
topography, 50
trade associations, 54, 265
Trader Joe's, 65
trade shows, 54
Trade Support, 229
trends, 9, 14, 22, 168, 201, 225, 377, 379–81, 393
TTB ID number, 279
TTB news release, 278
TTB provision, 278
TTB website and scroll, 42
*Two Buck Chuck*, 3, 64, 168

## U

United Parcel Service (UPS), 30, 96, 122
United States Department of Agriculture (USDA), 91
US Census, 375
US Compliant Labels, 91, 138
Utah, 127, 182

Utah Department of Alcoholic Beverage Services, 182

## V
verdelho, 300
verdot, 142
vignerons, 35, 49, 64, 217, 277
*Vinous*, 155
viognier, 15, 294

## W
Waiheke, 16
Walmart, 38
warehouse contracts, 33
warehouse manager, 265
warehouse personnel, 151, 355–56
Washington, 43, 84, 94, 238, 280, 359, 366
Washington State Liquor, 370
webinars, 125, 148
Whole Foods,' 359
Wholesaler's Permit, 42
*Wine & Spirits*, 55, 155, 157, 160
*Wine Advocate*, 199
*Wine Business Monthly*, 351
wine clubs, 360, 367, 370, 374
*Wine Companion*, 140
wine dinners, 67, 110, 233–36, 245, 251, 254–55, 291–93, 306, 315, 319–21, 347
Wine Dinners and Tasting Preparation, 291
*Wine Enthusiast*, 155–56, 158–59
wine law firm specialists, 125

winemaker, 15, 17, 136–37, 140–41, 143–44, 233, 236, 301, 303, 309, 317–18, 321, 325, 327–28, 378
winery, 24–25, 36–40, 52–54, 60–63, 66–71, 77–78, 80–83, 86, 93, 105–6, 123–26, 140, 153–54, 251, 259–61, 264–65, 267–68, 317–20, 365–70, 387–89
  large production, 4
  prospective, 42, 147
winery brochures, 235
wines, clearing, 385, 387
wine samples, 24, 158, 251
*Wine Spectator*, 8, 15, 50, 136, 155–56, 159–60, 230, 253
wine warehouses, 46, 203
Wyoming, 182

## Y
Yellow Tail, 168

Made in the USA
Columbia, SC
15 November 2023